LAWYERS' SKILLS

LAWYERS' SKILLS

Oral and Interpersonal Skills

Philip A. Jones LLM, MA, PG Dip PHE
Director of Legal Practice, Faculty of Law, University of Sheffield

Legal Research

Julian Webb BA (Hons), LLM, Dip Socio-Legal Studies
Principal Lecturer and Director of Postgraduate Programmes,
Faculty of Law, University of the West of England, Bristol

Legal Writing

Caroline Maughan BA (Hons), MA, Dip Law, Cert Ed, Barrister
Senior Lecturer in Law, University of the West of England, Bristol

and

Mike Maughan BA (Hons), Dip Applied Linguistics, Cert Ed
Lecturer in Organisational Behaviour, Cheltenham and Gloucester College
of Higher Education

Drafting

Marcus Keppel Palmer, BA (Hons), Solicitor
Senior Lecturer in Law, University of the West of England, Bristol

 BLACKSTONE
PRESS LIMITED

First published in Great Britain 1993 by Blackstone Press Limited,
9-15 Aldine Street, London W12 8AW.   Telephone 081-740 1173

© Philip A. Jones, 1993. The contributors hold the copyright for their respective Chapters.

ISBN: 1 85431 296 0

British Library Cataloguing in Publication Data
A CIP catalogue record for this book is available from the British Library

Reprinted 1993

Typeset by Style Photosetting Ltd, Mayfield, East Sussex
Printed by Ashford Colour Press, Gosport, Hampshire

CONTENTS

CONTENTS

CONTENTS

PREFACE

This Guide covers the lawyers' skills that are a central part of legal practice and which underpin the Legal Practice Course. It covers legal research, writing and drafting, and the interpersonal skills involved in interviewing and advising, negotiation and advocacy.

Legal Research

Legal research is quite clearly fundamental. You cannot be expected to carry all the law around in your head, but you should have both a broad picture of legal concepts, which you should have acquired in your academic studies, and the ability to research a point quickly and fully when it is relevant for a particular case.

This Guide adopts a structured problem-solving approach to legal research and provides clear advice on how to structure your research.

Writing and Drafting

Words are the fundamental tool that lawyers use to gain an advantage for their clients. Lawyers speak words, interpret them and write them. This Guide examines how to use words effectively in various contexts: when writing a letter, drafting a contract or will, or drafting documents in litigation.

We emphasise the need to use correct grammar, attend to structure and focus on the needs of your audience.

Oral and Interpersonal Skills: Interviewing and Advising, Negotiation, Advocacy

Oral and interpersonal skills are the very stuff of being a lawyer. You need to develop good oral communication skills if you are to interview a client or witness, if you are to negotiate on behalf of your client, or if you are to appear in court to present a case.

Negotiations permeate the professional life of a lawyer. Negotiations provide the primary mechanism for settling disputes and they are used to settle the terms of most transactions. Negotiations, at a less formal level, are a part of the life of all professionals.

Advocacy, is an important oral and interpersonal skill, which brings many of the other skills together in a formal setting. The ability to present a case to other people clearly, comprehensively and persuasively is so central to the role of the lawyer that you will benefit from learning how to do it even if you never venture near the courts.

The Nature of Social Skills Training

Many people are suspicious of skills training. They say that good lawyers are born not made. It may be true that greatness, in all areas, is born not made. But, in the Legal Practice Course, as in the early years of working as a lawyer, the concern is not with greatness but competence. You may not emerge as an artist, but you will be proficient.

This Guide to lawyers' skills is no substitute for practice. But it can provide a supplement to practice. It provides an account of what is involved in the major skills of being a lawyer.

The text adopts a broad approach to lawyers' skills. It focuses on the skills that are evident in communicating with and interacting with others. These skills are a central part of interpersonal communication and can be easily observed: listening, questioning, responding, probing, setting the scene, managing the agenda, producing a structure for the interaction.

Supporting these skills are the inner skills involved in decision making and problem solving. These inner skills are essential; they provide the mental structures without which it is impossible to act. The inner perspective and the cognitive skills determine the way you see a problem, they provide a framework which leads to the classification of the problem, and they enable you to develop a scheme of action that will help you solve the problem.

Finally, there are skills for creating a climate for effective communication. These too are inner skills: skills which are manifest in expressions of empathy, the adoption of a nonjudgmental attitude, respect for others and genuineness. These elements of communication may feel awkward. They are not like the hard analytical skills of legal reasoning. But these aspects of human relations are as central to being a lawyer as the critical faculties you develop at the academic stage. They lead to sensitivity, openness and warmth. They enable you and your client, or you and a witness, or you and a fellow lawyer, to establish rapport. Rapport, not the razor thrust of the critical intellect, may help you break through an impasse that is at the heart of a client's problem.

This Guide, then, provides an overview of the skills that lie at the heart of legal practice. But it also introduces you to some of the theories that underpin competent practice. These theories provide a set of working assumptions, accepted principles and ways of working. They provide one element, a guide, that will help you in the early years of practice.

Philip A Jones

LEGAL RESEARCH AND PROBLEM SOLVING

ONE

INTRODUCTION

In the Legal Practice Course the term 'legal research' carries a different meaning from that which is familiar to you from academic study.

Practical legal research encompasses not just library-based research techniques, but the skills of legal analysis and fact investigation and management. In this wider sense, legal research is central to the solicitor's work. Most central of all are the skills of fact analysis and management. Your ability as a lawyer will largely be measured by your ability to use the information underpinning your client's case. Fact management skills, as we shall see, play a part in most other skills the lawyer uses – interviewing, negotiating and advocacy must all be built on sound fact-handling. This means that your ability to find and use factual material is at least as important as your ability to find and use the law, if not more so.

The material in this part has been organised into six Chapters. The first provides an overview; the others focus on the principal skills themselves, namely:

  (a) Legal analysis.
  (b) Fact identification and analysis.
  (c) Fact management.
  (d) Doing library-based research.

For the most part, the topics are discussed in the context of litigation practice. This is not to suggest that research skills are unnecessary in non-contentious work, but the greatest difficulties of fact analysis and management tend to arise in the context of litigation. The methods of library-based research are essentially the same whether the work is contentious or not. Apart from that, detailed discussion of specific techniques for non-contentious work are discussed chiefly in **Chapters 2** and in **4.4**.

TWO

LEGAL RESEARCH – PROBLEM-SOLVING APPROACH

2.1   Introduction

Our task as lawyers is essentially to bring our working knowledge of the law to bear on a specific client's problem. The problem might be about virtually anything. With luck it will be well within the boundaries of our existing knowledge and experience, but that is not guaranteed. To use a medical analogy, every client requires a 'diagnosis' of a problem and advice on what to do next.

In common with other professional decision-makers we face a basic psychological problem in dealing with this situation. We possess information given by the client about the problem. We also possess certain professional knowledge. But we all suffer from certain limits in our ability to *use* those sets of information. This is primarily because, so psychologists tell us, we have a relatively limited working memory, by comparison with our long-term memory. This lack of memory capacity restricts our information processing capabilities. It means that we cannot work efficiently, in a relatively short time span, with all we know about a problem. So, we develop strategies to deal with this shortcoming. We process the information we receive serially, a piece at a time; we use that data selectively to construct a simplified model of the problem, and then we match that model with our own mental representations of legal problems – a sort of 'pigeon-holing' process. In this way we are able to produce an initial formulation and 'diagnosis' of the problem.

For an experienced professional these processes seem instinctive, but they are techniques we all develop from experience – essentially they are well-developed coping strategies. We suggest that you can try to short-circuit that learning process by using this 'instinctive' methodology to inform your own problem-solving approach.

The problem-solving approach depends upon recognising that problem solving involves a four-stage reasoning process:

  (a) *Information gathering*: we first obtain basic data by whatever methods are appropriate – interview, letter etc.
  (b) *Hypothesis generation*: we retrieve various possible formulations of the problem from memory, using basic cues (keywords or concepts) from the problem to access the knowledge we have stored in long-term memory.
  (c) *Information interpreting*: the information we have about the problem is interpreted in the light of our hypotheses to see if it confirms, denies, or is irrelevant to a particular hypothesis.
  (d) *Hypothesis evaluating*: we assess all the data by weighing up the pros and cons for each alternative problem formulation and then choose whichever hypothesis (if any) gives the best fit.

In lawyers' terms this method can be translated into six steps, each of which employs a range of legal research (and other) skills:

(a) Identify the facts.
(b) Classify your information in legal terms.
(c) Identify legal solutions.
(d) Use solutions to gather evidence.
(e) Evaluate solutions.
(f) Advise client of most appropriate solution(s); obtain and implement instructions.

It is important to recognise that these steps are not wholly discrete stages. In reality each level of analysis builds on and, in fact, tends to merge with the preceding step in the process. At the same time, it would be wrong to view legal research as a simple linear analysis, giving a single solution. Particularly in more complex cases you will be likely to identify a variety of alternative solutions, the viability of which must be determined. Your preferred solution is only likely to emerge after others have been researched and rejected, for example, because they do not coincide with your client's objectives, or because the evidence does not sufficiently support the legal argument you were proposing. In such cases research may involve you working on a number of parallel or overlapping lines of enquiry. Indeed, the process will often work in a cyclical fashion, whereby facts which you discovered and initially put aside as irrelevant to one analysis may lead you on to propose an alternative legal solution.

Each of the first five of those stages will now be considered in turn, though we have combined some of the categories where the connections are so close that it would have made the discussion too fragmented to have maintained the distinctions as listed above. The sixth stage will be touched upon briefly at various points in the analysis but, since it is a matter primarily of communication rather than research skill, it will not be treated in any depth here.

2.2 Identifying and Classifying Information

Your first picture of any client matter must be constructed out of the (factual) information obtained at the initial and subsequent meetings with the client, and from whatever written instructions and other documentation you have obtained. This information will form the basis for your case. In any matter you should have essentially three information-gathering and information-processing aims:

(a) to obtain the necessary client information to open a file;
(b) to establish your main reference points to the matter;
(c) to obtain sufficient information on the problem to proceed to a hypothesis, give initial advice and, if necessary, undertake further research and investigation.

The first of these, though obviously essential, is a matter of routine and office procedure rather than skill, and will not be considered at any great length in this Chapter (though see **2.2.2**).

2.2.1 ESTABLISHING REFERENCE POINTS

Casework does not take place in a vacuum. You need to understand what you are expected to do by your principal and/or by your client. Your perspective on any matter should therefore be informed by three reference points which, following Twining and Miers, *How To Do Things with Rules*, are usually termed standpoint, context and objectives.

2.2.1.1 Standpoint

When considering standpoint you are essentially asking the question: Who am I? On the face of it, this may seem a pretty silly question to ask, but it is significant once you recognise that your standpoint must change according to your objectives and the context in which you are operating.

So, it is not enough to say that your standpoint on a case is simply that of 'a solicitor' without also recognising that your standpoint must reflect your role in a particular matter and the experience that you bring.

For example, if you assume your standpoint is that of a trainee solicitor interviewing a client for the first time, then your perspective on the case will be substantially different from the standpoint of your principal, who may be a qualified solicitor of 10 years' standing. Similarly, your standpoint in a case is likely to be different if you are managing the casework as part of a team from that which you would adopt if you were working on it alone. By recognising your standpoint in a particular transaction you are focusing on different functions, different levels of skill and different expectations.

2.2.1.2 Context

The concept of context, or role as it is sometimes called, begs the question: At what stage in what process am I? The importance of determining process is self-evident, but the recognition of the stage you are at is equally necessary, for two reasons.

First, quality analysis and advice is dependent on an awareness of your starting-point. It is not possible to define your objectives unless you are sure what that starting-point is. To take an obvious point, do not assume, for example, that the client always approaches you about a matter *ab initio*. The client may already have taken some crucial step before consulting you. Some other agency may already have given advice – a Citizens Advice Bureau, or perhaps another solicitor. You need to consider how that different context can influence your approach to the matter.

Second, you should also maintain a continuing awareness of the stage you have reached in a case. This is not just a matter of good client care, it is basic common sense. As your volume of work increases it will become more difficult to keep tabs on individual matters unless you have a good diary system and your own routine of case reviews. This is important in all areas of your work, but it is absolutely fundamental in litigation where cases may be statute-barred because of failure to observe limitation periods.

2.2.1.3 Objectives

The most important reference point of all is your objectives. Your question should always be: What am I trying to achieve? It is a question which can be answered at a number of different levels. Ultimately your objectives are your client's. You must obtain a clear view of what your client wants (albeit in the light of what you advise could reasonably be expected). Your legal and fact analysis should keep those objectives in mind. You will inevitably have to determine your own intermediate goals in the context in which you are working, i.e. the things that you need to achieve at that particular stage in the process if your client's ultimate objectives are to be met.

2.2.2 GATHERING INFORMATION

It is axiomatic to say that your advice must be based on a thorough investigation of the facts involved; but, for the new trainee, fact investigation is a relatively untried skill. At the academic stage of training, facts are mostly presented as unproblematic. The facts are given to you, and it is up to you to provide a solution to the legal problem disclosed by those facts. Practice, of course, is not like that. The factual basis of the problem needs to be constructed or reconstructed by you. Much of your factual information will be derived from your first interview with the client, though the process of investigation will normally take you well beyond a single meeting.

In gathering information your concern is simply to find out as much as you can about what happened – or did not happen: do not forget that, legally, omissions may be as significant as positive acts. As a preliminary, therefore, you need to consider where you will obtain the information you need, and how you will begin to organise it (the main skill of fact management is considered more fully in Chapter 4). In this section, we will focus on two things: sources of information and categories of information.

2.2.2.1 Sources of information

Gathering information is primarily about finding sources of information. Potentially these are limitless, but in most cases your initial sources are going to fall into one or other of five categories: your client, other participants in the case, your colleagues, your 'opponent' and evidence of the *locus in quo*.

Your client is your most valuable information resource, and needs to be handled accordingly. Indeed, your client is often the only source for both oral and documentary evidence that you have in the early stages of case preparation. (In some non-contentious matters your client may be the only source you use.) The quality of your initial fact-gathering is largely dependent upon two closely connected things: your skills as an interviewer and your knowledge of the legal issues involved. Both of these will affect the utility of the information you obtain from the client. If you can maximise the quality, rather than just the quantity, of information you obtain at this stage, it will save you time and the client money later on. Do not forget that your client is not just a potential source for factual information. Many professional or commercial clients may have other knowledge you can exploit, for example, names of potential expert witnesses who could help in the case.

Other participants may also be relevant. Remember, the basic rule is that there is no property in a witness, which means that you have the right to approach any person (other than your opponent's client) for information. Though useful, this power needs to be used selectively for various reasons. It will increase costs (sometimes not just in terms of your own time – the police, for example, will charge a fee if you wish to interview the investigating officer of a road traffic accident). Sometimes it will be relatively unproductive – a witness may have already been interviewed by the other side and his or her perception of events may be coloured by that; in extreme cases, witnesses may have had pressure applied to discourage them from talking to you. Interviewing witnesses who may ultimately appear for your opponent may also carry a tactical cost, by disclosing elements of your strategy and direction in the case to the other side.

Other participants may also be a useful source of real or documentary evidence, for example, following a road traffic accident the police will produce an accident report which may be obtained either once they have decided not to prosecute, or once criminal proceedings have been completed. The report not only provides useful information for your investigation, but elements of it, notably plans of the scene and any photographs taken at the time, may be admitted as evidence at trial.

Members of your own firm should not be underestimated as a source of useful information. Most firms build up a network of contacts who may be useful – potential expert witnesses, private detectives etc. Much litigious work is run of the mill; someone is almost bound to have been there before you, and there is very little point in reinventing the wheel.

Opponents can also be very useful, albeit rather more reluctant sources of information, particularly in the later stages of a case. This is especially true of civil cases. The processes of pleading and discovery are extremely important. Intelligent use of the notice to admit facts (RSC, ord. 27, CCR, ord. 20), of interrogatories and requests for further and better particulars can lead to valuable information being disclosed (see the volume on *Civil Litigation* in this series). Even evasive answers will give you some indication of the other side's tactics and potential weak points.

A personal investigation of the *locus in quo* – the place where an event has, or is alleged to have taken place – may give you vital insights. Investigations are quite commonly used in personal injury cases, especially factory cases. In the latter it is useful to remember that the plaintiff's solicitor has the power under the County Courts Act 1984, s. 52, and the Supreme Court Act 1981, s. 33(1), to apply to the court for access to inspect any property relevant to the proceedings (e.g. the allegedly unguarded machinery). They will also have their place in criminal trials; for example, where a defendant alleges misidentification it may be helpful to make a site visit to ascertain lighting conditions, distances, potential obstructions of view etc. (See also **11.1** below.)

2.2.2.2 Categories of information

It is always helpful to have some system which enables you to categorise the information you are seeking at a particular point in time. There are no hard and fast rules on how you go about this, though most solicitors in practice will use a system of checklists. Many practitioners' texts now provide specimen checklists that you can adopt or adapt for your own use.

Some areas of non-contentious work require their own very specialised checklists, reflecting the information needs of those fields. Otherwise, much of the information you will be obtaining is reasonably standard across most areas of contentious or non-contentious work. Although it is pretty obvious that you will not be asking exactly the same questions of a client who wishes to sell a house as you would ask of one who wants a will drafted, the broad kinds of information required are not that dissimilar. In contentious work, your initial information needs are probably more standardised. It is suggested that any checklist you devise is likely to incorporate elements of the seven information categories developed by Sherr (1986) 49 MLR 323 and listed in table 2.1.

Table 2.1   Seven information categories

Personal information Name, address, phone numbers, family ties, work, age, nationality, income and health may all be relevant – though not necessarily in all cases.
Other parties Basic personal details; solicitor instructed (if any); connection with the client (if any).
Witnesses (if relevant) Basic personal details (though often these will not be known by the client and must be followed up by the solicitor at a later date); witness to what and for whom? Connections with the client.
Events Dates; times; place(s); persons involved; the cause and course of events; persons affected; property affected; precipitating incident to visiting the solicitor.
What the client wants Identify the main problem; desired outcome; difficulties in achieving outcome; persons to be affected by outcome.
Previous advice and assistance Anyone else consulted? Details of consultant; the advice given; action taken by consultant and by client; effects of any action taken. In Sherr's research this and the category following were the areas least often addressed by trainee solicitors when interviewing.
Existing legal proceedings Nature of the proceedings; parties; stage of process; past/future hearing dates.

2.2.3 CLASSIFYING THE ISSUES

Once you have identified the issues, you should seek broadly to categorise your information. This really constitutes the first step towards finding an appropriate legal solution (see further **6.3**). Such categorisation takes place on two levels.

At one level, we often try to fit the problems that come before us into our established framework of legal categories, so we identify problems as 'contract', 'tort' etc. After all, this is how we conceptualise academic legal problems. It is impossible to say that this is simply the wrong approach, but it does carry with it the danger that these sometimes artificial classifications of law will blinker you, so that you think purely along one line – contract rather than tort, for example, rather than looking across those subject divisions for the best solution.

As a way around this it is often more helpful to think first about your client's objectives and the legal remedy, or other outcome, that provides the best potential solution. The victim of an assault does not really care whether compensation is obtained via a claim in tort, a compensation order from a criminal court or an award of the Criminal Injuries Compensation Board. His or her concerns are more likely to be variations on the theme of: How can I get the most compensation for the least cost and in the shortest time? The managing director of a company is not going to be impressed by your advice to sue an errant supplier for breach of contract if the supplier is already on the verge of insolvency and your client is likely to be joining the queue of unsecured creditors. Adopting a remedial or outcome-led perspective can help you to maintain a more flexible approach to classification and hence to problem solving more generally.

Secondly, you may broadly classify the problem according to whether it involves matters of fact, law or procedure. This step is useful preparation both for constructing your hypothesis about the case (see **6.3.1**) and for preparing to undertake whatever library-based research is necessary (see **Chapter 6**). It may be helpful to explore briefly the nature and implications of these distinctions.

2.2.3.1 Law and fact

For the practitioner the distinction between law and fact can be expressed fairly simply: a question of fact is one which asks: What happened? It is determined by evidence, which may be either real (i.e. tangible things) or documentary, or the testimony of an eyewitness (or 'earwitness'). A question of law asks: What rules apply? It is determined by legal authority.

Although it is easy enough to provide an abstract definition of fact and law, they can be difficult concepts to apply. Given its significance, the difficulty we have in distinguishing between law and fact may seem rather surprising. At its root, it is difficult because English lawyers have traditionally treated the question 'What is fact rather than law?' as context-specific. In other words, different approaches have been applied in different situations. The following general guidelines may offer some limited assistance:

(a) *Normally, the question is resolved by the substantive law.* The statutory or common law rules governing a particular issue may well make explicit that a certain matter is a question of fact, rather than law, or vice versa. The issue is complicated by a lack of consistency. Thus, for example, for most purposes the issue of 'reasonableness' is treated as a matter of fact – as in the uses of the 'reasonable man test' in both civil and criminal law (see, e.g., *Qualcast (Wolverhampton) Ltd* v *Haynes* [1959] AC 743) but, on a criminal charge of malicious prosecution, the question whether the accused had 'reasonable cause' to bring the prosecution is a question of law for the judge.

(b) *Frequently cases raise mixed questions of fact and law.* For example, in cases of defamation it is necessary for a plaintiff to establish that the words used by the defendant had a defamatory meaning, and that they were defamatory to the plaintiff. The issue of defamatory meaning is a question of law, while the requirement of actual defamation of the plaintiff (ie proof that the defendant published the words complained of) is one of fact. Again, there are no general guidelines to recognising where an issue raises such mixed questions – it is a matter where we have to be guided by the substantive law.

Although processes of factual and legal analysis are closely interlocked, do not lose sight of the principle that factual and legal issues must be dealt with separately; each requires distinctive research strategies and methods of argumentation.

2.2.3.2 Procedure

The practitioner, unlike the academic, cannot overlook the significance of procedural rules. Questions of admissibility of evidence, of jurisdiction and of pre-trial or court procedure will provide a hidden agenda in respect of a client matter. For the trainee litigator, these can be the most difficult issues to spot, because they are the least familiar. You should not worry excessively about procedural issues in the earliest stages of a case unless there are major procedural problems looming – such as the expiry of a limitation period – or important tactical reasons for doing so (for example, where you might seek pre-action disclosure of documents to determine whether certain evidence exists prior to discovery – see RSC, ord. 24, r 7A; CCR, ord. 13, r 7). You will need to come to grips with them once it is clear that you are preparing a case for trial. You should bear in mind that decisions as to case strategy in particular can be influenced greatly by the effect of procedural rules (see **5.3**).

2.2.4 FROM ANALYSING TO ADVISING

Your normal aim at the end of the first interview will be to have obtained sufficient information to find a preliminary classification of the client's problems and to advise accordingly. Your advice at this stage is likely to be quite tentative, not least because there will be a significant amount of fact gathering, and possibly library research, to be done.

To be in the position to give any advice at all suggests that you will inevitably have had to identify a (set of) potential solution(s) to the problem. While it is important for the client to leave your office with some idea of what his or her position is, it is also important that your advice not only reflects what is achievable, but that it does not foreclose other potentially viable solutions, either in your own mind or in the mind of the client. Determining potential solutions must be distinguished from determining the *best* solution, which is the issue to which we turn now.

2.3 Further Reading

Anderson, T., & Twining, W., *Analysis of Evidence* (London: Weidenfeld & Nicolson, 1991).
Binder, D., and Bergman, P., *Fact Investigation: From Hypothesis to Proof* (St Paul Minn: West Publishing Co., 1984).
Holland, J., & Webb, J., *Learning Legal Rules*, 2nd ed. (London: Blackstone Press, 1993).
McElhaney 'The Trial Note Book' (1980) 1 *Litigation* 1.
Sherr, A., 'Lawyers and Clients: The First Meeting' (1986) 49 *Modern Law Review* 323.
Twining, W., and Miers, D., How To Do Things With Rules, 3rd ed. (London: Weidenfeld & Nicolson, 1991).

THREE

IDENTIFY THE LEGAL SOLUTIONS

Identifying a legal solution (or legal solutions) involves both analytical skills and research skills. Here we focus on analysis and, though research skills, in the narrow, library-based sense of the term, will be considered in passing, the main discussion of research skills has been left to **Chapter 6.**

3.1   Legal Analysis: Proposing a Hypothesis

Once you have established the initial factual framework of the case, attention shifts, in part, to the need to locate those facts within a hypothesis about the solution of the case. It may seem strange to suggest that your focus needs to shift to the law at such an early part of the process when the information relating to the case is likely to be incomplete. However, your initial hypotheses are nothing more than plausible explanations of what *may* have happened and its legal consequences.

You must never lose sight of this limitation. You are concerned at this stage with theory not *proof*. The whole purpose of developing a hypothesis (or hypotheses) is to provide you with something tangible which can then be used to assist further information gathering and evaluation. In short, it gives you a clear sense of direction. Developing a hypothesis itself involves two elements: the creation of legal and factual theories of the case.

3.1.1   THE LEGAL THEORY OF THE CASE

By legal theory we mean simply the construction of arguments for one or more potential legal actions, i.e., a claim for breach of contract, negligence etc. The creation of a legal theory itself presupposes two things.

First, it assumes that you have identified a legal right from the facts. To give a very simple example, you will have established that there is a contract, a term of which has been broken. You should also seek to identify the legal source of that right – in specific common law or statutory rules – a process which may involve you in some library-based research.

Second, it assumes that you can identify the cause of action accruing from that right, e.g. an action for damages for breach of contract. Again, this may involve research, but into remedies and procedural rules, rather than matters of substantive law.

It is also important to recognise that the relationship between legal and fact analysis is symbiotic. Although a legal theory is triggered by the factual information you have available, it also underpins the process of fact analysis. Your legal theory is crucial in determining how you organise and explain the facts of the case. To understand this point fully we need to recognise that a legal analysis has to incorporate a third feature, the *ingredients* of a cause of action (or of a crime), by which we mean the elements of the action which require proof. It is ultimately the ingredients which determine the manner in which you classify the facts. An example of this structuring can be found in figure 3.1, which is adapted from materials developed by the Law Society of Upper Canada.

3.1.2   CREATING A FACTUAL THEORY OF THE CASE

In developing a factual theory you are moving down a level from your legal analysis. You are now concerned more with the facts and evidence that must be mustered to establish the ingredients of a cause of action or crime (see levels 4 and 5 in figure 3.1).

Constructing a factual theory involves what Anderson and Twining call 'a creative process of using known data to generate hypotheses to be tested by further investigation' (*Analysis of Evidence*, p. 443). It requires a style of reasoning that is based on your ability to use existing knowledge and information to infer potential facts and explanations.

You are essentially asking yourself a series of very basic questions about a case:

(a)   What happened?
(b)   How did it happen?
(c)   Why did it happen?

Your answers to those questions will constitute your theory of the case. Your starting-point is, of course, the known facts of the case. Using that information, your attention shifts to what you have to prove to establish a particular legal solution. You can then identify gaps in the existing facts. This enables you to do two things:

(a)   Identify avenues for further research into what actually happened.
(b)   Identify reasonable inferences from the facts which may persuade a court that your explanation of events is correct.

The hypothetical elements of your case may be based upon your general knowledge, or on analogies with other cases – any solicitor will confirm that history does repeat itself, albeit not inevitably, but often enough to enable you to develop some reasonable hunches about cause and effect from past cases. These assumptions may then serve as guides to further fact investigation.

Before we move on, there are a few notes of caution. First, if you are going to use this technique it is terribly important that you do not lose sight of what is fact and what is speculation within your theory. Your aim must be to close as many of the gaps as possible by providing sufficient evidence to enable a tribunal of fact to make a reasonable inference about what happened. Secondly, it is not wise to reject facts as irrelevant early on solely on the basis of your theory of the case. As more evidence comes to light and your theory moves from the plausible to the provable, you can become more confident in accepting or rejecting facts on the basis of their relevance to your theory. Thirdly, it is also important to remember that what is 'known' to be fact by your client may well be contested by your opponent. The wisest basis on which (possibly) to develop and (certainly) to evaluate a theory of the case is an agreed statement of facts. At least by that stage it will be reasonably clear what facts are to be contested. These latter points also explain why we emphasise the need sometimes to develop a number of hypotheses.

3.2   The Relationship between Legal and Non-legal Solutions

As a final point, it is worth remembering that advice should take account of the legal and/or non-legal alternatives that are available. For example, where a client comes to complain that she is being harassed by her landlord, a potential legal solution might be to advise proceedings for breach of the implied covenant of quiet enjoyment. But a good solicitor should also recognise the limits

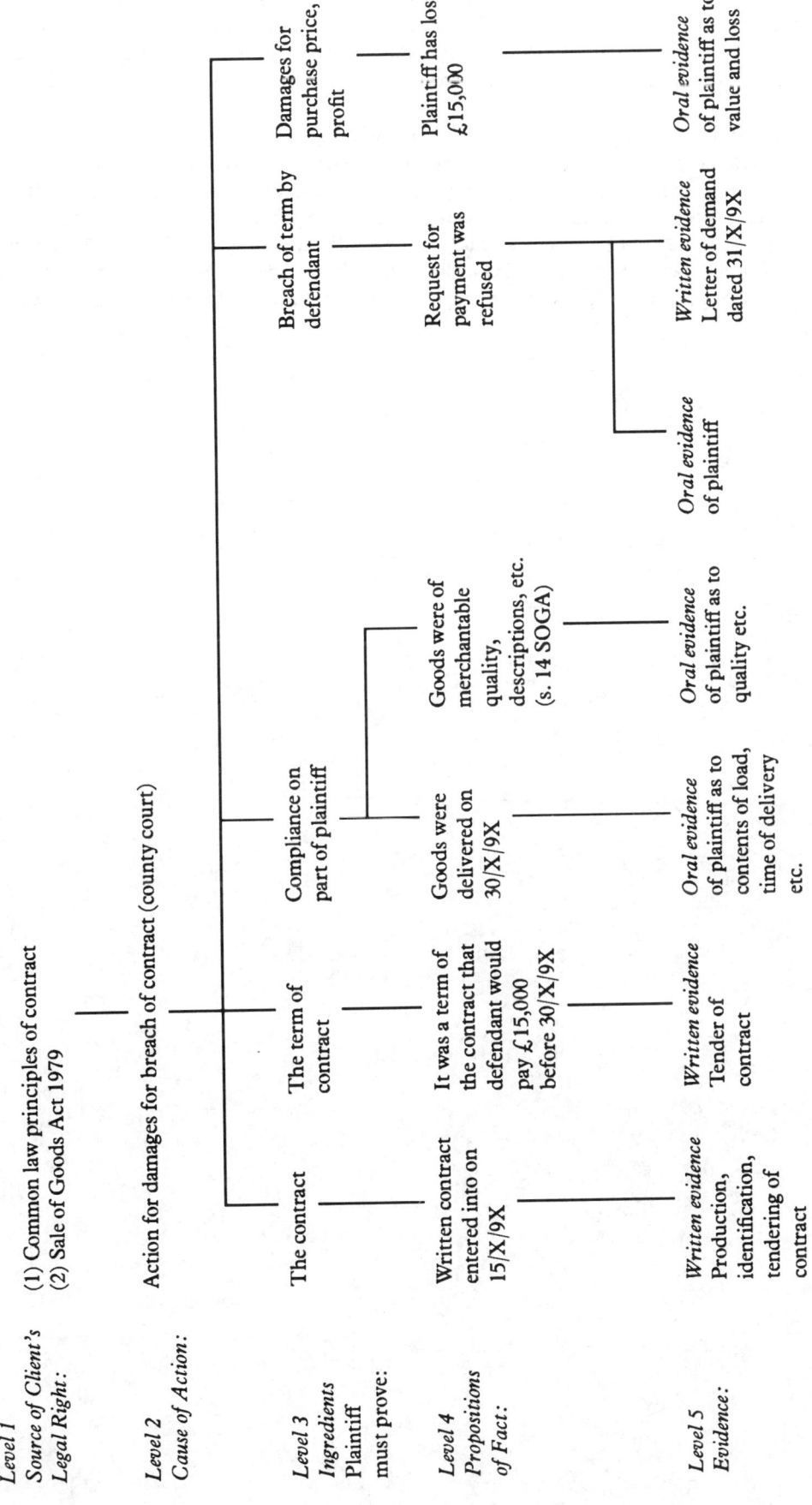

Figure 3.1

to such procedures, and that, in the longer term, the best solution for her physical or psychological welfare might be for the client to obtain alternative accommodation – clearly a non-legal solution. By focusing on legal solutions in this Chapter we are not underplaying the significance of non-legal alternatives. Where they are relevant, such alternatives should be considered.

What qualitative differences do potential non-legal solutions make to the analysis? The answer is, of course, that it depends! Often non-legal solutions need to be considered in tandem with legal solutions (as in the above example) and so the one does not necessarily displace the other. The analysis of a non-legal solution does not make the same technical demands on the lawyer; for one thing, you do not have to worry about the application of legal rules in the same way. But in terms of skills, there are few significant differences in approach. The appropriateness of any solution – legal or otherwise – must be determined in the light of the facts and of the client's objectives.

FOUR

ESTABLISHING THE EVIDENCE

In this Chapter we shall first consider the preliminary question of how we define and categorise the evidence. From there we shall identify three particular techniques that may prove helpful in identifying and managing the evidential data you need to obtain.

4.1   Distinguishing between Fact and Evidence

Once you have a basic hypothesis you must find the evidence to substantiate it. In so doing it is important that you recognise the qualitative difference between fact and evidence. The point of fact is the proposition you are seeking to prove; the evidence is the specific material presented in support of that proposition. The evidence is thus an entirely different entity from the proposition of fact. We can reflect this difference in the terminology we use, though there is some lack of standard terms, so that usage is not wholly consistent.

Fact propositions may be further categorised into the 'facts in issue' (or sometimes 'issuance' facts) and 'collateral facts'. Facts are in issue when they go directly to the proof of an ingredient of the cause of action or crime. Facts are collateral where they go to prove a fact in issue; i.e. they are removed one step further away from the ingredient, but are relevant because they make a fact in issue more or less likely. Evidence of character, for example, is normally brought in to prove a collateral fact – the veracity of the witness – rather than a fact in issue (unless it is admitted as similar fact evidence, when it will go to issue). The distinction between facts in issue and collateral facts is also reflected in the terminology used to describe the evidence brought to prove those facts. Thus we refer to items of 'direct' and 'indirect' evidence respectively.

The distinction between issuance facts, collateral facts and evidence can be illustrated by a simple example. Assume that you are prosecuting Marvin for participation in the robbery of the Wessex Bank on the High Street. Your case is that Marvin was driving the getaway car – a red Capri, registration D 123 ABC. Assuming for the sake of argument that no facts are admitted by the defendant, what propositions of fact do you need to prove to show that Marvin was implicated in this way?

There are three potential facts in issue here. First, you would need to establish that a red Capri, registration D 123 ABC was on the High Street when the robbery took place. Secondly you would have to show that Marvin was the driver at that time. Thirdly you would need to show evidence of participation – otherwise it would be open to Marvin to argue that he was simply an innocent bystander who got caught up in events.

The evidence adduced to prove those facts might be as follows. Diana is prepared to testify that she saw a red Capri parked by the bank with its engine running at the time of the robbery, and then saw two men run out of the bank and jump into the car, before it drove off at speed. Lionel will also testify that he saw Marvin at the wheel of a red Capri which was turning into the High Street about five minutes before the robbery took place. Which evidence here would go directly to the facts in issue, and which to collateral facts?

Diana's testimony that the car was there is direct evidence of the fact in issue. Lionel's identification evidence proves the collateral facts that Marvin was in a car of the relevant description that was approaching the High Street at a time consistent with the crime. It is not direct evidence of the fact in issue, but clearly renders it more likely to be true – to use terminology we shall return to in 5.2, it creates an inference in support of that hypothesis. So, what about the value of Diana and/or Lionel's evidence to the question of participation? Can you determine whether we have evidence to support the issuance fact, or evidence of a collateral fact here?

You should be aware that it is permissible to create quite lengthy chains of inference built upon collateral facts. It is not possible, however, to identify any general point at which such indirect evidence is too far removed from the fact in issue to be admitted. This point is determined by the judge on the basis of his or her assessment of the evidence's 'relevance'. The rules of evidence governing relevance therefore need to be understood before you can accurately determine what is likely to be provable.

4.2   Methods of Establishing Evidence – an Introduction

The process of establishing evidence involves skills of fact analysis and management. There is no single correct system for analysis and management. In essence, there are a variety of narrative and charting techniques. The most sophisticated of these involves procedures derived from Wigmore's chart method (see, e.g., Anderson and Twining, *Analysis of Evidence*). This is used in a variety of professional training programmes. It is a very powerful tool of analysis, but extremely complex and demanding to learn. In truth, it is probably too sophisticated to be of great assistance to the trainee solicitor or occasional litigator.

If the Wigmorean chart method is excluded, then there are essentially three evidence-gathering and managing techniques worth considering, though as Anderson and Twining point out, it is probably better to view these techniques as complementary rather than alternative. It is worth experimenting with various styles, until you find an approach that works best for you. This may be one discrete method or your own amalgam of elements from each. The three methods to be considered may be termed:

(a) Narrative technique.
(b) Simplified charting.
(c) The outline system.

4.3   Narrative Technique

There are a number of alternative narrative techniques. The one chosen here is adapted from one of the American 'trial notebook' methods (see McElhaney (1980) 1 *Litigation* 1). A trial notebook is a technique for providing total management of information in a case. The notebook itself can be pretty well whatever you want it to be – a single notebook, a ring binder, or a set of notebooks or files – which contains your notes and supporting documents on a case and is organised into a methodical set of materials which can be used in court.

Within the notebook you should have a copy of your working theory of the case and, whenever possible, a separate analysis of your opponent's case. The main mechanism for gathering and managing the evidence is a proof checklist. This will contain a record of evidence divided into three columns, thus:

Ingredients to be proved	*Supporting evidence*	*Source of evidence*

The organising principle is topical: you focus first on what you need to prove to succeed, for example, the need to prove the terms of a contract, compliance with those terms by the plaintiff, and a breach by the defendant which caused the plaintiff to suffer damage. The second column will then list the specific supporting evidence, and the final column will identify its source, together with a note of its page number in any agreed bundle of documents.

This is the simplest record to compile, but it does tend to overlook the conceptual differences, and the need to construct probative links between the ingredients (a matter of law), the facts and the evidence. Particularly in the evidentially more complex case, these distinctions may need to be followed through precisely – where, for example, one ingredient can only be proved by an accumulation of evidence supporting several facts in issue. It would of course be possible to insert an additional column between ingredients and supporting evidence to list specific issuance or collateral facts, but this would make the checklist significantly more cumbersome to construct.

The rest of the 'notebook' will contain the documentary evidence in the case and any research notes and skeleton speech you have prepared. All this material should be paginated or colour coded to distinguish the different sections.

4.4   Simplified Charting

Charting techniques are intended to provide a graphic representation of the law and evidence relevant to a case. The basis for our system of simplified charting is the Canadian material already considered in **3.1**. As we have seen, one of the strengths of this system is its capacity for representing the legal and fact analysis conjunctively. Another is the fact that it is one of the few systems capable of easy adaptation to support research of non-contentious issues (see **4.4.2**).

4.4.1   CHARTING LITIGATION

In litigious work, this system operates by representing the legal and fact analysis of a case on five separate levels:

Level 1. The source of the client's/Crown's right.
Level 2. The cause of action or charge.
Level 3. The ingredients of the cause or charge.
Level 4. The propositions of fact.
Level 5. Items of evidence.

This makes it a relatively simple system, though the charting can become quite complex if one takes account of two additional elements not represented in the chart in figure 3.1. The first of these arises out of the distinction between issuance and collateral facts discussed in **4.1**. Proof of collateral facts will introduce a new element into the chart between levels 4 and 5. This can change the form of the chart in a number of ways, see figure 4.1.

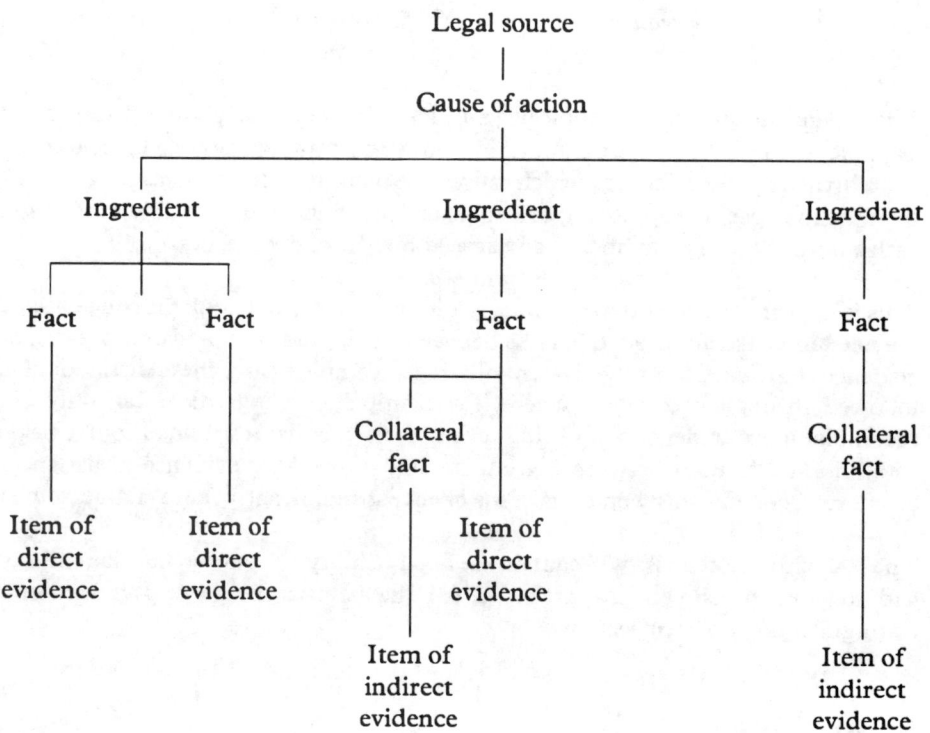

Figure 4.1

The second element reflects the desirability of attempting a chart analysis of your opponent's case. This enables you to note facts which, for example, are not admitted or are traversed by the other side, and thereby helps to highlight the points in dispute, and the nature of that dispute. For the sake of clarity, the analysis of an opponent's evidence is best done on a separate chart rather than superimposed on the chart of your own evidence, though the two could be presented in parallel on the same sheet of paper – provided you have a sufficiently large sheet, or can draw very small!

4.4.2 CHARTING NON-CONTENTIOUS WORK

The shift from contentious to non-contentious work creates a qualitative change in the nature of your analysis. Charting non-contentious cases tends only to be necessary where the legal and factual issues are sufficiently complex to demand particularly careful attention to the relationship between fact and legal issues; otherwise, simple narrative or checklist approaches tend to suffice. In essence, charting is useful in the drafting or analysis of the more complex legal documents, such as commercial contracts and leases, some wills, and other documents evidencing extensive transfers of property.

The system is once again based on a five level analysis:

Level 1. The source of legal rights and obligations needs to be identified, as in the litigious model, though, of course, our focus shifts to the nature of the transaction, rather than the substantive law. The primary source usually will be the document created by the parties identifying those rights and duties. Substantive law may still play a part (for example, where there are implied covenants affecting a sale of land), but often that role is secondary to the agreement.

Level 2. At the second level, it is necessary to identify the subject-matter to which the rights attach. This will normally be some species of property or personal obligation, e.g. in a conveyancing transaction it is inevitably the parcel of land being sold and purchased.

Level 3. At this level it is necessary to identify the fundamental rights and obligations attaching to the agreement, i.e. those things which are at the heart of the relationship between the parties. These are normally easily defined; to maintain the conveyancing illustration, the central obligations are for the vendor to give good title, and for the purchaser to pay the agreed price.

Level 4. At level 4 we should try to put some flesh on the bones of the agreement, so, if at level 3 we are concerned with *what* the fundamental obligations are, at level 4 we need to identify the details of their operation: *how, when* and/or *where* must each obligation be performed? So, e.g., what is the date and time for completion; how is the purchase price to be paid – electronic transfer or banker's draft etc? It is at this level that the analysis is likely to become complex, as one may end up with a long list of consecutive obligations. It is advisable to organise these both in chronological order and to reflect any dependency between the obligations on each party. To use the conveyancing analogy again, the time at which the purchase price is received will in turn determine when the purchaser is authorised to enter the property, so entry should be listed so as to reflect its contingency on payment.

Level 5. Finally, at level 5, we get down to the facts of the actual issue. The question before you is likely to involve some kind of problem: a potential delay in executing or performing the agreement; a disagreement about terms, even a complete breakdown of the transaction. You need to identify what the problem is; what obligations have and have not been complied with, and how the document (or the law) deals with that particular problem, that is, you need to identify the facts establishing both the breach of obligation and the remedy or action that can now be taken under the agreement. So, for example, where a purchaser pulls out of a house purchase it will be essential to determine whether contracts have been exchanged or not, since that will determine whether or not the legal obligations of the purchaser have been broken and therefore what action may be taken. If litigation is an option then, of course, we are right back where we started at the beginning of the previous section.

4.4.3 CONCLUSION

Simplified charting is a very helpful and highly flexible system of information analysis and management. Although the system works adequately by itself, and is sufficient for much legal work, it can be combined with other techniques to provide a more powerful tool. In Canada and New Zealand, for example, the system is combined with modified Wigmorean charting techniques, which enable the lawyer not only to track obligations and evidence but to incorporate an assessment of the probative value of that evidence. There is no reason why charting should not also be combined with the outline method. Outlines can provide a more detailed assessment of the probative value of the evidence than can the simplified chart alone, and may also offer a more thorough method of cross-checking the factual detail you have obtained.

4.5 The Outline System

The techniques described here reflect the system devised by David Binder and Paul Bergman (*Fact Investigation: From Hypothesis to Proof*). The strengths of their method lie in its simplicity, flexibility and power as a device for managing large quantities of complex information.

The purpose of an outline is twofold. First it is a means of marshalling your existing information. Second it is a mechanism for determining what additional information you require. The first is a prerequisite of the second. You cannot clearly identify what information you need (and what steps you need to take to get it) until you have a clear idea of the information you already have. It also follows that outlines must be amended or even completely rewritten as the case proceeds, to take account of the additional information you obtain.

Binder and Bergman's method is based upon five distinct outlines, which they call:

    (a) The story outline.
    (b) Outline of client's existing affirmative evidence.
    (c) Outline of opponent's existing affirmative evidence.
    (d) Outline of client's potential affirmative evidence.
    (e) Outline of client's potential rebuttal evidence.

These should be developed more or less contemporaneously, and together should provide you with a reasonably thorough and complete representation of the case.

4.5.1   THE STORY OUTLINE

The story outline provides you with an overview of the case. In it you should present the events leading up to the case in a chronological order. So far as possible you should represent both side's versions of events (for reasons which will be explained shortly) and identify inconsistencies in those versions which need to be explained. Gaps in the facts which are of importance and need to be filled can also be listed separately. The outline thus breaks down into three columns:

Gaps   *Events*   *Conflicts*

In putting together a story outline, it makes sense to begin with the events column, as this will provide the core of your case. It should focus only on the specific facts which constitute the parties' explanation of what happened. It is advisable to try to combine both your client's and your adversary's versions of events. This is not as difficult as it sounds. The odds are that they will agree on more of the story than they dispute. Attempting to combine the two stories serves as both a useful cross-check on your own client's version, and a means of identifying points of conflict, which should be separately noted in the conflicts column.

In developing the story outline you should bear in mind three general points:

    (a) Avoid including too much detail. It will make your outline cumbersome and threaten the coherence of the narrative you are seeking to establish. The place for (relevant) detail is in your evidentiary outlines.
    (b) It helps to be aware of problems of proof and probability even at this early stage, but do not be too quick to make judgments about the relevance or admissibility of certain facts. What seems irrelevant now may become relevant as more information becomes known. The extent to which you include evidence that may prove inadmissible is also a matter for your own judgment.
    (c) Following on from (b), you should keep in mind the importance of distinguishing between facts and inferences or conclusions derived from facts. Your outline should stick to the facts. Those are the only things provable in court, and if you start using conclusory statements, you risk overlooking the facts which go to justify the conclusion or inference. To take a rather simplistic example, assume you are acting for the plaintiff in a contractual dispute over terms of delivery. Your client has told you that he had assumed that delivery would be made on terms established in previous dealings with the defendant. This statement is not really evidence. It is merely conclusory. It begs a whole range of questions about the facts: how many times had the parties had dealings in the past? What were the terms your client believed would apply? What notice, if any, did your client receive of the terms? Had those terms in fact applied in all the previous dealings?

The stage at which you begin drafting your outline is also largely up to you. You could begin right at the outset, by outlining the events as described by your client in the initial interview. There is nothing wrong with such an approach. Though it may involve you in rather more correcting than a later start, it does at least mean you have started analysing rather than simply gathering the facts at an early stage. Equally, you may feel it is easier, especially for the purposes of identifying gaps and conflicts, to obtain responses from your main information sources first, such as police accident and hospital reports in a personal injury case.

It is a good idea to include some form of documentary reference to each statement (in respect of both events and conflicts) so that you can use the outline as a kind of index to your case file, and as a means of tracking key pieces of information or evidence.

4.5.2   THE EVIDENTIAL OUTLINES

The four evidential outlines are constructed around two dichotomies: the distinction between affirmative and rebuttal evidence, and that between existing and potential evidence.

Affirmative evidence is evidence which supports a party's version of events. Rebuttal evidence is that which weakens the affirmative evidence of an adversary.

Although the effect may look very similar, evidence which rebuts your opponent's case should not be described or used as evidence which positively affirms your case. To use our earlier robbery example (see **4.1**), evidence which proves that Lionel could not have identified Marvin as the driver of the car will rebut that allegation of identification, but it is not affirmative evidence proving the defence's assertion that Marvin was not the driver. Logically, proof of the one cannot be transmuted into proof of the other. This is not just one of life's academic niceties. As Binder and Bergman point out (at p. 16):

> That each party usually presents affirmative evidence regardless of the burden of proof is responsive to the way in which factfinders decide cases . . . they try to reconstruct history to learn 'what really happened'. Because of this, they typically expect a party to do more than poke holes in the opponent's story.

By contrast, the distinction between existing and potential evidence is rather more obvious. The existing evidence is that which is known to you when you begin the analysis; the potential evidence is that which you anticipate will be needed in the course of the trial – it is thus the evidential equivalent of the gaps in the story outline.

The evidential outlines can be marshalled on broadly the same principles. In each case the specific items of evidence should be listed under the ingredient it proves or disproves. If you are matching this up with the simplified charting techniques already discussed, then what you are doing is presenting the detail of levels 3 and 5 in narrative form.

One of the strengths of this system is the opportunity it provides to contrast your evidence very precisely with the contradictory evidence of your opponent. This is because two of the outlines can be presented as matched pairs. Binder and Bergman suggest one outline could contain both your client's existing affirmative evidence and the other side's existing rebuttal evidence. Similarly, the outline containing your potential rebuttal evidence can also be matched against the opponent's existing affirmative evidence. It might also be possible to outline the opponent's potential affirmative and rebuttal evidence in addition to your own potential rebuttal evidence, though in most cases this would greatly increase the workload beyond the minimum required to outline your own case and, given the level of supposition that could be required in some types of case, the effort might not be worth it.

The outline method can be quite time consuming until you are proficient at it, and does require some careful use of discretion and experience to determine just what level of detail should be incorporated. The system has its limits but offers a great improvement over less structured narrative methods.

FIVE

EVALUATING THE LEGAL SOLUTION

Once you have established a working hypothesis, or working hypotheses, you can use them to try to construct a case. But your ultimate aim must be to establish a single hypothesis or, at worst, a set of reasonable alternatives that will hold up in court. This means that, once you feel you have sufficient additional information, you should begin to evaluate your hypothesis or hypotheses. This is unlikely to be a one-off exercise, as it will usually be desirable to evaluate your case analysis at various points. There are no absolute answers to this one, as the most appropriate points for review, particularly in non-contentious work, tend to differ according to the nature of the transaction. In contentious work, many litigators would tend to suggest that there are three potentially critical review points. These are, first, just before the first pleadings are filed (e.g., the summons or defence in a county court action); the second is just prior to discovery; and the third is just before the trial itself, but once again there are no hard and fast rules.

In evaluating the case, you need to take account of four things:

(a) The existing information in your possession.
(b) The inferential strength of your explanations.
(c) The external (legal, ethical, procedural or personal) constraints on a course of action.
(d) Your objectives.

5.1 The Existing Information in your Possession

In evaluating a hypothesis you must, of course, contrast it with the known facts. As we said before, your initial framework should be provided by the agreed facts, but in evaluating your hypothesis you will also need to take into account those facts which are disputed. When assessing your hypothesis, try considering the following questions:

(a) Is the hypothesis consistent with the facts as presented by my client?
(b) Is there any evidence known to me which is inconsistent with this account?
(c) If so, can that inconsistent evidence by accommodated by the hypothesis, or must it be challenged or explained away?
(d) If the latter, do I have the evidence to mount a successful challenge?

5.2 The Inferential Strength of your Explanations

Insofar as your hypothesis is built on inference rather than fact, you should make some assessment of the inferential strength of your hypothesis.

We have already used the term 'inference' a couple of times without any real explanation. By inference we mean the process whereby evidence is treated as proving a particular proposition. For example, if A testifies that he saw B leave C's house carrying a bloodstained knife, that evidence could support the inference that B killed C. Inferences necessarily use an inductive form of reasoning (for a simplified explanation of the reasoning processes in legal and fact analysis, see J. A. Holland and J. S. Webb, *Learning Legal Rules*, 2nd ed. (London: Blackstone Press, 1993), ch. 9). This means that no inference is logically conclusive and may be viewed as more or less strong or weak. The less convincing the connection between the evidence and the proposition to be proved, the weaker the inference.

For example, B in the above case might explain that he found C already injured, possibly dead, and pulled the knife out of C before attempting to plug the wound, then, in his panic, he ran out of the house to get help, while still carrying the knife. This could weaken the inference that B killed C, but that in turn would depend on our willingness to find B's explanation plausible, i.e., on whether his evidence enables us to infer an innocent explanation in place of the guilty one. All litigation necessarily involves the use of such inferences. In assessing your hypothesis you need objectively to assess the strength of the inferences involved. How credible would your version of events be to an independent observer?

5.3   External Constraints

Your choice of solution will also depend upon your ability to recognise external constraints on any course of action. The illegality of certain activities, the constraints of professional ethics; rules governing the disclosure or admissibility of evidence etc., will all influence your proposed solution to the case. Of all these elements, however, it is often the personal constraints that are the most difficult.

It is often said, quite rightly, that lawyers are not trained social workers and should not play a part for which they are unqualified. Nevertheless, as a solicitor you will be seen by clients as a trained problem-solver, and, given the traumatic context in which many private *and* commercial clients come into contact with lawyers, it will almost certainly be impossible to avoid responding to their 'non-legal' needs also.

In essence, you need to be aware that the legal aspects of a client's problem cannot be considered in isolation, and this reality must inform your relations with the client, your problem-solving strategy and your advice. For example, there is little point in recommending a client to take a course of action which the client cannot cope with either financially or emotionally, and in such cases your advice may have to go beyond that which is strictly legal. At the same time, you must remain conscious of your own limits and recognise that a stage may be reached where it would be appropriate to advise a client to obtain other forms of professional advice or assistance.

5.4   Your Objectives

Any solution you propose must be matched against your client's objectives. If there is a lack of fit, you need to consider whether to drop a particular hypothesis. If in all other respects that hypothesis constitutes the best fit, it is probably time to suggest to the client that his or her objectives may not be achievable, and to obtain further instructions.

SIX

DOING LIBRARY-BASED RESEARCH

It may seem strange to include a section on library-based research when you may feel that one skill you definitely have by this stage is the ability to do legal research. Certainly, your existing research skills are by no means irrelevant. However, they are unlikely to be enough. The jump from the academic to the practising environment involves the development of some rather different research skills, and the use of research resources with which you may have little or no familiarity.

The actual process of research can be broken down into four phases (see further Price, Bitner and Bysiewicz, *Effective Legal Research*):

(a) Analysis of the problem.
(b) Preliminary review of the subject-matter.
(c) Search of primary and secondary sources.
(d) Updating of search.

6.1   Analysis of the Problem

The starting-point for research must inevitably be the client's problem. But clients' problems may be presented in very different ways.

During your training contract research problems will be presented to you by your principal and, increasingly, by your own clients. Inevitably, therefore, the form in which these problems are presented will vary, but they will typically fall within a broad continuum, which goes something like:

Can you find out when class 1A national insurance contributions will be payable on a company car?

I read an article a while ago which mentioned a recent case on the jurisdiction of national courts to apply the competition rules under art. 85(2) of the EEC Treaty. I think the name was *Auto* something or other. Can you find a law report for me?

Mrs Smith called in to see me about the house we exchanged contracts on last week. Apparently it was damaged in the storm the other night. The vendor is now saying that responsibility for repairs has passed to her. Can you work out what the position is on that, please?

I own a shop in the High Street. The cellar of the shop runs under the road. About six weeks ago, part of the cellar roof collapsed. I've had it shored up, but now part of the road surface over the cellar has started to sink and crack. Today I got a letter from the council informing me not only that immediate repairs to the cellar must be carried out, to their specification, but also that they intend to charge me for the cost of repairing the road surface. What should I do?

What is it that makes the last of these problems more difficult to research than the first? The answer should be obvious. In the first, the problem is discrete and already reasonably well-defined; we know the basic subject-matter, and it is sufficiently narrow to enable us to find a solution quite easily – assuming we know where to look. The second problem is only marginally more difficult. In such cases, we can go straight to the library and commence a search using the subject indexes of the appropriate sources. There is little need for problem analysis. The third problem requires a little more problem analysis, but is still fairly well-defined, though here our research strategy would need to be rather different because of the greater reliance on factual as opposed to legal criteria for defining the problem. In the last, the problem is *unfocused*. It is not particularly clear what the issues are, or how, or where, the answers will be found.

One of the key skills in practice is to identify and research unfocused problems quickly and efficiently. It is important because clients simply do not walk into the office with a neatly packaged problem labelled (for example) 'enforceability of covenants over land', or 'powers of highway authorities'. To be sure, the lack of focus will not always create difficulties. Your knowledge of the law may be sufficient for you to identify the problems and either give advice then and there, or to at least identify the issues sufficiently to make the process of research relatively straightforward. But this will not always be the case.

In determining what needs to be researched, you must first depend on the basic skills of analysis and classification already discussed. Your first job is to determine what your client wants advice on. Take another look at the last of our four research scenarios. The problem raises a number of potential issues: is your client in breach of any common law or statutory duty? If so, what? If so, can the council require your client to make immediate repairs? Can it legally charge him for the damage to the road? Even if these rights exist, has the council used the proper enforcement procedures? If your client has employed contractors to shore up the roof, have they done the job adequately? Could there be a case of negligence here, with the possibility of an action or set-off against the contractors? And so on. Each of these issues may centre upon substantially different questions of fact, law or procedure. Before you commence research it is therefore essential to separate problems into their constituent parts: to identify the factual issues and both the substantive law and procedural issues which arise.

Your capacity to identify the issues will depend in part upon your existing knowledge of the field. If you already have a reasonable knowledge of the area, you will probably be familiar with the research resources you need to use. You may have already identified key primary sources that you might need to look at. But at least some of the problems you will be confronted with will involve what are, for you, novel issues. In this sort of situation, you need to develop a capacity for researching problems from scratch – a technique that is often referred to as 'cold starting' (see, e.g., Tunkel, *Legal Research*). Cold starting involves the use of keywords to formulate a research strategy. Keywords are terms which you have identified from your client's story which you consider to be significant in identifying and structuring the problem. These keywords may be based on either the specific facts of the case, or on any legal concepts which you have identified as relevant. For simplicity we shall call these techniques 'key-fact' and 'key-concept' searching.

6.1.1   **KEY-FACT SEARCHING**

If you have little idea of the law involved, you will be forced to rely on key-fact searching. The trick in picking out keywords from the facts of an issue is to try to select those terms which are most likely to provide useful keywords. A simple technique which helps in this is to look for 'PEPT words'.

The acronym PEPT stands for parties, events, places and things. Together these four groupings provide the categories of facts which, in the majority of cases, will yield useful keywords. This does not, of course, mean that each category will yield relevant terms in every situation. For example, it will not be significant in determining criminal liability for burglary that the person you are defending is unemployed – though that fact may be significant if the issue you are researching is one of sentencing. You need to use some common sense, and your knowledge of law, to determine broadly what words are most likely to produce results. Relevant points you should consider when using the PEPT categories are:

Parties. Do the persons involved belong to a particular class – independent contractors, minors, lessors or lessees, company directors etc? Are they in a significant relationship – e.g., as cohabitees, vendor and purchaser, doctor and patient, solicitor and client?

Events. What event(s) created the problem – e.g., selling shares, driving a car, conveying a flat etc?

Places. How important is the place (and/or time) where (when) the event happened? For example, did an accident take place on the street, at work (during or out of normal working hours), on private property etc?

Things. Does the case involve a specific object (a van, house, computer or 50 tonnes of sheet steel) which might be relevant to the legal issue?

Keywords discovered using PEPT can form the basis for any subsequent literature or case searches that you might wish to perform. Key-fact searching is a useful device in its own right, particularly if you are using your facts to try to identify a potential cause of action. However, in most cases you will probably have enough knowledge of the area to identify relevant legal concepts so that it is possible to integrate key-fact and key-concept searching to provide a more precise search strategy.

6.1.2 KEY-CONCEPT SEARCHING

Key-concept searching involves identifying the legal concepts involved in the problem. In so doing, it is advisable first to distinguish between issues of substantive and procedural law.

In substantive law terms, keywords can be established by thinking about three things:

(a) The cause of action or crime charged.
(b) Any defence available.
(c) In civil cases, the remedy sought.

So, to give a simple example, in a civil action for personal injuries the cause of action would be negligence, for which the plaintiff would be seeking the remedy of damages; the facts might disclose some assumption of risk by the plaintiff, thereby raising a *volenti* defence. Thus each of the terms 'negligence' 'damages' and '*volenti non fit iniuria*' could be used for key-concept searching.

Key-concept searching can similarly be used to help research procedural issues. The main difference from researching substantive issues lies in the fact that we not only need to think about the cause of action, defences and remedies, but also about *context* – the stages of the process in which we are engaged. Does a problem arise before or after exchange of contracts, at trial or pre-trial, for example? So, if a client wanting a divorce from her husband is concerned that he might attempt to avoid a substantial settlement by transferring assets overseas, there are a number of research issues you could follow up. You might want to explore whether the court determining the settlement has the power to take assets into account if they are outside the jurisdiction; but it could be more important to try to prevent those assets leaving the country in the first place, so are there orders available that would do this? Thus, your key concepts could involve the obvious terms, such as 'divorce', 'family property' and 'financial relief' (which are so general as to cover both substantive and procedural issues), and the more specific procedural concepts such as 'emergency procedures' or 'injunctive relief', or, if you have sufficient grasp of the area already, '*Mareva injunction*'.

6.2 Review of the Subject-Matter

The simplest way to begin researching a problem is to find a book about it. Books about law, as opposed to books of law, which contain just the legislation or case reports, are often referred to as 'secondary' sources, to distinguish them from the latter, which are 'primary' sources.

At this stage in your research you should be attempting to obtain an orientation to the problem. Depending on your knowledge of the area, you may be seeking to obtain an overview of the law (the principles, concepts and language used) as well as basic references to primary (and possibly other secondary) sources. The purposes of review reading may therefore be:

(a) To familiarise yourself with the legal principles involved.
(b) To enable you to refine and/or extend your keyword search.
(c) To obtain references to primary authority which will form the basis of a search.
(d) To obtain references to other secondary sources which may form part of the review.

Academic treatments of the subject, including established student texts, may be an adequate starting-point, but they do have some limitations.

First, they are often organised according to conceptual criteria which do not always relate easily to the kind of fact-centred problems which will confront you in practice. This means, for example, that their indexes tend to be structured around concept as opposed to fact keywords, which may limit their utility.

Secondly, they may not be updated as frequently as key practitioner texts – especially the loose-leaf volumes. You may therefore need to do more updating than would be necessary had you gone to a practitioner text or encyclopaedia.

Lastly, they will not necessarily give sufficient (or any) weighting to practical or procedural issues which could be relevant in determining your strategy in a particular case.

As a result, it may make better sense to go straight for an encyclopaedia or other practitioner text at the outset. We will identify the general sources you are likely to use as a practitioner, and offer some comments on their strengths and weaknesses. Advice on particular search techniques for these different sources can be obtained from more specialist works on legal research, such as Tunkel, *Legal Research*; Clinch, *Using a Law Library*; or Dane and Thomas, *How to Use a Law Library*.

6.2.1 LEGAL ENCYLOPAEDIAS

These take a number of forms and serve a variety of functions. Perhaps the best known, and most widely available, are the three Halsbury works: *Halsbury's Laws of England*, *Halsbury's Statutes* and *Halsbury's Statutory Instruments*. The two legislative series will be discussed later in this Chapter. The Halsbury volumes are not the only major encyclopaedic works worthy of some mention, and we shall briefly consider a few other important resources before discussing *Halsbury's Laws of England*.

6.2.1.1 Specialist encyclopaedias

Most major areas of legal practice have their own encyclopaedic work. Most are in loose-leaf format and many are multi-volume sets containing the full text of legislation as well as commentary.

6.2.1.2 Words and phrases

The growth of legislation has meant that questions of statutory meaning are increasingly the dominant issues of law coming before the higher courts, to the extent that there are a number of specific resources identifying accepted judicial usage. *Stroud's Judicial Dictionary of Word Phrases*, 5th ed. by J. S. James (London: Sweet & Maxwell, 1991) and *Words and Phrases Le Defined*, 3rd ed. (London: Butterworths, 1988–90) are among the more commonly used.

6.2.1.3 *The Digest*

For researching points of case law, *The Digest* may sometimes be useful. It provides brief case notes, organised under quite detailed subject headings, on decisions from most common law jurisdictions outside the United States. It is not the easiest of encyclopaedias to use, and it can be misleading in some circumstances, but is particularly useful if you need to find older cases (which might not appear in *Current Law*, for example) or material from the Commonwealth.

6.2.1.4 *Halsbury's Laws*

One of the most valuable starting-points, particularly if you are researching a topic about which you have little or no existing knowledge, is *Halsbury's Laws of England*. The current edition (the 4th) was only completed in 1991, and some of its 56 volumes have already been revised and reissued. The whole work is regularly updated by a loose-leaf current service volume. *Halsbury's Laws* covers all areas of English law, by summarising the present state of the law with references to the relevant case law and statutes. The quality of its coverage is generally good, but it is not exhaustive! Its other great advantage is the detailed level of indexing, which makes it particularly easy to use for key-fact searches. For example, assume that you are interested in problems related to arsenic poisoning contracted at work, you could actually look up 'arsenic' and find:

> ARSENIC
> control, **18**, 1111
> importation in food, **18**, 1181
> poisoning, factory in, notification of, **20**, 514

Each of these references gives us an indication of the context in which arsenic is being discussed, followed by the number of the volume in which it appears, and then the paragraph – not page – number.

Apart from the two-volume index, searching *Halsbury's Laws of England* involves using three separate elements of the work. From the index you can go direct to the subject volume which is relevant and make a note of what appears there. Updating that text can be done using the cumulative supplement and current service volumes. The supplements are published annually and contain all updates to the main volume, up to their own date of compilation. It is therefore only necessary to use the latest supplement. The current service provides an update on everything that has happened since the publication of the last supplement, in the form of monthly reviews and a noter-up section.

6.2.2 FORMS AND PRECEDENTS

The use of precedent books will be discussed in relation to drafting in **11.4**. Briefly, there are two major encyclopaedic works on forms and precedents, the *Encyclopaedia of Forms and Precedents*, 5th ed. (London: Butterworths, 1985–) and *Atkin's Encyclopaedia of Court Forms*, 2nd ed. (London: Butterworths, 1961–). Both can be extremely valuable starting-points for drafting, but some of the precedents do need to be approached with a little caution as, stylistically, they have aged rather badly and reflect drafting standards that have fallen somewhat into disuse.

Forms and precedents may also be obtained from a variety of other sources, such as specialist practitioner texts (e.g. Pettit's *The Will Draftsman's Handbook*, 6th ed. (London: Longmans, 1990)) and journals (e.g., *The Conveyancer and Property Lawyer, Legal Action*). In addition, many firms now carry their own computerised precedents database for commonly used forms and standard letters. A small but growing number of commercial software packages are also available on the market. Some of these may be limited to precedents for quite specific transactions, such as debt collection, for example, though there is also a more generalist database available called *Magna Precedents*. The advantages of being able to call up a precedent on screen and customise it then and there are obvious. As more firms computerise their law office functions, this is likely to be one of the key growth areas of legal information technology in the 1990s.

6.2.3 COURT PRACTICE BOOKS

Most of these contain a mixture of commentary, primary sources and precedents. They tend to be published annually, or at least regularly updated. The best established are the *Supreme Court Practice* (the 'white book'); the *County Court Practice* (the 'green book'); Archbold's *Criminal Pleading, Evidence and Practice* and *Stone's Justices' Manual*.

6.3 Searching Primary and Secondary Sources

Your preliminary review of the subject-matter should have given you some references to primary authority, either legislation or case law, and possibly some references to books or journal articles also. Your first decision, therefore, must be where to go from here. It is not easy to determine just how much research is enough, and no book can give you anything other than a rather glib answer to that problem. For what it is worth our glib answer is that you should always do sufficient to convince yourself that you have the right solution. Whether this means you must plough through copious cases or rely on a textbook summary and analysis is for you to determine in the context of each problem. For the litigator it is important to remember that the best authority for a point of law is always primary authority, particularly in the higher courts and the more legalistic of our tribunals (such as the Inland Revenue Special Commissioners and the Employment Appeal Tribunal), and this factor, together with your own self-confidence, may ultimately determine your approach.

Assuming you consider it necessary to return to primary sources, there are one or two useful principles that are worth bearing in mind.

6.3.1 SEARCHING LEGISLATION

Unadorned versions of statutes are published by Her Majesty's Stationery Office and in the *Law Reports: Statutes* series. If you can get access to them, however, there are three series which are potentially of greater practical value.

Halsbury's Statutes is a partner series to *Halsbury's Laws of England*, containing an annotated version of all legislation presently in force, organised by subject. It is therefore the main resource for discovering whether legislation exists on any topic.

The fourth edition of *Halsbury's Statutes* was finally completed in 1991. The techniques are similar to those employed in respect of *Halsbury's Laws*. Begin with the general index, which gives you a wide range of keywords, each of which will refer you to a volume and paragraph within the main collection. If you are looking for a specific statute by title, you can take a short-cut by referring instead to the alphabetical list of statutes at the beginning of the Table of Statutes and General Index. Any revisions which post-date the publication of the relevant main volume will be found in the cumulative supplement and the noter-up. The text of very recent legislation will appear, alphabetically by subject, in one of the five binders of the *Current Statutes Service*; it can be found by reference to the alphabetical list of statutes at the front of the *Service*.

In *Current Law Statutes Annotated* all Acts are published in a loose-leaf format soon after enactment. Those which the editors judge to be sufficiently important are annotated by someone who is a specialist in that area of law. The annotations are not part of the Act, and do not, of course, have any legal force, though they can still be helpful in explaining the background, scope and operation of the Act. The current loose-leaf volumes are supplemented each year by bound volumes of the statutes, printed in order, according to the Chapter numbers of the Acts.

Statutes in Force should be a useful collection as it is published by HMSO in both microfiche and loose-leaf formats and is therefore easily and quickly updated when new legislation comes into effect. Material within the collection is organised under subject headings, but these are not always well indexed, so *Statutes in Force* can be rather difficult to use unless you have a very good idea of what you are looking for. The series is not annotated by any commentary on the provisions.

We are less well served when it comes to secondary legislation. HMSO issues all statutory instruments (or Statutory Rules and Orders as they were termed before 1948) individually and in annual bound volumes. Again, few libraries have the resources to maintain a full collection of these. The only other substantial source is *Halsbury's Statutory Instruments*, but this is by no means complete, and contains only a selection of the regulations in force, chosen on the basis of their perceived importance to the practitioner, and their unavailability elsewhere in the library. As with the other Halsbury series, the set is organised by subject-matter and the bound volumes are supplemented by a loose-leaf service. A number of practitioner texts carry the key SIs in their subject, sometimes in an annotated form (see, e.g., *Butterworths Family Law Service; Harvey on Industrial Relations and Employment Law* and J. Mesher, *CPAG's Income-Related Benefits: The Legislation*).

Local authority by-laws, which can be of considerable importance in some contexts, such as planning law, can only be obtained direct from the promulgating authority.

6.3.2 SEARCHING CASE LAW

There are a variety of indexes you can use to track down cases. *Current Law*, which is issued in monthly parts and then consolidated into the *Current Law Year Books*, is indexed by case name and subject. The *Law Reports* series also publishes cumulative indexes which are organised by case name and subject. These contain not only references to the *Law Reports*, but also to the *Weekly Law Reports*, the *All England Law Reports* and a number of specialist series as well (such as the *Industrial Cases Reports*).

If you are engaged in litigation, particularly before the higher courts, then, strictly speaking you should bear in mind that the *Law Reports* series (Appeal Cases, Chancery, Family and Queen's Bench) take precedence of citation. It makes sense in such situations to use those (if possible) from the outset, as it could save rechecking references later.

6.3.3 SEARCHING EC LAW

The primary sources of Community law remain generally less easy to access than their English counterparts.

For the practitioner, the main sources for the Treaties tend to be vol. 50 of *Halsbury's Statutes* or Sweet & Maxwell's *Encyclopedia of European Community Law*. These are perfectly adequate for most purposes.

EC secondary legislation (i.e. Regulations, Directives and Decisions) is more of a problem. All secondary legislation is recorded, from draft to final stages, in the EC's *Official Journal*. The great advantage of the *Journal* is its speed of publication. It is by far the most up-to-date source on Community legal and fiscal issues. This strength is partly offset by the search strategy required to use it, which is nearly as complicated as some of the EC's legislation (for concise explanations of the strategy, see Holland and Webb, *Learning Legal Rules*, or Tunkel, *Legal Research*). As it is, few practitioners will have direct access to the *Official Journal* (unless they are close to a European Documentation Centre or other university law library). There are essentially two commercially published alternatives: Sweet & Maxwell's *Encyclopedia of European Community Law*, and CCH's *Common Market Reporter*, both of which are multi-volume loose-leaf works.

The case law of the EC is best accessed by reference to the *Common Market Law Reports*, which are published far more quickly than the official *European Court Reports*.

Commentaries on the case law and legislation appear in a wide variety of generalist and specialist encyclopaedias, including *Halsbury's Laws of England* (vols 51 and 52), as well as more specialist textbooks.

6.3.4 SEARCHING FOR JOURNAL ARTICLES

If you wish to find an article on a particular subject there are three possible sources to use.

The *Legal Journals Index*, which only commenced publishing in 1986, contains full details of a very wide range of legal journals published in the United Kingdom, and so provides an extremely valuable research resource. It is indexed according to both subject-matter (with a brief summary) and name of author. Cases and Acts of Parliament which have been the subject of a commentary are also indexed under their title. *Legal Journals Index* is issued monthly, though some libraries take only the quarterly and annual cumulative issues. An on-line version is available for access through a computer terminal with bibliographic details downloadable to disk or paper copy.

Current Law lists recent articles under each subject heading, and each *Current Law Yearbook* contains a separate index thereto. The range of journals covered is not exhaustive and so it is less useful than the *Legal Journals Index*. It does, however, provide some assistance in tracing articles before 1986.

Very exceptionally it may be helpful to look further afield, in which case there is the *Index to Legal Periodicals* and the *Index to Foreign Legal Periodicals*. These are both American publications. The former is an index to all American journals, plus a selection from Britain, the Republic of Ireland and the Commonwealth; the latter indexes articles on international and comparative law, and on the municipal law of all countries which do not appear in the *Index to Legal Periodicals*. They tend to be available only in the larger and more specialist libraries.

6.4 Updating the Search

Publication time lags mean that most research will need occasional updating to check its accuracy. Updating techniques will be considered under the same headings as the initial search strategies.

6.4.1 UPDATING ON LEGISLATION

For general updating purposes, there are a number of sources that can be used. As we have already seen, these include the noter-up features of the Halsbury works, and other loose-leaf sources. *Current Law* is also a useful general source in finding out what has happened, as it contains a brief description, under the relevant subject heading, of any legislation passed during the year. It is not sufficiently detailed to be of substantive help, but it can make you aware of primary or secondary legislation which you might not otherwise have known about.

When updating legislation, however, we tend to be concerned with two specific questions: (a) Is the legislation in force? (b) Has the legislation been amended or repealed?

In determining whether legislation is in force there are several sources to be used if you are to be completely up to date. Your usual starting-point should be a copy of *Is It in Force?* This is part of *Halsbury's Statutes* and is published annually covering statutes passed in the last 25 years. The implementation (or non-implementation) of every section is listed there, alphabetically by the year and short title of the Act. To complete the update it is necessary to go to either *Halsbury's Laws of England*, where commencement orders are listed in the noter-up, or to the *Current Law* monthly parts, where commencement orders appear under the relevant subject heading. This will bring you up to date within a matter of weeks. Any final checking beyond that becomes more difficult. HMSO publishes a *Daily List* incorporating such information, but this is not carried by all libraries. Otherwise it is a matter of checking the pages of journals such as the *New Law Journal* or *Law Society's Gazette*. If all else fails, a phone call to the House of Commons Information Service may succeed, provided your inquiry is sufficiently specific.

If you wish to discover whether legislation has been amended or repealed, the quickest technique is to use *Halsbury's Statutes* if you are looking for detail on amendments or partial repeals, or the *Chronological Table of Statutes* if you just wish to know when an Act was wholly or partly repealed or amended. The *Chronological Table of Statutes* is published in two volumes by HMSO. It contains details on all Acts passed since the Statute of Merton in 1235. Its one substantial weakness is that it is published every other year, so that it is always at least a year behind and cannot be relied on for totally up-to-date information. The *Current Law Legislation Citators* may also be used in respect of post-1947 changes, but they do not give the full legislative history of Acts passed before 1947. The *Citators* contain information on all legislation passed in 1947–71, 1972–88 and 1989–91 respectively. Each citator is organised chronologically by year and Chapter number (it also gives the title). Any changes to an Act are then listed *section by section*. This is important; it means that to use the citator most effectively you need to know not only the short title and Chapter number, but also the specific sections of the Act that you wish to trace.

Suppose, for example, you wish to discover what has recently happened to s. 1 of the Criminal Evidence Act 1898 (c. 36). The latest changes (if any) will be contained in the 1972–88 and 1989–91 citators, and subsequent *Current Law Year Books* or monthly parts. The first of these citators has the following entry:

s. 1, amended: 1979, c. 16, s. 1; repealed in p. 1982, c. 48, sch.16; 1984, c. 60, s. 80, sch.7.

This shows that part of the section is no longer in force and that other elements of the wording have been amended. To work out the detailed effect of those amendments you would, of course, have to compare the various texts. The titles of those later Acts can either be found elsewhere in the citator, or you could go direct to the relevant volumes of *Halsbury's Statutes*, or *Current Law Statutes Annotated*. More recent checks can be made using the statute citator in the monthly parts of *Current Law*.

6.4.2 UPDATING CASE LAW

The best method of updating case law involves finding the citation in the *Current Law Case Citators*. There are two bound volumes – the first covers cases reported from 1947 to 1976, the second from 1977 to 1988 – and a third soft-cover volume covering the period from 1989 to 1991. All reported cases are listed in the citator in alphabetical order, based upon the first-named party to the case. The citator will then give a list of all citations of that case, and a reference to a summary of the case in the relevant annual volume of *Current Law*.

In addition to the citations of the case named, the citator also charts its subsequent history. If a case predates 1977, it is still worth checking the later citators, as they will tell you when the case has been most recently considered. If it appears, it will still be necessary to go back to the earlier citator, as the whole history will not be given in the latest entry. The form of reference in the citators is broadly the same so, to give an example, in the 1989/91 citator you will find (approximately) the following entry:

R. v. Secretary of State for Transport, *ex p.* Factortame [1990] 2 AC 85; [1989] 2 WLR 997; [1989] 2 All ER 692; [1989] 3 CMLR 1; [1989] COD 531; (1989) 139 New LJ 715, HL; reversing (1989) 133 SJ 724; [1989] 2 CMLR 353; (1989) 139 New LJ 540, CA ....*Digested*, 89/3081: *Considered*, 90/9, 2125; 91/70

This gives us quite a lot of information about the *Factortame* case. In addition to the references to the various reports, we know that it appears in the *Current Law Yearbook* of 1989 at para. 3081 and that it has been considered judicially in three later cases (two in 1990, one in 1991), which are also digested in *Current Law*. Note that where a court has done more than merely consider a case, the citator will say so, using the conventional terminology of approving, distinguishing, overruling etc., so we can begin to assess the importance of those later decisions directly from the citator.

For very recent cases, it may be sufficient to use the monthly parts of *Current Law*, by searching through either the abbreviated case citator, to be found near the centre of each monthly issue (if you know the case name), or the relevant subject headings. However, there is also a publication called the *Daily Law Reports Index*, which, since 1986, has carried digested notes of all cases reported in the broadsheet newspaper law reports. Cases can be accessed by subject-matter, case name, or the name of any legislation referred to in the case. The *Daily Law Reports Index* is normally up to date to two weeks preceding publication.

6.4.3 UPDATING EC LAW

Probably the most up-to-date source after the *Official Journal* is Butterworths *EC Brief*, which is published as a weekly newsletter covering the whole range of EC legal activities, together with a telephone support service. A number of the large law firms also publish their own briefing papers on EC matters. The coverage in these tends to be far more selective and in the form of news items or short articles, rather than the more basic legal intelligence of the Butterworths publication.

For some years, *Current Law* contained an EC law section. However, since the beginning of 1992 this has been replaced by a separate publication entitled *European Current Law*, which covers every country in Europe, except Turkey. The format is essentially the same as for *Current Law*.

More generally, the noter-up to *Halsbury's Laws* will also provide you with a general update of the issues covered by vols 51 and 52 in the work.

6.5 Using Electronic Information Retrieval

To date, the impact of legal information retrieval on solicitors' offices seems to have been fairly limited, though it will probably continue to expand as the technology becomes more affordable, and is increasingly used to support other lawyering functions.

Anyone intending to use a database system is advised to get trained on the system first. There is no substitute for that hands-on experience. Accordingly we will not attempt to teach you how to use the systems here but merely outline their uses.

Practitioners tend to be fairly divided about their usefulness. They are certainly efficient tools for updating cases or legislation, or doing specific 'words and phrases' definitional searches. Because of the way the search commands are implemented, however, they are less effective at more conceptual searching, and the onus is very much on the user to find an appropriate research strategy, as there tends to be little conventional indexing of the databases. Useful guides to search technique are published by the system suppliers, though P. Clinch *Using a Law Library*, (London: Blackstone Press, 1992), also contains a valuable section on search techniques.

6.5.1 LEXIS

The LEXIS database is probably the most extensive. It includes full text case reports of most cases reported in England and Wales since 1945 (tax cases since 1875); all public general Acts and statutory instruments in force; a small range of English periodicals; certain Scottish, Irish, Australian and New Zealand law reports; decisions of the Court of Justice of the EC; some French cases and legislation (in French) and extensive American materials. For more manageable searching this material is broken down into two tiers of segments. At the first level, these are called libraries. Each library is then subdivided into a set of files. It is only possible to search one file of one library at a time. Thus to search the English case database it is necessary to enter first the 'ENGGEN' library and then the CASES file. The system prompts you with on-screen commands, so accessing files is not difficult. Searches are then performed by typing keywords on to the screen and transmitting them as a 'search request'. The volume of information carried by the system does mean that the system is not updated as rapidly as some practitioners might like, with delays of up to two months on some parts of the system.

6.5.2   LAWTEL

The LAWTEL database contains a wide range of material, much of which is not available on LEXIS, including the progress of Bills through Parliament, decisions of social security commissioners, and white and green papers. This is in addition to the 'normal' fare of leading cases, and primary and secondary legislation. The limitation of the system is that the material is summarised, rather than full text, which rather restricts LAWTEL to an updating or initial research function. The system, however, is generally well indexed, cross-referenced and quite easy to use. However, it is by far the most rapidly updated, having a daily update feature.

6.5.3   JUSTIS

The JUSTIS software was developed in the late 1980s to run Context's series of databases either on-line or using the relatively new CD-ROM technology. CD-ROM (compact disk read only memory) uses essentially the same technology as the music CDs with which most of us are familiar. It is a major advance in legal database technology since it has a far greater storage capacity than conventional software – the equivalent of about 250,000 typed A4 pages of text can be stored on one disc. CD is faster than on-line searching, and since it does not require a modem, can be rather more portable.

In the early days of CD-ROM, cost prevented regular updating, but this is becoming less of a problem than it was, with most systems now offering quarterly updates. This does mean, however, that CD databases still tend to be less up to date than on-line systems.

The main Context databases of interest to practitioners are: (a) JUSTIS (on-line), (b) JUSTIS WL-CD, (c) JUSTIS-CELEX.

JUSTIS contains a full-text version of cases reported in the *Weekly Law Reports* after December 1984 and the indexes of the *Law Reports* (1981 to 1986) and the Criminal Appeal Office list of judgments (from 1982 to the present). It also has all cases reported in *The Times* and *Independent* newspapers (from December 1989 and October 1987 respectively).

JUSTIS WL-CD is a CD database containing both the full text of the *Weekly Law Reports* from January 1985 to date and the *Law Reports* index.

JUSTIS-CELEX contains an English language version of the EC's Celex database. It contains the full text of the *Official Journal*, which is subdivided into four sections: treaties, proposals, legislation and cases. JUSTIS-CELEX is available in both on-line and CD-ROM forms, and search procedures vary slightly between them (see Clinch, *Using a Law Library*, p. 183).

6.5.4   *CURRENT LAW YEARBOOKS*

In addition to the various JUSTIS systems, the *Current Law Yearbooks* have been published by Sweet & Maxwell on CD-ROM. The first disc was published in 1991, and contained the text of the *Year Books* from 1986 to 1990; updates maintain that basic database and will incorporate each *Year Book* after 1990.

Exercise 6.1

Consider the four problems identified in **6.1**. Using the research strategies and sources identified, see if you can provide an answer to each of them.

With the fourth problem confine yourself to the question whether, on the facts, the council could require the owner to undertake the required repairs.

You should cite full authority for any proposition of law. If you consider the facts are insufficient to advise, please say so and identify what further facts you consider it necessary to obtain before advising.

6.6   A Legal Research Checklist

To conclude, our library-based research techniques can be summarised in the form of a legal research checklist. This particular checklist has been designed so that it can be used, either as it is or in an amended form, as a standard research proforma.

LEGAL RESEARCH CHECKLIST

Background information
Researcher. . . . .
Memorandum for. . . . .
Commenced. . . . . Completed. . . . .

Strategy
Material facts. . . . .
. . . .
. . . .
Legal issue . . . .
. . . .
Keywords:
Fact. . . . .
Concept. . . . .

Database search? YES/NO

Encyclopaedias and digests
... *Halsbury's Laws*
... *Halsbury's Statutes*
... *Halsbury's Statutory Instruments*

... *The Digest*
... Other loose-leaf
. . . .
. . . . (name)
... *Words and Phrases*

Checked:
... Cumulative supplement
... Noter-up
Updated to: . . . .

Checked:
... Supplement
... Service
. . . . (dates)

Other secondary sources
Books:
Name. . . . . Date published. . . . .
Name. . . . . Date published. . . . .
Name. . . . . Date published. . . . .

Name. . . . . Date published. . . . .
Journals:
Legal Journals Index checked?   YES/NO
Current Law checked? . . . yearbook . . . monthly parts

Primary Sources

Legislation	*Case law*
. . . HMSO copy	. . . *Law Reports*/WLR etc.
. . . *Current Law Statutes*	. . . Specialist series
. . . *Statutes in Force*	. . . Daily law reports
. . . *Halsbury's Statutes*	
. . . Other source	
. . . .	
. . . .(name)	
. . . SI/SR & O	
Updated by:	
. . . *Is It In Force?*	. . . Case citator
. . . Statute citator	. . . *Current Law* (monthly)
. . . *Current Law monthly parts*	. . . *Law Reports Index*
. . . *Halsbury's Statutes* (noter-up)	. . . *Daily Law Reports Index*
. . . HMSO *Daily List*	
. . . Journal source	
Checked to:	. . . .(latest dates)

European law
General
. . . *Encyclopedia of European Community Law*
. . . *Common Market Reporter*
. . . *Halsbury's Laws*
. . . *Official Journal*
. . . Other source
. . . .
. . . .(name)

Legislation	*Case Law*
. . . *Official Journal*	. . . *Common Market Law Reports*
. . . *Halsbury's Statutes*	. . . *European Court Reports*
. . . *Encyclopedia of European Community Law*	. . . Other law report
. . . *Common Market Reporter*	. . . .(name)
Supplement or service checked?	
. . . . (latest date)	
Updated by:	*To date:*
. . . *Official Journal*	. . . .
. . . *EC Brief*	. . . .
. . . *Halsbury's Laws of England noter-up*	. . . .
. . . *Halsbury's Statutes noter-up*	. . . .
. . . *Current Law*	. . . .
. . . *European Current Law*	. . . .

Forms and precedents; court practice

Title	*Supplement or service date or date of publication (if not updated)*
. . . *Encyclopaedia of Forms and Precedents*	. . . .
. . . *Atkin's Encyclopaedia of Court Forms*	. . . .
. . . *Longman's County Court Precedents*	. . . .
. . . Other precedent book(s):	

Title. . . . .
Title. . . . .
Title. . . . .
. . . Journal precedent (ref:)   . . . .
. . . Database search   (ref:)
. . . White Book   . . . .
. . . Green Book   . . . .
. . . Stone   . . . .
. . . Archbold   . . . .
. . . *Blackstone's Criminal Practice*   . . . .
. . . Other
. . . .
. . . .(names)   . . . .

SUMMARY OF RESEARCH FINDINGS

6.7   Further Reading

Clinch, P., *Using a Law Library* (London: Blackstone Press, 1992).
Dane, J., and Thomas, P. A., *How to Use a Law Library*, 2nd ed. (London: Sweet & Maxwell, 1987).
Price, M., Bitner, H., & Bysiewicz, S., *Effective Legal Research*, 4th ed. (Boston: Little Brown, 1979).
Tunkel, V., *Legal Research* (London: Blackstone Press, 1992).

LEGAL WRITING

SEVEN

LEGAL WRITING

7.1   Introduction

You have been writing for 20 years or more, and you have been highly educated in a system in which writing played a crucial part. Why, therefore, do you need to work through this Chapter?

We think there are several possible reasons:

(a)   You will probably have done most of your writing in school, college and/or university, and while that seems like quite a lot of writing, it is quite different from the kind of writing you will need to be a competent legal practitioner.

(b)   Have you really had many years' writing experience, or have you had a year's experience repeated many times? In other words, you may have developed bad habits.

(c)   You may not have a clear idea about what makes effective writing. You need this in order to be able to vary how you write, depending on what you write and who you are writing to.

(d)   Your recent experience of writing will have been as law students. You will have written essays and answers to problems for other lawyers to read and evaluate. This means that you will have got used to the discourse of law (the language and method of reasoning used by lawyers) and will probably use it automatically in your legal writing. As a practising solicitor, however, much of your writing will be aimed at lay people.

The purpose of Chapters 7 to 9 is to enable you to become a competent writer in professional practice. When you have worked through it you will be able to:

(a)   list the strengths and weaknesses of your own writing;
(b)   identify and put into practice strategies for improving your writing;
(c)   plan your writing to take account of the needs of your reader;
(d)   vary your language to suit the needs of the content and your reader;
(e)   use reference books and other aids to effective writing;
(f)   write so as to avoid using discriminatory language.

7.2   Why Write?

Why did human beings invent writing? Consider the following documents:

(a)   a will,
(b)   a TV licence,
(c)   a letter to a client on holiday abroad, informing her of the date of her court appearance,
(d)   a degree certificate,

(e)   *Cheshire and Fifoot's Law of Contract,*
(f)   an inventory,
(g)   a diary entry,
(h)   an arrest warrant.

Why do you think we need to have these documents in writing?

Try to think of at least two purposes of writing and note them below:

(a)
(b)
(c)

You may have thought of others, but here are the reasons we came up with:

(a)   Writing enables you to communicate accurately through time. What you write can be stored and read later, either by you or others.
(b)   Writing enables you to communicate at a distance. Documents can be published, and so read by large numbers of people.
(c)   A written document may authenticate certain actions by being signed, witnessed, stamped, or marked in some other way, e.g. a will, certificate or licence.

Note that a will fulfils all three of these purposes; it is communicated over time in that it is written by someone who will never see it enacted. It is authenticated by being signed and witnessed, and is stored in a public records office for anyone to see.

These are the reasons why people write, but the purpose of writing these documents will only be fulfilled if their meaning is clear to those who read them. The information must be accurate and clear; writers may not get a second chance to communicate their meanings in the way they intended them to be communicated.

Lawyers need to communicate through time, over distance and to create permanent records. But the fact that their education and training immerse them in 'legal language' often leads them to forget that many of the people they write to find such language very difficult to understand. The effect of this has been to distance the law from the people and lawyers from their clients. Moreover, this distance between lawyer and client can lead to poor relationships, resentment and a feeling of powerlessness on the client's part, whilst lawyers may feel frustrated that they are unable to get their message over.

7.3   Know your Reader

One of the main aims of this Chapter is to make you aware that different readers require different approaches from writers. Imagine you need to convey the same information about an industrial injury to three separate people:

(a)   your client, the plaintiff,
(b)   the defendant's solicitor,
(c)   the client's doctor.

Consider how you would communicate this information in the three different cases.

Each of these recipients is an individual with whom it is important to establish and maintain a fruitful relationship. You will therefore need to vary your language and style not only to suit the status of the recipient, but to show your awareness of their individual requirements. The way you write will be determined by a number of factors:

(a) how well you know the person,
(b) how easy they find it to grasp the issues involved,
(c) their likely attitude towards the message,
(d) their attitude towards you, the writer
(e) their reading ability,
(f) their understanding of English, if English is not their mother tongue,
(g) what the outcome is likely to be for them.

To practise varying your style, try writing the following for a non-lawyer:

(a) The legal definition of theft.
(b) The effect of a derogation from an EC Directive.
(c) *Volenti non fit iniuria*.

Check how well your non-lawyer has understood your explanation.

It will have become obvious from this exercise that in order to get your meaning across effectively you need to be clear about the meaning yourself. Because we are familiar with and constantly use technical language and jargon, we no longer need to think about their meaning. It then becomes difficult to express the meaning in everyday language. The ability to write effectively begins with an appreciation of the needs of your reader.

7.4   Further Reading

Our aim in writing this section has not been to provide you with a comprehensive course in legal writing. Instead we have tried to draw your attention to some of the features of poor writing that have frustrated, infuriated or confused us as readers. Writing well is a skill worth developing for both professional and personal reasons. If you want to commit yourself to further development, here is a list of useful (and, we hope, readable) titles to help you.

Crystal. D., *Rediscover Grammar* (Harlow: Longman, 1990).
Fowler, H. W., *A Dictionary of Modern English Usage*, 2nd ed. revised by Sir Ernest Gowers (Oxford: Oxford University Press, 1983).
Garner, B. A., *Dictionary of Modern Legal Usage* (New York: Oxford University Press, 1987).
Garner, B. A., *Elements of Legal Style* (New York: Oxford University Press, 1991).
Gowers, Sir Ernest, *The Complete Plain Words* (London: HMSO, 1986).
Greenbaum, S., *An Introduction to English Grammar* (Harlow: Longman, 1991).
Quirk, R., et al., *A Comprehensive Grammar of the English Language* (Harlow: Longman, 1985).

The books by Garner, though based predominantly on the usages of the American legal system, are nevertheless invaluable as guides to writing good English.

The National Consumer Council, Plain English Campaign and Clarity (a movement for the simplification of legal English) have produced guidelines on plain English for letter writing and drafting. Useful publications are:

Adler, M., *Clarity for Lawyers* (London: Law Society, 1990).
National Consumer Council, *Plain English for Lawyers* (London: National Consumer Council, 1984).
Wydick, R., *Plain Engish for Lawyers* (Carolina Academic Press, 1985).

EIGHT

STRATEGIES FOR EFFECTIVE
LEGAL WRITING

8.1   Planning

To ensure that your message is clear and precise you must *know exactly what you mean to say and how you mean to say it to this particular recipient.*

Begin by clarifying the purpose of your communication. Are you merely giving information or are you attempting to persuade someone to a particular course of action, or perhaps responding to a complaint? Decide what you want to happen as a result of what you write.

Think carefully about the content. Do you have all the information you need? Is it accurate? Remember, others will rely on what you say.

Decide the most logical and appropriate structure for your content. For example, if you want to persuade the recipient to respond in a particular way, you must indicate the benefits of following such a course of action and the likely drawbacks of failing to follow it. You may therefore wish to present the information little by little, slowly building up a persuasive case. If on the other hand you are providing information, you must organise the content so that the information can be quickly and unambiguously understood. Look for an obvious logical order, for example, a sequence of events over a period of time. If you cannot find one, decide how best to order the content and present the information clearly, accurately and concisely.

Remember that each paragraph should deal with one main topic. The most common structure for a paragraph is to begin with a word or phrase linking it to the previous one and then to go on to introduce the new topic. The rest of the paragraph explains, illustrates, modifies or otherwise develops this topic.

Moreover, you should vary the length of your paragraphs to add variety and interest, just as you would vary the sentence length.

Consider how your writing will look on the page. There is nothing more daunting for the reader than closely spaced, undivided blocks of print. If you are providing a lot of information, use headings, subheadings and a numbering system to break up the information on the page and to indicate the relationship between various pieces of information.

To summarise: planning involves

(a)   *Knowing your purpose.*
(b)   *Knowing your content.*

47

(c)   *Knowing your structure.*
(d)   *Deciding your layout.*

8.2   Say What You Mean to Say

No doubt you are aware that there are differences between the spoken and written language. Make a note at this point of what you think those main differences are.

(a)

(b)

(c)

You may have noted that the spoken language has a number of features that are absent from the written. If you watch people talking you will see that not only do they use the vocabulary and grammar of the language to communicate their meaning, they also convey meaning by using body language (gesture, posture, facial expression). Body language tells each of the participants the state of mind and level of understanding and interest of the others. Moreover, you will hear the speakers emphasise certain points in what they say by the tone of voice that they use. Speakers and listeners utter 'wordless' sounds from time to time, for example, 'ugh', 'um', 'phew', 'ouch', which convey disgust, agreement, sympathy, the need for time to think and so on. It is this combination of body language, intonation and wordless sounds which make the spoken language so much easier to understand than the written.

Furthermore, a conversation allows the participants to respond immediately to what is said, and it allows for modification of what is said in the light of that response. With writing there is no immediate response, so you need to get it right first time. It is therefore hardly surprising that competent writing is thought to be such a difficult skill to master.

Another difference you may have noted is that in writing we use less frequent words and phrases than we would use in speech. Adherence to this practice is probably the main source of much of today's obscure or unintelligible 'officialese'! For example:

My client is seeking a figure in the region of £25,000.

I have given implicit instructions to my staff to keep noise to an absolute minimum due to the close proximity of residential properties.

Since clarity is your main aim, try to avoid the appearance of pomposity and unnatural, unnecessary formality which infrequent words and phrases give to writing. For the same reasons you should avoid long-windedness, unnecessary jargon and overlong sentences.

Criticism of lawyers' communication skills is not new. In 1702 Daniel Defoe wrote that the English of the clergy, physicians, academics and lawyers: 'has been far from Polite, full of Stiffness and Affectation, hard Words, and long unusual coupling of Syllables and Sentences' (*Essays upon Several Subjects: or, Effectual Ways for Advancing the Interest of the Nation*, p. 234).

As we noted earlier, competent written communication involves recognising and anticipating the needs of your reader. This involves more than explaining complex legal terminology to the lay person, which you attempted to do in 7.3. The degree of 'stiffness' you select for your communication may determine whether your relationship prospers or not. You need to select language forms (grammar and vocabulary) which not only make the meaning clear as rapidly and straightforwardly as possible but which do so with an appropriate degree of formality.

We suggest you adopt the *three Cs* as your starting-point: *be clear, concise, correct.*

    (a)   Use frequently used words and phrases instead of infrequently used ones (see above).

    (b)   Avoid clumsy and inelegant words and phrases.

    (c)   Use active verbs instead of passive.

    (d)   Omit redundant words and phrases.

    (e)   Avoid using jargon and technical terms unless:

        (i)   there is no alternative, and

        (ii)   the reader will understand them.

    (f)   Avoid long and complex sentences.

8.2.1   INELEGANT WRITING

Some formerly infrequent usages have now become common in both speech and writing. Writers pad out their communications with additional words to avoid using a single word. For example:

At a later date (later).
Until such time as (until).
In the event that (if).
Prior to (before).
Subsequent to (after).
On a regular basis (regularly).

In letter writing this padding device is often used to link paragraphs:

So far as this matter *is concerned*, we will deal with it *as a matter of urgency*.

We would prefer something like:

We will deal with this matter urgently.

Clarify your thoughts when planning your communication so as to link your paragraphs concisely and avoid these clumsy devices. Using concise language will bring elegance to your writing.

8.2.2   ACTIVE V PASSIVE

The use of the passive is one of the most common reasons for over-formality in writing, because it concentrates on what happened, treating the people involved as less important. Here is an example:

When you arrive at the court you WILL BE MET by my clerk. You WILL BE TAKEN to court 2 where the case WILL BE HEARD by Judge Jeffries.

This may be acceptable if you have a very formal relationship with your client, but the effect is to de-personalise the communication. It would be more direct and friendly (and probably more reassuring) to write:

My clerk, Brian, will meet you when you arrive and take you to court 2. Judge Jeffries will be hearing the case.

8.2.3   REDUNDANCY

Redundancy is an important part of the language. It conveys the same message in more than one way so as to ensure understanding. For example, when you ask a question, the fact that it is a question may be conveyed:

    (a) by the use of a question word,
    (b) by a change in word order, and
    (c) by intonation, or in writing by punctuation: WHAT time SHALL WE meet tonight?

The redundancy that is built into language in this way is unavoidable and useful. However, the kind of redundancy that is not acceptable is the insertion of unnecessary words and phrases. These have the effect of padding out your writing, reducing its clarity and conciseness and diluting the force of the message. Here are some examples:

FORWARD planning, CLOSE proximity, DULY incorporated, I enclose HEREWITH, TRIED and tested.

8.2.4   JARGON AND TECHNICAL TERMS

All occupations and professions have words and phrases which the members of those groups understand. As we noted earlier, outsiders often have difficulty with this and it can act as a barrier to good communication. Lawyers have often been accused of mystifying the public with their insensitive use of jargon and technical legal terms. Consider this example from a letter to a client:

So far as your house purchase is concerned I enclose herewith a copy of a Deed of Grant dated 1967 which conveys to the Water Board in fee simple a right of easement to enter in and upon the lands.

The solicitor will have lost the reader long before any explanation is given, if indeed any is forthcoming.

8.2.5   LONG AND COMPLEX SENTENCES

What makes a 'long sentence' is quite difficult to define because readers have different levels of reading ability. While one person might find a 12-word sentence difficult to cope with, another might regard it as simplistic and patronising. The average reader seems to be happy with sentences of 15 to 20 words, but this is a rough estimate. The degree of understanding will also depend on the complexity of the sentence. By this we mean the number and length of subordinate clauses. Subordinate clauses are 'sentences within sentences' and consequently make more demands on the reader's memory. Consider the following (subordinate clauses in capitals):

Mr Smith, WHO IS WHEELCHAIR BOUND AS A RESULT OF A RECENT ACCI-DENT, is unable to come to these premises, ALTHOUGH I HAVE SEVERAL TIMES OFFERED TO SEND A TAXI, WHICH THE FIRM IS HAPPY TO PAY FOR, and would prefer to meet us at his home IF YOU ARE AGREEABLE.

You will see that there are seven separate ideas in the sentence, each of which could be written as a simple sentence. However, if you were to do that you would find that what you wrote appeared childish. Nevertheless, we do not consider the sentence satisfactory. One effect of subordinate clauses is to alter the chronology of events, so one way to approach rewriting is first of all to work out the actual sequence of events. Then rewrite the sentence taking care not to confuse your reader about the order of events, though you do not have to keep strictly to the chronology. Here is the sequence of events:

Mr Smith has recently had an accident and is confined to a wheelchair. He is unable to come to the office. We have offered him a taxi at our expense, but he is still unable to come. If you agree, we can meet at his home.

We suggest that the paragraph could be worded as follows:

> Mr Smith is unable to come to the office because he has recently had an accident and is confined to a wheelchair. We have offered to send a taxi for him at the firm's expense, but he is still unable to come. He is happy to meet us at his home if you agree.

You do not need to avoid subordinate clauses altogether, but remember that the more you have in a sentence, the more difficult it becomes to understand it.

8.2.6 USING 'CORRECT GRAMMAR'

There is a debate in educational and professional circles about what constitutes 'correct grammar'. See if you can write down in a few sentences what you understand by the term.

The word 'grammar' has many meanings, some popular, some technical. For linguists and others who understand language the main meaning of 'grammar' is a *description* of the rules that underlie a user's ability to understand, speak and (possibly) write a given language. In its popular sense, 'grammar' is a set of rules which *prescribe* how users should speak and write. Thus we have the distinction between 'correct' and 'incorrect' English. Bear in mind that there are many varieties of English (such as American English, Cockney, Glaswegian) each of which can be described and therefore can be said to have a grammar. However, most varieties of English are spoken varieties. The written form is expected to be usable by all speakers of English no matter which variety they learned as children. This written form of English is often referred to as 'standard English'. It is the variety of English used by all the national institutions, taught in schools, learned by non-English speakers and used in international communication.

We often import aspects of the variety we learned as children into the standard variety. Typical examples would be the restricted forms of the verb 'to be' – 'they was', 'you was', 'we was' – or the double negative, 'You don't know nothing about it'. While these utterances in no way obscure the meaning of what is being conveyed, they are not regarded as acceptable in standard English, particularly in writing. Standard English has prestige because it is perceived as the language of the educated. Many people therefore believe it is superior to other varieties, so that non-standard forms are 'incorrect'. However, we prefer to think of grammatical forms as *appropriate* or *inappropriate*, rather than 'correct' or 'incorrect'.

Moreover, since the rules of language are constantly adapting to changes in language use, what is considered 'correct' at one time may be out of date some years later. For instance you may have been told at school that the word 'different' should be followed by 'from'. Modern usage has replaced 'from' with 'to', so that 'different to' could now be considered appropriate. Although it would make life a lot simpler if there were a hard-and-fast set of rules, the effect would be to freeze the 'official' language in time, and it would not take account of the process of continuous change that language is undergoing. In the end the 'rules' would simply be disregarded. Compare the fate of spelling in English! (More on this later.)

When a language change is identified, it is usually difficult to know when it becomes appropriate to incorporate it into the standard language. A good example is the distinction between 'less' and 'fewer', as in

> There are less people here than there were last year.

In the traditional, prescriptive view of grammar 'fewer' is the 'correct' form. However, the use of 'less' is now so prevalent that we cannot be sure whether it may safely be used or not. David Crystal in *Rediscover Grammar* (Harlow: Longmans, 1990) says that the use of 'less' instead of 'fewer' is 'widely criticised' (p. 119).

Reactions to new usage can be so extreme as to make people ill! For years now there has been debate about the word 'hopefully', used as in 'Hopefully this case will soon be settled' instead of the traditionally acceptable 'I hope that . . .' or 'It is hoped that . . .'. In *Good English and the*

Grammarian, Sidney Greenbaum tells of the responses of members of a panel of authors and editors to this usage:

> It is barbaric, illiterate, offensive, damnable, and inexcusable.

> The most horrible usage of our time.

> I have sworn eternal war on this bastard adverb.

> 'Hopefully' so used is an abomination and its adherents should be lynched.

> This is one that makes me physically ill.

Fortunately, help is at hand. There are several useful reference books you can turn to for advice. The best known is H. W. Fowler, *A Dictionary of Modern English Usage*, 2nd ed. (Oxford: Oxford University Press, 1983). *Rediscover Grammar* by David Crystal (Harlow: Longman, 1990) is an up to date, readable grammar book. If you want to look into contemporary English grammar in detail, we recommend R. Quirk et al., *A Comprehensive Grammar of the English Language* (London: Longman, 1985). *An Introduction to English Grammar* by S. Greenbaum (Harlow: Longman, 1991) is more accessible, and also includes useful sections on punctuation, spelling, usage and style, together with exercises.

You will find a complete list of books in **9.2**.

How comfortable would you feel about using the following in your writing?

    (a)   Anyone who thinks THEY have reasonable grounds for complaint should send THEIR objections to . . ..
    (b)   If you require any further assistance, please contact MYSELF or my assistant.
    (c)   I shall be unable to meet you on the 17th DUE TO circumstances beyond my control.

    (a)   The traditional rule is that pronouns ('they') or determiners ('their') which refer back to a singular indefinite pronoun ('anyone') must be singular: therefore 'they' and 'their' must be replaced with 'he' and 'his'. Greenbaum considers this rule the 'traditional choice for formal writing' (p. 144).

Fowler, *A Dictionary of Modern English Usage*, rejects the use of the plural pronoun and determiner 'they' and 'their' because it 'sets the literary man's teeth on edge' (p. 404). He says further: 'Have the patrons of *they* etc. made up their minds yet between *Everyone* was *blowing their noses* (or *nose*) and *Everyone* were *blowing their noses*?'

Today, however, many writers use 'they' and 'their' because they are commonly used as singular pronoun and determiner in the spoken language. Unfortunately this usage is far from being generally accepted.

Fowler goes on to reject 'he/she' and 'his/her', which, although 'correct', are 'so clumsy as to be ridiculous'. He recommends 'he' and 'his': 'where the matter of sex is not conspicuous or important the masculine form shall be allowed to represent a person instead of a man'.

This is a convention you will be familiar with from the interpretation of statutes and other legal documents. However, as Mark Adler says in *Clarity for Lawyers* (London: Law Society, 1990), men generally do not realise how irritating women find this traditional assumption that everyone is a man. 'Nor are they mollified by the answer that the Law of Property Act provides that the "masculine includes the feminine"' (p. 71). Today many writers prefer to use the gender-neutral 'they' and 'their', etc. where possible. You might choose instead to use roughly equal numbers of 'he', 'his' etc. and 'she', 'her' etc. in your writing, or alternatively to rephrase the sentence to avoid the problem altogether.

So sentence (a) above might be rephrased thus:

If you think you have reasonable grounds for complaint you should send your objections to . . ..

(b)   The reflexive pronouns (-self, -selves) may be used to give emphasis, as in:

Are you sure he received the letter? Yes, I took it round there myself.

The traditional rule prohibits their use as a substitute for the object pronouns 'you', 'me', 'him', 'her', 'us', 'them', though this usage is now quite common in both spoken and written English and is often found in solicitors' letters. It is a usage which makes many people feel particularly uncomfortable.

(c)   Prescriptive grammar requires 'owing to' after a verb phrase, as in 'The match WAS CANCELLED OWING TO the bad weather', and 'due to' after a noun phrase, as in 'THE CANCELLATION OF THE MATCH was DUE TO bad weather'. However, many speakers and writers now regard these usages as interchangeable. If you are in doubt about either of them you can always play safe and use 'because of'.

You are lawyers, not language experts, but the way you use language is crucial to your professional success and standing. You will therefore want some certainty about what is and is not acceptable. We recommend that you select a work of reference and keep to the advice that it gives. Remember, however, that it may be updated from time to time to reflect changes in acceptable usage. You will need to update, too.

8.2.7   THE SENTENCE

Failure to write complete sentences is a common feature of poor writing. Here are three examples in letter-writing:

THANKING you for your kind attention.
ASSURING you of our best attention at all times.
With reference to your letter of 16th May.

These phrases fail to observe the basic rules governing the grammatical make-up of sentences. But what is a sentence? You probably think you know one when you see one, but could not provide a satisfactory definition. In fact the 'sentence' is very difficult to define. Some of you might say it begins with a capital letter and ends with a full stop. This (inadequate) definition fails to appreciate that we do not signal capital letters when we speak, and only indicate the existence of a sentence end by our intonation. Moreover, the words between the capital letter and the full stop still may not form an acceptable sentence.

Others will define a sentence by saying that it must be grammatical, so that 'The cat sat on the mat' is a sentence whereas 'Sat cat the on mat the' is not. Yet others think the sentence expresses a complete thought and so can stand on its own. This can also cause problems. For example, are these sentences? 'Yes!' or 'Not guilty'. And are they grammatical?

The 'grammatical' definition is the least inadequate of the three we have mentioned, and therefore we will use it as our starting-point. In general all written sentences should contain at least a subject and a verb.

8.2.7.1   The subject

This usually appears before the main verb in statements and after the main verb in questions. For example:

THE COURT ordered her to pay a £50 fine.
How much did THE COURT order her to pay?

The following can be subjects:

A noun	LOVE is a many splendoured thing.
A noun phrase	THE COST OF PETROL is going up.
A pronoun	IT shouldn't be allowed. WHO killed Cock Robin?
A subordinate clause	WHAT SHE SAID was taken down in a statement.

In some formula sentences the subject is implied rather than stated, for example:

[I] Thank you.

Commands also omit the subject, which is usually 'you', for example:

When you arrive, (you) GO up the stairs to my office.

8.2.7.2   The verb

This must take an appropriate form to suit its subject. Fortunately in English there is little variation in the form of verbs, with the exception of the third person singular of the present tense. For example:

I KNOW, she KNOWS.

The exceptions to this are:

(a)   The verb 'to be', which has several forms, which we assume you are familiar with!

(b)   Some modal verbs – must, can, may, might, shall, will, ought, should, would, could – which do not change at all.

Look again at the phrases we gave at the beginning of **8.2.7**:

Thanking you for your kind attention.
Assuring you of our best attention at all times.
With reference to your letter of 16th May.

Both are unacceptable sentences. It would be possible to say 'Thank you for your kind attention' (where the subject, 'I', is implied) but 'thanking' does not imply the subject, 'I', and is therefore not a verb. We have seen that 'thank' is a special case and implies the subject. 'Assure' is not a special case, so a subject must be expressed. In this case the subject would be 'I' or 'we', but the word 'assuring' is not a form of the verb which can follow these subjects. In the third example there is neither subject nor verb.

It would be possible to put a comma at the end of any of these phrases and continue with a subject and another main verb, though this is a cumbersome way of expressing yourself:

Assuring you of our best attention at all times, I look forward to hearing from you in due course.

You probably know most of this already, even if you are not in the habit of articulating the rules. However, if you think that you need to go into more detail, consult the books listed in **9.2**.

8.2.8   PUNCTUATION

Punctuation helps the reader understand written language by breaking it up into smaller units. Understanding of the spoken language is helped by pauses, intonation and emphasis on particular words and syllables. (Language experts refer to these features as 'prosody'.) This is a very subtle and sophisticated process. As we noted earlier, these features are absent from writing. Punctuation is one way of compensating for this absence. See how this sentence can have its meaning altered by punctuation:

The judge said the accused was the most heinous villain he had ever met.

The judge, said the accused, was the most heinous villain he had ever met.

If either of these sentences were spoken, the meaning would be clear from the intonation and emphasis.

Punctuation alone is inadequate compensation for the loss of prosody. This is where intelligent planning comes in. Some words and phrases which are clear in speech may be ambiguous in writing. For example, the use of 'only' can cause serious problems. 'I only spoke to the officer' may mean:

(a)   The officer was the only person I spoke to, or
(b)   I spoke, but did not do anything else, to the officer.

Careful planning of the word order would prevent ambiguity: 'I spoke only to the officer' gives meaning (a). To get meaning (b) you may need to make more radical alterations:

I did nothing to the officer except speak to her.

How well do you think you know the rules of punctuation? When would you use:

(a)   a full stop,
(b)   a comma,
(c)   a semicolon,
(d)   an apostrophe?

8.2.8.1   Full stops

These are used, followed by an initial capital letter, to separate sentences, for example:

The court ordered the defendant to pay £750,000 in damages. Her solicitor advised her to lodge an appeal immediately.

8.2.8.2   Commas

Commas separate words, phrases and clauses. They usually take the place of short pauses and changes in intonation in the spoken language.

Lock, stock and barrel.

Please forward your cheque, together with any documents for sealing, and the completed tear-off slip.

Where a policy of assurance has been charged to the society by way of deposit, please inform the insurance company following repayment that the society has no further interest in the policy, quoting the above roll number.

Too many commas interrupt the flow of your writing and can be an obstacle to understanding. Here is an example:

> I am writing to inform you that I have carried out a mining search on the property you are proposing to purchase, 14, Denning Walk, Wilberforce, Nottinghamshire, which is, as you know, situated in the heart of a mining area, and, I regret to report, there is evidence of serious subsidence to the neighbouring properties.

This text demonstrates that an overzealous user of commas may be prone to extend the length of the sentence to accommodate new thoughts as they come to mind. The comma is not a substitute for thinking and planning. To make the text more readable, you would have to do more than cut out a few commas. Here is a possible alternative:

> Dear ——
>
> Purchase of 14 Denning Walk
>
> This property is in a mining area, and I have therefore carried out a mining search. Unfortunately, this has revealed serious problems of subsidence in some neighbouring properties.

Some writers mistakenly use the comma to function as a full stop. Unless a coordinating conjunction is used (such as 'and', 'but', 'or'), the sentence will be ungrammatical:

> (a)   The court ordered the defendant to pay £750,000 in damages, her solicitor advised her to lodge an appeal immediately.
> (b)   The statute covers two different situations, one applies to those on income support, the other to those with an income of more than £7,500 p.a.
> (c)   You must put your application in within three months, otherwise you lose the right to claim compensation.

You can replace the commas in (a) and (b) with full stops.

> (a)   The court ordered the defendant to pay £750,000 in damages. Her solicitor advised her to lodge an appeal immediately.
> (b)   The statute covers two different situations. The first deals with those on income support and the second with those who earn more than £7,500 p.a.

Alternatively you could use a stop which is not quite as full: a semicolon or colon. You can use a semicolon where you think that a clause is too closely related to what has gone before to be cut off by a full stop. A colon is used to precede an explanation (as above), or introduce a list, for example:

> English law is largely derived from two sources: common law and statute.

You should also split (c) into two independent sentences:

> (c)   You must put your application in within three months. Otherwise you lose the right to claim compensation.

8.2.8.3   Apostrophes

You find these in all sorts of places where the rules say they should not appear at all. We use apostrophes most frequently with noun phrases to indicate possession. In spoken English possession is indicated by adding 's' to 'the possessor'. The 's' is retained in writing, but with an apostrophe added. This is an example of redundancy, which we discussed in **8.2.3**. The rules are:

(a)   Singular nouns and plural nouns which do not end in 's': put the apostrophe before the 's'.

John's books.
The judge's wig.
The men's room.

(b)   Plural nouns ending in 's': put the apostrophe after the 's'.

The judges' wigs

(c)   Singular nouns ending in 's': put the apostrophe after the 's', and you can add another 's'.

Ms Jones' last case, or
Ms Jones's last case.

We also use the apostrophe to measure a period of time:

three weeks' holiday, five years' schooling,

to refer to places and premises:

We will eat at Quaglino's.
I'll meet you at the doctor's.

Furthermore, the apostrophe is frequently used to mark elision. This occurs where subject and verb are combined to make one word, for example:

HE'S arriving late.
KATHY'S had her car stolen.
WHO'D like a custard tart?
WHO'S next?

Many people think the apostrophe is old-fashioned and unnecessary. It is left out of many notices and shop signs, such as:

St Pauls, Earls Court, Menswear.

It is probably because attitudes are changing that some people are not sure how to use apostrophes and mistakenly add them to plural nouns and verb endings:

Potatoes' and fresh beans' on special offer.
Nobody love's me.

According to Crystal this usage is 'universally condemned by educated writers'. (p. 111).

The rules for using the apostrophe are straightforward, yet it is probably the most misused of punctuation marks. Our advice is that you should learn to use it correctly if you want to be considered an 'educated writer'.

8.2.9   SPELLING

Mark Twain remarked that he could not respect a man who could only spell words one way. English spelling is difficult because words are not always spelt as they are pronounced. There are two main reasons for this. One is that the spelling system introduced by the Normans was mixed with the system we used before the Norman Conquest. This accounts for two spellings of the same sound, for example, '-se' and '-ce' ('mouse' and 'mice') and two sounds for the same spelling, for example 'g', as in 'get' and 'gem'.

The other reason is that spellings have generally not changed, while pronunciation has. During the Middle Ages the few people who could write spelt words in different ways. A fixed and uniform spelling system only began to be established in the 15th century with the introduction of printing. The standard system developed by printers was adopted in the 18th century by the most important dictionaries. This is largely the system we have today, unaffected by the significant changes in pronunciation which have taken place since the 15th century.

The effect of this fossilisation is that, for instance, we preserve letters in words that are no longer pronounced:

niGHt, Know, deBt, SaLmon.

We use different spellings for the same sound, such as 'ee' and 'ea' in meet and meat, because in the past ee and ea were different sounds. If you compare greet and great you will see that we cannot count on this 'rule'. Similarly, when you consult books on spelling you will find that the 'exceptions' often outnumber the 'rules'.

Some people see poor spelling as a sign of intellectual incompetence. Since there are so few rules, however, learning to spell involves memorising rather than exercising your intellectual skills of judgment, discernment and reflection. These are the skills you need to learn the complex linguistic skills of grammar and punctuation, where even a small error can cause misunderstanding. Poor spelling is rarely responsible for a breakdown in communication.

Nevertheless you have to recognise that poor spelling may make your reader think you are uneducated, incompetent or unprofessional. Be sure to use a dictionary or spell checker.

8.3 The Importance of Self-Editing your Writing

We can summarise this Chapter with a list of questions you should answer honestly every time you have composed a written document. Since this is a method of looking at it through the eyes of the reader, you may prefer a friend or colleague to read it and answer the questions.

8.3.1 SELF-EDITING CHECKLIST

Purpose:

(a) What is the purpose of the communication?
(b) Have I adapted style and content to suit the reader's needs?
(c) Have I dealt with the issues?
(d) Have I answered all the questions?
(e) Have I answered them in enough depth?

Content:

(a) Is the information accurate?
(b) Is it relevant?

Humanity:

(a) Will my tone produce the desired response?
(b) Is it friendly, courteous, helpful, frank, forceful?

Layout:

(a) Is the layout appropriate for the purpose and content?
(b) Is it set out in manageable blocks?

Structure:

(a) Are the sentences short enough?
(b) Does the order of sentences and paragraphs make sense?
(c) Does each paragraph contain just one main idea?
(d) Is there a link between each paragraph and the next?

Language:

(a) Have I used plain language, that is, clear, concise and correct language that can be easily understood by the reader?
(b) Have I omitted words and phrases which are:

(i) infrequently used,
(ii) inelegant,
(iii) redundant,
(iv) unneccessarily technical,
(v) verbose,
(vi) vague.

(c) Is the grammar appropriate for the purpose?
(d) Are punctuation and spelling correct?

NINE

THE CONVENTIONS OF LETTER-WRITING: AN EXERCISE

9.1   Exercise

Here is a solicitor's letter which contains many of the characteristics of poor writing we have discussed. Note down in detail what you think is wrong with it. If necessary, use the self-editing checklist to help you. Then compare your comments with our 'annotated' version. Finally, rewrite the letter clearly, concisely and correctly.

Dear Both,

> Re: 14 Denning Walk, Bingham, Oxfordshire OX13 4QC
> Sao Miguel, Bridge St, London SW13 9JJ

Further to previous correspondence on this matter, we now enclose herewith the enquiries and fixtures and fittings list, to be duly completed by yourselves and returned, forthwith, to this office.

As regards title to the property. It is registered at the Land Registry with absolute freehold title. You will observe from the Land Registry plan that there is a small area of land, coloured pink, and within that land there is a Water Main and I am enclosing a copy of a Deed of Grant dated 10th May 1966 which gave the right to the Water Board to lay and maintain a water pipeline through that land. Therefore the Water Board have a legal easement, which means the main can remain there.

It follows from that, if the Water Main ever needs to be repaired then the Water Board has the right to enter upon the land in order to maintain and repair the said pipe.

They would have to cause as little damage as possible and put right any damage caused afterwards, in so far as such is possible. It also follows that you would not be able to build over the Water Main. There are no Covenants which affect this property other than those contained in the aforementioned Deed of Grant dated 10th May 1966 related to the Water Main.

As far as exchange of contracts prior to completion is concerned, you will be required to pay a deposit to the Vendors Solicitors. As yet, we are not entirely clear how much Deposit will be received on the Sale, but should be able to provide the same amount on your purchase of this property. However, it is not inconcievable that, the same sum will not be able to be provided, or that the amount will be insufficient. Should this be the case, it will be brought to your attention with all speed and alternative arrangements will be put into effect.

You should contact this office if there are any difficulties arising from this letter.

This is to keep you informed.

Yours faithfully,

_____
?

Dear (Both,)

redundant
(omit)

(Re:) 14 Denning Walk, Bingham, Oxfordshire OX13 4QC } full address necessary?

Sao Miguel, Bridge St, London SW13 9JJ

Is this phrase necessary?   stilted   What matter?   not needed   redundant and archaic

Further to previous correspondence on this matter, (we) (now) enclose (herewith) the enquiries and

no explanation of lists — fixtures and fittings list, to be (duly) completed by (yourselves) and returned, (forthwith,) to (this

(office.) <- impersonal   passive   ?   passive   ?

Unnecessary and not a sentence   ungrammatical   pompous   ?   ?   ?

[As regards title to the property.] It is registered at the Land Registry with absolute freehold title.

formal   ?

long and confused sentence — meaning?

You will observe from the Land Registry plan that there is a small area of land, coloured pink,

Why capitals? we? tense? ? ?

and within that land there is a Water Main and (I) am enclosing a copy of a Deed of Grant dated

water company

10th May 1966 which gave the right to the Water Board to lay and maintain a water pipeline

through that land. Therefore the Water Board (have) a legal easement, which means the main can

remain there.   What is this? Explanation correct?

from what?   unnecessary

Poor paragraphing

It follows from that, [if the Water Main ever needs to be repaired] then the Water Board (has) the

right to enter (upon) the land in order to maintain and repair the (said) pipe.

archaic   ugh! Legalese

Who?   clumsy

(They) [would have to cause as little damage as possible] and put right any damage caused

What does this mean? What is not possible?

vague and ambiguous

afterwards, [in so far as such is possible.] It also follows that you would not be able to build over

New topic! Paragraph?   unnecessary

the Water Main. There are no Covenants which affect this property other than those contained

meaning?

in the aforementioned Deed of Grant dated [10th May 1966] related to the Water Main.

Clumsy, inelegant phrase, poor link   redundant, legalese   verbose   Why repeat?   Uncle? Aunt?

[As far as (exchange of contracts) prior to (completion) is concerned,] you will be required to pay a

meaning known? Assume yes   passive

deposit to the Vendors Solicitors. As yet, [we are not entirely clear] how much Deposit will be

clumsy   redundant }   passive

wordy phrase

62

[handwritten: subject of verb?] *[handwritten: which?]*

received on the <u>Sale</u>, but <u>should</u> be able to provide the same amount on your purchase of <u>this</u>

[handwritten: passive] *[handwritten: unnecessary, clumsy phrase]* *[handwritten: even more obscure and ugly!]*

property. However, [it is not inconceivable that] the same sum [will not be able to be provided,]

[handwritten: ? ? ?] *[handwritten: sp.]* *[handwritten: Is this appropriate language for reader? (complex)]*

or that the amount will be insufficient. [Should this be the case,] it will be brought to your attention

[handwritten: meaning?] *[handwritten: passive]*

with all speed and alternative arrangements <u>will be put</u> into effect.

[handwritten: Why this unusual phrase?] *[handwritten: verbose and clumsy phrase]*

You should contact <u>this office</u> if there are any <u>difficulties</u> arising from this letter. *[handwritten: Peremptory ending]*

[handwritten: impersonal] *[handwritten: meaning what?]*

This is to keep you informed. *[handwritten: (!)]*

   Yours faithfully,

Many of the problems with the letter arise from the failure to consider the needs of the reader. The sentences are full of verbose, redundant and technical words and phrases. Poor structure and layout reflect the writer's failure to think and plan.

Furthermore, it is not clear how formal or informal this relationship is supposed to be. We know there is a relationship between lawyer and client already established through previous correspondence, if not through personal contact. The use of 'Dear Both' suggests that the relationship is fairly informal, whereas 'Yours faithfully' at the close of the letter is a formal closure which normally follows the opening 'Dear Sir or Madam'. Twice in the letter the client is asked to contact the office rather than the writer personally or another named person. This, together with the use of the passive, makes the tone impersonal and peremptory.

The writer is inconsistent in other ways. In the first paragraph the writer is 'we', but 'I' in the second. Again the readers may be confused about the kind of relationship they have with their solicitor, and who is actually doing the work: the solicitor or some other person in the firm? You can clarify this by using 'I' if you want to encourage a fairly informal, friendly relationship, and 'we' when writing about the general undertakings of the firm, for example:

  We aim to provide a quick and efficient service.

To be consistent you should then sign personally at the bottom. You can sign in the firm's name if you want to keep the recipient at a distance, though you should give the name of someone in the firm to contact.

Like newspapers and magazines, firms of solicitors have their own 'house style'. Your firm's style may therefore determine how you sign letters and the level of formality you adopt.

The letter writer is also inconsistent in the use of capital letters. These are not confined to names and titles but are sprinkled liberally throughout the text for some unknown purpose – perhaps to venerate some noble legal institutions: 'Solicitor', 'Deed of Grant', 'Vendor', 'Sale'? This cannot account for 'Water Main', however.

Tinkering with this writer's prose will improve it, but not much. The whole text needs radically rethinking. You could probably get the message across more clearly by dealing with sale and purchase in separate letters.

Compare our rewritten version with yours:

THE CONVENTIONS OF LETTER-WRITING: AN EXERCISE

Dear Mr and Mrs

<u>Sale of 14 Denning Walk</u>

<u>Purchase of Sao Miguel, Bridge St</u>

Before we can agree a contract of sale with the purchasers, we have to give them some more information. I therefore enclose two forms for you to complete.

The enquiries before contract form provides the purchasers with important details about the property. The fixtures and fittings list tells them which items you are taking with you and which you are leaving behind. Could you therefore complete both forms and return them to me as soon as possible in the envelope provided.

I also enclose a Land Registry plan of Sao Miguel. The house is registered with absolute freehold title. This means that you will be the owners of the house from the date of completion.

You will notice on the plan that a small area of the property is coloured pink. This marks a water main running through the property. You may not build anything over this pipe. Moreover, the water company has the legal right to enter the property to repair and maintain the pipe. This right is given by a deed of grant dated 10 May 1966. The deed also protects you by insisting that any work the water company carries out causes as little damage and inconvenience as possible. Any damage caused by work on the main must be put right by the company. This is the only right over the property granted to someone other than the owner.

When I exchange contracts on your behalf I have to pay a deposit to your vendor. I expect to use the deposit I receive from your purchaser to do this. If your vendor considers this amount too small, you may have to arrange a loan for the shortfall. This is normally not a problem and I will be happy to advise you.

Please telephone me if there are any points in this letter you wish me to clarify.

Yours sincerely

DRAFTING LEGAL DOCUMENTS

TEN

INTRODUCTION TO DRAFTING

10.1 Introduction

'What do you get if you cross the Godfather with a lawyer?' enquired Don Henley on his album, *The End of the Innocence*.

Such is the confusion often sown into the minds of lay clients by a consideration of legal documents that the response to the question should come as no surprise: 'A man who makes you an offer you can't understand!'

Legal drafting has often been the source of amusement and the central aspect of many plots of confusion. Take for example the central plot to the Gilbert and Sullivan operetta, *The Pirates of Penzance*, in which a youth, Frederick, is indentured to be an apprentice to the Pirate King. Frederick interprets the document as releasing him from his bounden duty upon him reaching his twenty-first year, whereas the document states the release to occur on his twenty-first birthday – a grave concern as Frederick's birthday was on 29 February and thus he only has a birthday every leap year. 'A paradox, a most ingenious paradox' and a clear illustration of the ramifications of infelicitous and thoughtless drafting.

The skills of drafting legal documents are in essence similar to the skills of legal writing set out in **Chapters 7 to 9**. However, the purpose of the draft being produced may be different to the purpose behind legal letter-writing. The completed document will often reflect an agreement or accord between parties, often separately advised and represented, and regulate the legal relationship between those parties. The drafter should be able to sit back and relax secure in the knowledge that the document finally produced for signature has married together the relevant facts and law in a clear and concise manner and encapsulates the final agreed instructions or negotiations.

But all too often the document fails in its purpose. As in the indenture from *The Pirates of Penzance* the wording may not have been chosen correctly. Perhaps the agreement overlooked an eventuality which the drafter should have considered. Perhaps the document is so obscurely drawn that only a court can construe it and find its meaning.

The purpose of a well-drafted document is to provide a touchstone which governs the legal relationship and which keeps its signatories away from the expenses of litigation. However, a glance at any legal text, e.g. *Words and Phrases Judicially Defined* would indicate that lawyers have not enjoyed success in this modest aim.

In setting the written standards for the Legal Practice Course, the Law Society has identified that students should, in developing the basic skills of drafting, be able to prepare a range of documents and to formulate and present a coherent piece of writing based upon facts, general principles and legal authority in a structured, concise and, when appropriate, persuasive manner. Students should be able to draft documents that:

(a) meet the client's goals, carry out the client's instructions or address the client's concerns;
(b) accurately address all relevant legal and factual issues;
(c) where appropriate, identify relevant options;
(d) where appropriate, demonstrate a critical use of precedents;
(e) are logically organised;
(f) form a consistent and coherent whole;
(g) follow the rules of grammar;
(h) demonstrate appropriate use of language;
(i) are succinct and precise;
(j) meet any formal requirement;
(k) maintain a standard of care which protects the interest of the client.

Here drafting will be looked at primarily in the context of the non-contentious core subjects, but the criteria for good drafting are also relevant in the context of litigation and indeed the option subjects.

This part will introduce you to the relevant skills and matters relating to drafting by considering the various stages in drafting a document:

(a) Preparing to draft.
(b) Who drafts.
(c) Getting down to drafting.
(d) Style and content of drafting.
(e) Your draft in their hands.
(f) Use of grammar and language.
(g) Making amendments.
(h) Engrossment and completion.
(i) Some points of construction.

10.2   Further Reading

Atkin's Encyclopaedia of Court Forms.
Blake, S., *A Practical Approach to Legal Advice and Drafting*, 4th ed. (London: Blackstone Press, 1993).
Encyclopaedia of Forms and Precedents.
Garner, B. A., *Elements of Legal Style* (New York: Oxford University Press, 1991).
Melville, L., *The Draftsman's Handbook*, 2nd ed. (London: Longmans, 1991).
National Consumer Council, *Making Good Solicitors* (London: National Consumer Council, 1989).
National Consumer Council, *Plain English for Lawyers* (London: National Consumer Council, 1984).
Shurman, L., *The Practical Skills of the Solicitor*, 2nd ed. (London: Longmans, 1985).

ELEVEN

PREPARING TO DRAFT

As with any of the other lawyerly skills, preparation is essential to a successful outcome. Unlike advocacy or negotiation, it is true that the drafter will have the option to reconsider a document before presenting it for public consumption. However, it is certainly true that without adequate preparation the document will take longer to prepare and, even on reflection, is likely to omit matters material to meeting the client's goals or addressing the client's concerns.

The Law Society recognised the value of preparation in points (a), (b), (c) and (d) of the written standards (see **Chapter 10**). Unless the drafter is clear about the purpose of the document being drafted then the proper outcome cannot be achieved.

11.1   Identify the Client's Goals, Concerns, Instructions

All documents produced by a lawyer will be produced at the instigation of the client. That is not to say that the client is necessarily aware on giving instructions that certain documents must be prepared – in the conveyancing process the client is not necessarily aware that both a contract of sale and subsequently a conveyance or transfer are required.

The taking of instructions is often determined by the solicitor's knowledge of the client and the latter's expertise in the legal arena. In the business sphere, the solicitor should be familiar with the whole range and objectives of the client's business to understand precisely the agreement desired to be drafted. On the other hand, meeting for the first time a client wanting a will to be prepared would entail the solicitor obtaining background information about family, dependants and property for which the client may see no need but which the experienced solicitor recognises to be necessary to attain the client's objectives.

When taking instructions, do not assume that the person instructing you knows the law. It is for you to clarify the legal position and ask for instructions in the light of the law.

Consider whether you have taken instructions from the appropriate person. Does an employee have the authority to instruct you? Is the person instructing you the legal owner of the property? If not, make sure the instructions are checked with the appropriate person or people.

Can you actually take instructions from the client? If you were to prepare the document would there be a conflict with an existing client's interest? Is the document you are being instructed to prepare illegal? You must of course consider whether you can accept the instructions in the light of the Solicitors' Professional Conduct Rules.

Instructions may of course be taken over the telephone, in person or received in writing. It is up to you to be satisfied that the instructions you have are sufficient for you to commence drafting.

When taking instructions it is for the solicitor to appreciate that there may be more than one outcome. The solicitor must identify with the client the client's primary goals and concerns. The client may approach the solicitor wanting an agreement to buy Blackacre completing in one year's time when the client can obtain planning consent. This can be achieved by entering into an option agreement, a conditional contract or an unconditional contract, each with its own advantages and disadvantages in relation to the client's goals and concerns.

Before drafting it may be desirable to make a site visit. As there will be expense involved, the client should consent to this beforehand, but often, especially in relation to complex commercial property matters, it is of enormous assistance to make a site visit and subsequently recall to mind the layout of the land when drafting a lease or agreement. It may also be beneficial to the solicitor drafting commercial agreements to visit the client's business to form a clearer view of it.

Summary

(a) Take your client's instructions.
(b) Do you have all relevant background information?
(c) What is your client's prime goal or concern?
(d) Can you put your client's instructions into a legal context?
(e) Refer to the Chapter on interviewing for further consideration.

11.2   Analyse All Legal and Factual Issues

This should be basic common sense. After all, your client has come to you in the belief that you know the law and are thus able to prepare the requisite document. You must assimilate and analyse the actual factual context according to your instructions. Only then can you formulate a clear idea of what the draft document should contain.

Before setting pen to paper, consider your instructions. Are they clear to you? What is the objective of the draft? If it is, say, a contract, can you identify the parties, the consideration, the obligations of each party, any conditions, warranties and representations, any provisions which take effect after a breach of contract and any other material matters on which you have instructions? If there are gaps, ask yourself why there are gaps. Perhaps the gap is filled elsewhere? Perhaps it is a matter which neither you nor your client may have considered. Do you need further instructions?

If you conclude that you need further instructions, consider whether it is necessary in order to prepare the first draft to require these additional instructions or whether you can produce a draft and afterwards ask your client to fill in the missing piece. Remember your client is likely to be busy as well.

Equal importance should be afforded to a mature consideration of the law affecting the agreement to be prepared. This is the area in which you are the expert. You must get this right. This is why you are being paid by the client. Are there any restrictions to what is being proposed? Supposing you are drafting a director's service agreement; is it lawful to bar the director from working anywhere in the UK for five years after dismissal? Check up by researching the texts and original sources.

Has the law altered recently? Using precedents as a base is no safeguard if they are out of date. Taxation is an obvious area where there is a constant change in the law. Is what is proposed tax-efficient or should the client's affairs be ordered in a different manner? Solicitors should of course update themselves regularly with new developments, but in drafting an agreement for a client you must ensure your draft is right in line with the current law.

In particular, you must be aware of any provisions which imply obligations into certain types of contract and whether you can override them. Consider the Partnership Act 1890. Section 24 provides that the interests of partners in partnership property and their rights and duties in relation to the partnership shall be determined by the rules contained in that section unless there is a special agreement between the partners. Thus, for example, if partnership profits are not to be shared equally, the partnership agreement should specify the contrary agreement. Consider the Carriage of Goods by Sea Act 1971 which provides that the Hague–Visby Rules shall automatically apply to certain bills of lading. If the rules apply to the bill of lading there are minimum duties and liabilities which cannot be excluded or reduced by agreement. It is otiose to attempt to prepare a bill of lading for a client which would be void.

Time spent before drafting analysing the factual situation and the legal context into which it is to be set is never time wasted.

Summary

(a)   What are the facts which provide the bones of the draft?
(b)   What is the law that is applicable?
(c)   Carry out all further research into any aspect which may affect the draft.
(d)   For further consideration see the Chapter on legal research.

Exercise 11.1

Consider the position of Frederick in *The Pirates of Penzance*. You are instructed to prepare a contract whereby Frederick is to be an apprentice to the Pirate King. He is to be apprenticed until he is 21. By further enquiry you establish that Frederick was born on 29 February. What is your analysis of the information available to you? Can you draft the agreement or do you need further instructions? Do you think the parties have considered all the problems? Should you bring it up?

11.3   Where Appropriate, Identify any Options

Preparation by analysing the law and the facts may well reveal to you that there may be various ways of drafting part or parts of a document. The primary goal must be to achieve what the client wishes in a legal context. However, if this can be achieved in various ways, consider adopting an option which saves on stamp duty, or one which may be tax-efficient, or one which may attain the client's wishes without incurring inappropriately large costs.

Summary

(a)   Think laterally through the problem.
(b)   Think about any costs implications.

11.4   Critical Use of Precedents

11.4.1   LIMITATIONS OF PRECEDENTS

Of all the preparatory tasks, selecting precedents is the most crucial and often solicitors feel that once it is done, no other type of preparation is necessary. A precedent should be seen as a checklist against which your draft can be checked for completeness. A precedent is not a replacement for a solicitor. It should not be merely copied without thought. Indeed there is a school of thought, primarily in the litigation field, which suggests that trainees should draft without reference to precedents. In the non-contentious sphere, it is suggested that you as a trainee should learn to draft by using precedents so as to avoid reinventing the wheel, negligent and material omissions, and delay and cost to the client.

11.4.2 WHAT PRECEDENTS ARE AVAILABLE?

There are many excellent books of precedents and access to them is vital to most solicitors. Chief amongst these in the non-contentious sphere is the *Encyclopaedia of Forms and Precedents* which is currently in its 5th edition, although some volumes of the 4th edition have not yet been replaced. Containing 42 volumes together with an index, the work is ordered alphabetically and covers topics from agency to landlord and tenant, from copyright to shipping, from acknowledgements to wills and administration. It is also regularly updated in a loose-leaf format in the service volumes. In addition to precedents, there is a concise statement of the relevant law for each subject area, and most precedents have comprehensive footnotes citing law, cases and common variants on the precedents. In addition the work includes many codes of practice and rules which are of assistance to the practitioner. For example, vol. 1 contains the Advertising Standards Authority Code of Practice, while vol. 3 contains the rules for a number of arbitration venues such as the UNCITRAL rules.

Some of the volumes of the *Encyclopaedia of Forms and Precedents* are being reissued throughout 1993 as new law outdates the first volumes of the 5th edition, which were published from 1985 onwards. The aim of the work is stated by the editor-in-chief, Sir Peter Millett, as meeting the needs of the drafter who must 'carry into effect his client's often half-formulated intentions, and to do so in language which is not only legally effective and unambiguous, but also simple and concise'.

Other excellent precedents may be found in:

(a) *Practical Conveyancing Precedents* and *Practical Lease Precedents* both by Trevor Aldridge.

(b) *Precedents for the Conveyancer* (London: Sweet & Maxwell), a loose-leaf two-volume work which has been published since 1970 in this form with regular updating issues. While primarily dealing with a conveyancer's requirement it also has sections on business transactions and charities, amongst others.

(c) *Parker's Modern Conveyancing Precedents*, 2nd ed. by Eric Taylor (London: Buttworths, 1989) which in its 1st edition pioneered the use of plain English in drafting conveyancing documents.

(d) *Practical Commercial Precedents*, which again has a loose-leaf format and in particular contains precedents for City-type agreements of a specialised nature.

(e) *Kelly's Draftsman*, 15th ed. (London: Butterworths, 1986), Pettit's *Will Draftsman's Handbook*, 6th ed. (London: Longmans, 1990) and *Practical Will Precedents* (London: Longmans), which specialise in probate and will drafting.

In the contentious field, the primary source of precedent material for pleadings and forms is *Atkin's Encyclopaedia of Court Forms* which is now in its 2nd edition. It comprises 41 volumes together with index. The areas it covers in the contentious field are similar to those covered by the *Encyclopaedia of Forms and Precedents*. The 2nd edition was published from 1961 to 1971 and has been reviewed twice since. Many of the volumes are currently being updated and reissued. There are also annual service volumes. Many of the court forms are prescribed and these can be found in the white book (the *Supreme Court Practice*) and the green book (the *County Court Practice*).

In addition to specific precedent books, many textbooks and journals have directly linked precedents. W. J. L. Knight, *Acquisition of Private Companies*, 4th ed. (London: Longman, 1985) has, for example, drafts of a share purchase agreement. *The Conveyancer and Property Lawyer* often has conveyancing-related precedents. Knowing where to find a precedent is half the battle.

Most firms will also keep a more or less formal system of precedents developed over the years to avoid reinvention of the wheel. Especially now with the word processor it is easy and quick to adapt precedents already available rather than create them from scratch. Be familiar with the precedents available in your firm, especially those such as leases which will be frequently required in practice. Familiarity will allow you to adapt these documents to suit the client's purposes more easily and cost-effectively. But beware of churning out surplusage, simply because it is stored on the word processor, to cover some circumstance so remote it is not likely to happen.

Precedents are also available as software for computers, including *Practical Commercial Precedents*, the book form of which was referred to above. *Magna Precedents* is available solely as a software package.

11.5   Using a Precedent as a Base for Drafting

If you need to use a precedent as a base for your draft, find the precedent or precedent clauses most appropriate to your needs. Clearly, before you can do that you must have analysed the precise factual and legal context. Then read the precedent. Never simply reproduce it.

If the precedent you are working from is on your firm's word processor ask the operator to run off a full copy. Comparing this with a reference copy, you may find that the precedent has become corrupted with clauses altered, added or deleted either deliberately or erroneously. You may have to recreate the original version. Never assume that an old draft still remains on the word processor.

If the precedent you are working from is contained in a book, you should photocopy the clauses. Some writers suggest that you should rewrite by hand and seek to rephrase a precedent. This forces you to think about each clause. However, a clause or part clause may often be omitted when working this way and cannot be easily picked up once the draft has been to the word processor operators and come back. Working from a photocopy ensures that you always have the full draft of the basic precedent available. Secondly, it will generally be easier for the word processor operators to read the printed text than your handwriting. Thirdly, time and thus expense to the client may be saved.

    (a)   Using precedents is an assistance.
    (b)   Be familiar with precedents available to you.
    (c)   Always work from a full and up-to-date precedent.
    (d)   Precedents are your tools not your masters.

Exercise 11.2

Consider which precedent or precedents in the *Encyclopaedia of Forms and Precedents* would be most appropriate to use when preparing the indenture of apprenticeship between the Pirate King and Frederick. Are there any clauses which may help you from any other precedents?

Exercise 11.3

Consider precedent 16 on p. 414 of vol. 4 of the *Encyclopaedia of Forms and Precedents*, 4th ed. and compare it with precedent 10 on p. 91 of vol. 7 of the 5th ed. Both are declarations of trust of a clergy rest home. Note the modernisation of style and form in the latter precedent; but also note the continuing use of words from the former to the latter, e.g. 'the Trustees shall stand possessed of (trust monies) upon trust to apply the same'. There has been little attempt to rewrite in plain English words which have legal effect. Are there any substantive differences between the precedents? Is one or other drafter relying on the Trustee Act 1925 or other legislation?

TWELVE

RESPONSIBILITY FOR DRAFTING AND GETTING DOWN TO DRAFTING

12.1 Responsibility for Drafting

There are certain conventions about which party produces the first draft document:

(a) In conveyancing, it is generally the case that the seller's solicitor will prepare the draft contract, whilst the buyer's solicitor will prepare the draft conveyance or transfer.

(b) In share purchase transactions, normally the purchaser's solicitor will prepare the agreement and deed of indemnity and by incorporating various warranties require disclosure by the vending shareholders.

(c) The landlord's solicitor will prepare the lease and any licences deriving therefrom.

In other instances the parties should agree where the responsibility for the production of the first draft lies. It can be embarrassing explaining to the client in say a joint venture that you are awaiting the draft from the other partner's solicitors, only to find out that they have been awaiting your draft.

Summary

Establish at the outset whether by agreement or convention who produces the first draft.

12.2 Getting down to Drafting

Once your preparation is complete, you can begin to draft. Try to find a quiet place and period in which you can devote time to producing a coherent complete draft. Trying to do so on the run in five-minute bursts between fielding phone calls, seeing clients and appearing in court will only produce certain disaster, it being most unlikely that a cohesive draft will result.

Shut your office door or find a vacant room. Ask your secretary, telephonist and receptionist to ensure you are not disturbed.

Before drafting substantively, it is worthwhile to prepare a skeleton of the agreement to ensure that you do not omit any material facts or legal points. Certainly if there are complex factual or legal questions, having a skeleton prepared would enable you to see the coherent and logical whole at the outset.

Opinions vary as to whether the drafting should be done by hand on a fresh piece of paper, by dictation or by marking up a precedent. L. Melville in *The Draftsman's Handbook*, 2nd ed. (London: Longmans, 1991), recommends the first course of action including the copying out of any precedent clauses used as this will force you to consider every word as you proceed, enable you to see the draft emerging, and will also enable you to break off at any point to research a further point. L. Shurman in *The Practical Skills of the Solicitor*, 2nd ed. (London: Longmans, 1985), recommends dictation as this will have the merit of speed although he admits that complex clauses should first be written out. Melville rejects this approach as not carrying any of the benefits of handwriting the draft. As it is increasingly unusual that dictation is given to a secretary but instead machines are used, it is easy to play back the tape to consider the draft and to hear it emerging, and nobody's time will be wasted if you wish to research further.

It is probably most common to mark up a precedent, especially if the document is already on the word processor. Using the basic photocopy or draft the amendments should be clearly inserted by coloured pen and the deletions should also be clearly indicated by a single line being drawn through the relevant text. Any new clauses should be written out in whole or marked up from a photocopy of a precedent clause and firmly attached to the main draft either as a marked and numbered rider or by being stapled to the relevant page and clearly indicated where in the draft the clause is to be inserted.

If a word or few words only are to be inserted do so above the line with an arrow indicating the position of insertion. If a long phrase or sentence is to be inserted it is generally clearer to set the phrase out in the margin and mark it with an asterisk, or cross or circle, and indicate the place of insertion by marking the text with an arrow and the appropriate asterisk or mark.

Drafting by hand whether afresh or by marking up a precedent has the further advantage over dictation that whilst your draft or your tape can be lost, only a tape can be accidentally erased.

Remember that your draft will be transcribed on to word processor by someone to whom the sense of the draft may not be clear. Make sure that your draft is clearly legible and that crucial words such as 'not' cannot be confused with 'now'. If your writing is difficult to read, try drafting double-spaced, spell clearly in capitals any names or unusual words, and use blue, red or black pen and not some other exotic colour or pencil.

Summary

(a) Set aside time to draft.
(b) Do not be disturbed while drafting.
(c) Work from your precedent in a manner that is clear to whoever will type out your draft.
(d) Use a skeleton draft.

THIRTEEN

APPEARANCE, STYLE AND CONTENT
OF THE DRAFT

Most documents produced in draft will now be produced by the word processor and thus be printed double-spaced on A4 paper. Rarely now will a draft appear on foolscap paper, and the prevalence of the word processor means that the final document is likely to be printed on quality A4 paper. There is a diminishing use of judicature paper.

There should be a generous margin set at the side, and at the top and bottom. This profligacy in paper will be seen as worthwhile when the ease of making amendments is contrasted with the prospect of amending a document submitted in single spacing. Such is the perversity of human nature that faced with the latter document one is more inclined to carp at the draft.

13.1 Does the Draft Form a Consistent and Coherent Whole?

Generally, each clause should be given an appropriate heading, especially in drafting a lease or a commercial agreement, and each clause and subclause should be consecutively numbered. For no good reason conveyancers prefer to number subclauses in parentheses, e.g. clause 2(23), whereas company and commercial lawyers prefer to number clauses and subclauses with stops, e.g. 2.1, 2.1.1 etc. Provided the numbering (or even lettering) is consistent and internal references correct, adopt the style you find most comfortable.

Numbering clauses also assists an index to be compiled to the document. Beware as this will often not be amended when the substantive document is being negotiated and the final document may be engrossed with an incorrect index.

The draft should follow the prepared skeleton outline to which your client's instructions have led. Try to ensure that the clauses drafted from scratch fit stylistically with the precedent used as a base. You should ensure that the words and phrases defined in the draft are consistent throughout, e.g. 'seller' and 'buyer' should not be mixed with 'vendor' and 'purchaser'. However, the lessons of writing clear plain English should not be forgotten just because one is preparing a legal document.

When drafted read through the document to make sure that clauses do not conflict with each other, especially if you are not familiar with the precedent you are using as a base.

Summary

(a) Be consistent on style and numbering.
(b) Consider Chapters 7 to 9 for points of style.

13.2   Is the Draft Logically Organised?

To a large extent the contents of the draft document will be dictated by the subject-matter:

(a)   A transfer should comply with the Land Registration Rules;

(b)   A pleading or writ in the High Court should comply with the Rules of the Supreme Court.

(c)   A statutory demand should comply with the Insolvency Rules 1986.

On the other hand a partnership agreement, commercial agreement or trust deed will follow no prescribed format other than the basis provided by any precedent used.

Traditionally, a document starts with a description of itself, e.g. 'This deed' or 'This agreement' followed by the date to be inserted, although traditionally a will is dated at the end. The parties to the document are generally then described and defined for ready reference throughout the draft. It is often better to describe them by their legal function in the document, e.g. 'Vendor', 'Purchaser', rather than by a shortening of their name, e.g. 'Jones', 'Brown'.

Try to identify the parties clearly as any inaccuracy may have repercussions, for example, leading to a search in the Central Land Charges Registry against an incorrect name in a conveyancing transaction. You should ensure that you refer to each party's full name and address. In addition, you should ensure that every person who is entitled under an agreement is a party to that agreement otherwise there may be problems enforcing the agreement through the courts. Companies should be identified by their registered numbers as well as names to avoid any doubt or later confusion about subsequent changes of name.

Many commercial agreements will then recite a definitions clause pulling together to the beginning all the definitions in the document. This is particularly prevalent in commercial leases and share purchase agreements especially defining important concepts such as 'Demised Premises' or 'Service Charge', the full impact of which can only be discovered when reading the substantive document. Such a definitions clause should be handled with care by the inexperienced drafter. On the subject of definitions generally, you should be aware of statutory definitions such as those contained in the Interpretation Act 1978, the Law of Property Act 1925, the Administration of Estates Act 1925, and the Companies Act 1985. Definitions therein can be easily incorporated into your draft, especially in relation to questions of gender, whereby every reference to 'he' can also admit of 'she, it or they'.

Other recitals may then follow giving details of the history or purpose of the transaction or reciting an agreement pursuant to which the parties are entering into a deed. In conveyancing, recitals assumed an importance (now reduced) under s. 45(6) of the Law of Property Act 1925. In a share purchase agreement details of the target company are often contained in recitals.

Following any recitals, the main agreement or operative part of the deed should be set out and this will be dictated in the main by subject-matter. See in particular the *Conveyancing Guide* on drafting a conveyance. Do not forget that you are preparing a document for your client. Its purpose is to protect your client. But it will also generally have to be agreed by the other party and the other party's solicitor. So be careful to tread a fine line, protecting your client whilst not placing intolerable conditions on the other party. After all, an agreement is often the aim and objective of all parties. It is not your job, unless so instructed, to throw insuperable obstacles into the path to accord.

The operative part of the agreement may often depend on the type of document being drafted. If it is substantially prescribed there is less scope for deviating from the precedent than if it is a commercial agreement produced anew. However, all the points to be incorporated in accordance with your client's instructions should be set out clearly and logically.

Consider also any matters which your analysis of the law may have pointed up. It is in relation to such considerations that you must work from as up-to-date a precedent as possible:

(a)   In a trust deed, ss. 31 and 32 of the Trustee Act 1925 relating to powers of maintenance and advancement will apply, unless there is an express contrary provision.

(b)   In a contract for services consider the terms implied by the Supply of Goods and Services Act 1982, ss. 13 to 15 and any prospect of contracting out.

(c)   In a consumer credit agreement, be aware of the extortionate credit bargain provisions under the Consumer Credit Act 1974, ss. 137 to 139.

(d)   In an employment agreement, note the minimum notice periods required to terminate the employment under the Employment Protection (Consolidation) Act 1978, s. 49.

(e)   Note that you cannot contract out of liability for death or personal injury under the Unfair Contract Terms Act 1977, s. 2(1).

(f)   In a lease, if consent to an assignment may be given by the landlord, note that under the Landlord and Tenant Act 1927, s. 19, such consent may not be unreasonably withheld.

After setting out the parties' relevant obligations and rights, there may be matters of a 'what if' nature which should be incorporated. Typically in a share purchase agreement there are many provisions dealing with eventualities if the vendors are in breach of warranty. These would deal with matters limiting liability, conduct of claims and any taxation adjustments. It is not always possible to foresee and make provision for every consequence arising from the parties' subsequent dealings, but the good drafter should have, when taking instructions and advising on the law, raised with the client certain matters.

Although it is not the function of this guide to deal with substantive legal matters which are more properly addressed in the core and option subject guides, the drafter should expect to deal with the following:

(a)   In a Will, to make provision in the event of legatees or devisees predeceasing or there being a partial or total intestacy.

(b)   In a lease, to make provision for the consequences of the tenant paying rent late.

(c)   In a partnership deed, to make provision for the status of the partnership and its assets in the event of a partner retiring or dying.

(d)   In an option agreement, to make provision in the event of the option not being exercised.

(e)   In a joint venture agreement, to make provision if either party is in breach of its obligations.

(f)   In a mortgage, to make provision in the event of the mortgagor defaulting.

The above list is by no means exhaustive and the matters to be considered will vary depending on the client's instructions and the solicitor's own experience. Many precedents provide a basic checklist of future events which could be considered, whereas others may have special precedents to attend to certain events.

The main body of the document should then be brought to an end reciting the signatures to be appended. Care should be taken to ensure that if the document is a deed then it is executed as such. If the signatory is under a disability or an attorney is signing, the appropriate testimonium and attestation clauses should be affixed. A person who is named as more than one party should execute the document once only. For provisions relating to execution in special circumstances, see the *Encyclopaedia of Forms and Precedents*, 5th ed. vol 12, pp. 369–72. Check also any special requirements for witnessing the execution of the document. Certain statutes and statutory instruments dictate the requirement for witnessing signatures, such as the Companies Act 1985 in relation to the memorandum and articles of a company, the Trustee Act 1925 relating to powers of attorney, and the Land Registration Rules 1925 relating to dealings in registered land.

The modern tendency in drafting, one brought on by the word processor, is for the operative part of the agreement to be concise, referring to lengthy schedules containing the bulk of the draft. This tendency is not necessarily laudable, but its onrushing tide can be turned back no more easily than did Canute turn back the seas. In considering whether to schedule or not to schedule, you should consider whether removing a discrete part of the agreement to a schedule will aid or hinder the logical organisation of the whole, and whether it will render the agreement any more or less coherent.

Taking the commercial lease as an example, it being a document which has in the past 20 years become expanded to epic proportions, the rent review clause became the first to find its way into a separate schedule. This was in a way logical as it would make provision for a special procedure occurring outside the main leasehold relationship. Shortly after, in leases of shopping precinct units, the description of the services being offered or made available or charged for in the service charge formed a second schedule. This was an attempt to keep the reader's interest in the important mechanics of the service charge and not to deflect it with a two-page recitation of services in the main body. Also, it is less likely that a list of the services in a schedule would be amended than if it were in the main body of the lease.

As these shopping precinct leases required standardisation, the next step was to remove the description of the demised unit and any rights and reservations from the main body into another schedule, which only need be altered on the word processor of the lessor's solicitors, leaving the main bulk unamended. From there the floodgates opened, and more or less discrete areas are finding their own schedules, so that some leases now have an operative part which does no more than introduce the schedules.

It must be stressed that it is not wrong for that to be the final outcome, so long as you are happy with the draft, the client is happy with the draft, and the draft meets the client's goals. What must be stressed is that any schedule must be properly incorporated into agreement.

Summary

(a) Draft in a style that you find comfortable and is appropriate to the client.
(b) Make sure the order of the document is logical.
(c) Identify the parties.
(d) Deal with the substance.
(e) Cover any required eventualities.
(f) Check the law.

Exercise 13.1

In relation to the apprenticeship agreement between himself and Frederick, the Pirate King now instructs you that any inventions made by Frederick during his apprenticeship are to belong to the Pirate King. How would you incorporate this provision into your draft? Are there any statutory provisions which may affect this?

FOURTEEN

YOUR DRAFT IN THEIR HANDS

Many people may pore over the fruits of your labours. Chief amongst these must be yourself checking that the draft meets the client's objectives. Moving on, the draft may also be looked at by your secretary or word processor operator, your principal or partner, the client, the solicitor 'on the other side', the other party, and possibly the solicitor on the other side's secretary or word processor operator. Of course one hopes this is as far as it goes – though there must be at the back of your mind the potential for disagreement and litigation which may result in your drafts being considered by other solicitors, counsel and a judge.

14.1 Your Secretary or Word Processor Operator

If you are blessed with a secretary or word processor operator who is legally trained and interested in and devoted to your work, treat that employee as gold dust. If not, try to explain kindly and carefully the draft document you want prepared. A few minutes at the outset explaining names and the purpose may save hours of later frustration. This may enable the secretary or word processor operator to make educated guesses in the event of doubt, rather than chase you up.

Secondly, when handing the work in for typing try to explain genuinely when you require it. Everything in practice is always 'urgent', and such designation cuts no ice. If you have a deadline, make it known at the outset. If the deadline is one of enormous urgency, do not expect perfection to be handed back to you.

Policy differs from firm to firm. Everyone should take pride in work, but some firms may prefer work to be turned over swiftly at the expense of accuracy. Whatever the policy, it is up to you to check carefully and proofread the draft produced on the word processor not only for spelling but also against your handwritten or dictated draft. Also it is worthwhile to reread the draft *de novo* to see whether it still makes sense to you.

If there are errors in what has been handed to you, clearly indicate on the typed draft the amendments to be made, preferably in red pen, and indicate insertions, deletions and spelling corrections. You should ensure that the typed draft is dated and the amended typed draft is also dated. This may be automatically generated by the word processor, but it does not hurt to indicate somewhere the draft number and the date it is created.

Keep a copy of the draft once it is typed correctly on the file and do not write on it. You should as a matter of course keep all drafts in order on the file even when they are superseded.

Summary

(a) You are legally trained; your secretary may not be.
(b) Write or dictate clearly.

    (c)   Explain the draft.

    (d)   Check what is typed carefully.

14.2   Your Principal or Partner

Generally as a trainee solicitor, you will be closely supervised and your principal or supervising partner should check your drafting closely. As with any skill, you can always pick up tips from those around you and ideally, time permitting, your draft should be considered together by you and the partner. If that is not possible, ask for the return of the draft to you with his amendments and comments so you can digest them. Note points which are substantive, and ask yourself why they were omitted or incorrect in your draft. Note the points of style and consider whether these are an improvement on your own.

Do not automatically adopt your principal's style. One style is not better than another; you should use the style with which you feel most comfortable.

Always try to make time to discuss matters about your drafting with your principal and ask for regular feedback. As with everything, familiarity with the subject-matter of a type of document will lead to an improvement in your drafting.

Summary

    (a)   Discuss amendments with a senior solicitor.

    (b)   Learn from the comments and drafting of others.

14.3   Your Client

As has been emphasised before, a solicitor produces documentation at the request and expense of the client. It is therefore sensible to send a draft of an agreement to the client for the client to comment on. It is not for the client to check that you have got the agreement right; it is expected that you will have the law correct. This is the opportunity for the client to give you the missing pieces of information that may not have surfaced at the interview, or for you to ask the client what is to occur in a certain eventuality to which you have not previously drawn the client's attention.

How this process occurs often depends on the client and the nature of the documentation. If the client is sophisticated, used to reading documents drawn by your firm and familiar with the type of transaction, it is more sensible to send the draft with a few pointed comments. On the other hand, if the document and/or the legal contextual language is likely to be unclear, it may be better to discuss the document in a meeting with clients.

Of course, not every document needs to be checked with the client before submission to 'the other side'. For example, it would be unnecessary for the client to see a standard conveyance. On the other hand, the client should always have an opportunity to see and comment on a draft will. But, needless to say, you are acting on your client's instructions and if you have confirmation that your draft document conforms to those instructions, this will diminish the prospect of the transaction going wrong.

Summary

    (a)   Explain the draft to your client in plain English.

    (b)   Obtain any further instructions.

    (c)   Check your client approves the draft.

14.4　The Solicitor 'on the Other Side'

Drafting in the non-contentious sphere is mainly a collaborative exercise, enabling parties to come to an agreement. This suggests a meeting of minds, a fair outcome, and relative equality of bargaining power. Although this is the case, the process is often seen by the participants in confrontational terms, with each side scoring points off the other. Presumably, this is because most people perceive the legal process to be a confrontational system with the public image being of the courtroom rather than of the drafter. Hence, the other party is described often as being 'on the other side'.

It must be remembered that your client will want an identical outcome to the other solicitor's client providing that there is no detriment to either.

Take a domestic conveyancing situation. Your client wants to buy a house and move in. The other party wants to sell and move out. Both parties should have an identity of interest. There will be almost inevitable confrontation between the solicitors over the rate of interest for late completion. It is too high for one solicitor and too low for the other. Never mind that neither client has the slightest intention to complete other than on the fixed date. This confrontational aspect can then all too often spill over into the whole transaction.

So it is best to try to avoid unnecessary discord which may be a bar to agreement. Usually, within reason, the final agreement entered into will be fair to both parties; there is little to be gained by preparing a first draft that is unduly restrictive and one-sided. Time, money and effort can be saved if the first draft prepared can be used as a basis for final agreement.

Remember always, though, you are acting for your client and on your client's instructions and it is your primary duty to protect your client's position.

Mention was made above about equality of bargaining power. You may find yourself acting in cases where there is clearly an inequality of bargaining power. In such cases, especially when preparing contracts in the entertainment industry, you must warn your client of the possible consequences of any agreement which is one-sided or restrictive being overturned.

So, once you have instructions from your client to submit the documentation to the other solicitor, it is courteous to do so by sending clean word-processed copies in duplicate, enabling the other solicitor to retain a file copy. The drafts should be accompanied by a letter and, if appropriate, any comment on unusual provisions should be made there. If the reasons for such provisions can be seen from the outset, it is less likely that wholesale revision will be proposed.

One of the drafts submitted will then be used as the travelling draft by the other solicitor and returned to you with any amendments. It may be disconcerting to find one morning that your pristine draft agreement over which you slaved for many hours has been returned with red amendments on every page. Suppress the natural reaction of outrage and remember that the other solicitor is not being confrontational (even if that is the case) but is merely providing his or her client's input in order to reach a final agreement.

Consider the amendments carefully, and see if they are not a help to your own drafting skills. How are points of substance worded? Are there any stylistic amendments? In particular, has the other solicitor spotted any inconsistencies or imprecision in your draft which you failed to pick up?

Summary

(a)　Send drafts out in duplicate.
(b)　Highlight the precedent used and any unusual points.
(c)　Do not provoke delay by being unnecessarily unfair.

(d) Remember your duty to your client.

(e) Learn from the amendments made.

14.5 The Other Solicitor's Client

Remember that just as you would refer your draft to your client for confirmation of instructions, expect the solicitor receiving your draft to send a copy to his or her client for comment. As a matter of common sense, do not refer in derogatory terms to the other party nor word any provisions in inflammatory terms which would detract from finding the final agreement.

For example, in a mortgage it would be preferable not to define one party as 'the Debtor' and the other as 'the Creditor'. Rather use 'the Mortgagor' and 'the Mortgagee'.

Summary

Draft courteously.

14.6 The Solicitor on the Other Side's Secretary

In commercial matters, the process of amendment often occurs not by use of the travelling draft, but by retyping on the word processor. If this happens, check the retyped amended version sent to you carefully, not only to see the amendments but also against any transposition or omission of your original text. Remember, any error your office may make can also be made anywhere else.

Summary

Check every draft.

14.7 Others in the Event of Dispute

This is the situation which by your skill you are trying to avoid – the time when the parties are in dispute over the provisions of the document you prepared. This may also lead to accusations that you did not produce what your client wanted.

A good agreement should be watertight to prevent litigation. Even if it is, this is often no bar to litigation. Often, the litigation may take place many years after the agreement was negotiated.

Make sure at the time that your file is in good order. You should endeavour to keep your first draft and any precedents you used as a basis, the first word-processed draft, a draft incorporating your client's comments, the draft as submitted to the other side, the travelling draft with all comment or amendment, all word-processed versions as redrafted, the final version as approved by your client, and a copy of the completed document. Whilst this may appear to be unnecessarily bulky, it is far more useful than relying on your recollection. These drafts can prove that you proposed amendments which were rejected, and that your client approved the final draft without your amendment. It can also assist in rectifying any mistakes.

More comment on this will arise in the context of interpretation and construction of documents.

Summary

(a) Keep copies of all drafts and amendments.

(b) Check all drafts and amendments with your client.

FIFTEEN

USE OF GRAMMAR AND LANGUAGE

A lawyer must be skilled at communication to be truly effective. A lawyer must be able to interpret the facts of a matter to fit into a legal context and communicate the legal conclusions to the client. Interviews, negotiation and advocacy all depend on verbal communication. Drafting and legal writing depend on written communication, which relies upon the written word solely to convey meaning.

Verbal communication encompasses more than reliance on words. Tone, volume, inflection and body language, for example, add greatly to the listener's understanding of the words. On the page, the words stand naked, shorn of all nuance, save for their direct meaning and context. Written communication needs to be more precise than its verbal counterpart.

Take the words 'John did it'. In speech, this can be an accusation, an expression of surprise, an expression of delight, a questioning phrase, or a statement of fact depending on inflection and emphasis. On the page, one cannot be sure of the precise meaning to be conveyed without more of the context.

'John did it', he yelled as the winning runs sped to the boundary.

Now at least the words are in some context. However, this could still show surprise or delight, unless one knew more of the context.

Words written on paper require interpretation and if the interpretation is open to ambiguity there may be potential for dispute. Part of the lawyer's drafting skill is to ensure the document prepared means what the client has instructed the lawyer to prepare.

The concerns for writing plain English, using proper grammatical constructions and choosing appropriate language detailed in **Chapters 7 to 9** in the context of legal writing generally are equally applicable to the formal agreement.

However, you must always bear in mind the subject-matter of the document being prepared. There is a certain amount of formal necessity in many agreements and deeds, and this wording, even if it seems arcane, has been judicially or statutorily approved. That is one of the purposes and comforts in using precedents. If the words have already been approved by the courts, then if used again in the same context they should bear the same meaning.

The pace of evolution of formal legal language is slow in comparison to the change in spoken and written English. The plain English movement is likely to triumph ultimately, but until then there can only be a slow integration of wording into documents that have been previously judicially approved.

In such circumstances, it is not wise to depart from the approved wording simply to assuage the thirst of the gods of modern and plain English, as your paraphrase or rewording may be ambiguous and uncertain where before there was legal clarity and certainty. Take for example the forfeiture provision in the Rugby Borough Council tenancy agreement commented on in [1984] Conv 325. Here the plain English does not convey the legal meaning of the original and it also falls foul of the problems raised by the Common Law Procedure Act 1852, s. 210.

Traditional drafting eschewed punctuation for no good reason. It appears that this was a consequence of Acts of Parliament being passed in manuscript without any punctuation, and thus judicial interpretation had to disregard any subsequent punctuation inserted by printers. See, for example, *Inland Revenue Commissioners* v *Hinchy* [1960] AC 748. Modern drafting should be properly punctuated with appropriate use of comma, full stop, colon and semicolon. For a discussion of proper usage of punctuation see Melville 'The Draftsman's Handbook' or Fowler 'Modern English Usage'.

Beware incorrect punctuation which is worse than no punctuation at all. Inadvertently, a comma may parenthesise a clause that was meant to be read conjunctively, rendering a wholly unexpected meaning.

Summary

(a) Write clearly and concisely.
(b) Use proper punctuation.
(c) Make sure the words are unambiguous in the context.
(d) Bear in mind wording that is formal but legally appropriate.
(e) See **Chapters 7 to 9** for further points on grammar and punctuation.

SIXTEEN

THE PROCESS OF AMENDMENT

We have already considered the question of production of a draft document and submitting it for consideration. Unless the document is solely for the client, such as a will, it is likely that it will be considered on behalf of another party. Almost invariably there will be some amendment.

The art of amending documentation is part of the skill of drafting and can be seen as being analogous to the skill of adapting a precedent. In this case, however, the precedent is the draft document into which you have to fit your client's instructions.

You receive a draft document. It is likely that you will already have preliminary instructions from your client, even if it is merely a phone call warning you to expect the draft. You will now need full instructions from your client as this will provide the context in which the draft must be read. This may of course be obvious and you may be able to read the draft and consider amendments before you have full instructions, but you cannot carry out the task of amendment without full instructions any more than you can the task of drafting.

Secondly, read the draft document supplied. Do not assume that as you are familiar with documents of this type, the draft will contain provisions in the terms you expect to see them. Do not assume, if you have already received similar documents from the same firm or same client, that the draft will be the same as that previously supplied. In courtesy, the firm submitting the draft ought to point out amendments or similarities to the draft previously supplied, but do not assume anything from absence of comment. Your duty is to your client and you must read the draft carefully. Read not only what is included in the draft, but consider what has been omitted. If the source of the draft is clear, return to the original precedent and look at what has been amended or omitted.

Thirdly, go through the draft with your client pointing out and explaining the provisions including omissions. Take instructions on every point and note those instructions carefully. Advise the client on any points or clauses you would propose to amend and the reasons for amending. Does the client agree? Take instructions on the strength of feeling that the client has for the amendments in case they are not accepted. Suggest possible compromises which you might propose in the event of your amendment being rejected.

Often this will reveal three types of amendment to be made:

(a) Matters of principle relating to the transaction which your client understood would be incorporated, but have been omitted or not incorporated in the terms the client agreed.
(b) Matters to which you as a lawyer cannot permit your client to agree, as these would not afford appropriate protection in the transaction.

(c)   Matters of flexibility to which both sides will readily compromise, but which are used as negotiation tools or initial 'try-ons', being matters not previously discussed or agreed, but ones on which you endeavour to ensure favourable treatment.

Each of these categories of amendment should be dealt with by you with equal precision, but in terms of negotiation of the finally agreed document you should attribute differing weight.

Take for example a commercial lease. Consideration of the document with your client reveals that interest on a late payment of rent is at 5 per cent above base rate, the demised premises do not have a specific right of access over stairs to them, and a provision entitling the client to pay only 50 per cent of the service charge has been omitted.

Your client's instructions should inform you of the agreement on the service charge which will no doubt have been one of the factors influencing the client's decision to take a lease of the premises. It is thus very important to make and insist upon the appropriate amendment. If indeed this is a matter that the parties have agreed upon, your amendment will be readily accepted. If it is not, clearly it is a matter for further negotiations by your client.

No doubt your client would be grateful if you could reduce the interest rate in the event of rent default. But if you are unable to achieve a reduction this is unlikely to affect the client's decision to proceed. No doubt the landlord will be surprised that you would seek to amend such a provision. You would probably suggest 3 per cent over base rate and compromise at 4 per cent over base rate. Such a compromise can be seen as a hard-won point sacrificed to achieve a more meaningful agreement elsewhere.

The absence of any legal right of way to the premises would also probably not concern the client unduly if it were clear on the ground that access could be had without obstruction. But this is where the client relies on your expertise, and you must stress the importance of such a defect and of insisting upon a proper solution to the problem in the completed document.

Summary

(a)   Before amending, read the draft thoroughly.
(b)   Take your client's instructions.
(c)   Check the draft with your client.

16.1   Making Amendments

Essentially there are five ways of making amendments and negotiating documentation. These are:

(a)   By travelling draft.
(b)   By retyping.
(c)   By letter.
(d)   By telephone or meeting negotiation.
(e)   By disk.

The traditional method still favoured by conveyancers is for one copy of the draft document to be sent from firm to firm with subsequent amendments shown by coloured pen. The first amendments are generally shown in red pen, the second in green, the third in violet and the fourth in yellow. This is the same as the order for amending pleadings in litigation. Other amendments are made in whichever colour is most readily to hand.

Ensure that an amendment by way of travelling draft is clearly written, showing precisely where the amendment is to be made, and not obscuring the original text. If possible delete by a thin line and make amendment in the margin. Also make any notes on amendments in the margin.

To reinsert a deletion it is traditional to mark 'stet' next to the deleted wording and/or ' " ' on the line deletion.

Before returning the travelling draft, it is wise to mark up a copy for your file which mirrors the travelling draft and to mark every subsequent amendment on it. When receiving the travelling draft, mark up your file copy with the other side's comment and amendment before reamending. It is important to remember that at the end of the day the travelling draft will be kept by the solicitor who is engrossing the final document and so the file copy must be kept by the other solicitor not only to check the final engrossment copy but also as a record in the event of later dispute.

In commercial matters, it is usual for each amended draft to be retyped by the receiving party and the retype submitted duly reamended. Unless the amendments are clearly flagged (for example, by underlining the relevant changes) this can put the other solicitor to an enormous amount of unnecessary work rereading and checking each new draft. Only use this method of amendment if you are prepared to point out all the new or deleted wording.

The third method is to amend by letter. The letter should refer clearly to the page number, clause and subclause number, and line number and quote the wording to be amended and indicate the amendment to be made. This can often be helpful as you can show your reasoning in context with the amendment. All too often, the other solicitor may read the amendment in the draft and form a view on it before coming to your reasoning in a covering letter. However, it may be awkward to read the amendments without the draft and there is room for subsequent error when transcribing the finally agreed amendments from correspondence to the draft.

This method is used in conveyancing, although the amendments are often proposed in the form of preliminary enquiries and requisitions.

In some circumstances, it may be appropriate to propose and discuss amendments by way of negotiation over the telephone or in a meeting, rather than by the transmission of written amendments. The process of substantive amendment is the same as in drafting, but the techniques involved are those of negotiation for which see **Chapters 23 to 27**.

The suggestion that the amendment process occurs by disk is merely an extension of the retyping scenario. Instead of producing a fully retyped draft a word processor disk is sent from firm to firm and amendments can be printed out at the receiving office.

Summary

    (a)   Make amendments clearly.
    (b)   Amend substantive points only.
    (c)   Keep the travelling draft.
    (d)   Consider further the Chapters on negotiation skills.

16.2   Some General Principles about Amending

Whichever method of amendment and negotiation you adopt, make sure that your amendments are obvious both as to content and position. Always check that your amendment has been considered.

When making amendments it is courteous to inform the receiving solicitor of the reason for amendment, especially if it is a matter of principle which your client believed was previously agreed.

Do not amend simply for stylistic reasons. Do not change designations simply because you prefer to use your own appellations.

If you delete a provision, ensure that any consequential renumbering is also amended in the text and cross-references suitably amended.

If there is more than one document under consideration – for example, in a share purchase with deeds of indemnity, schedules of warranties and option agreements – ensure that your amendment operates consistently throughout the documentation.

Confirm your amendments with your client and continue to seek appropriate instructions. Your duty is to act in your client's best interests.

    (a)   Amend in an obvious manner.
    (b)   Explain amendments.
    (c)   Amend pursuant to your client's instructions.

Exercise 16.1

You are Frederick's solicitor. The draft indenture provides: 'The Apprentice shall be indentured to the Pirate King until midday on the day of his 21st Birthday whereupon he shall be so released and offered a post of Pirate on terms to be agreed'. What amendments would you make?

SEVENTEEN

ENGROSSMENT, COMPLETION AND CONSTRUCTION OF DOCUMENTS

17.1   Engrossment and Completion

Once a document has been agreed in draft by both parties, it will be ready to be entered into so as to create the appropriate legal relations. Generally speaking, the creator of the first draft will print out the final signatory document which is known as the 'engrossment'. Originally documents were written or printed on vellum or parchment. Nowadays with word processing, the final print will be on judicature paper or stiff quality A4 paper.

Before the engrossment is run off, you should ask your word processor operator to let you have a final draft, which you should check word for word against the travelling draft, and which you should also consider for spelling and general coherence. Only if this conforms to the agreed version should you ask for an engrossment to be run off.

Invariably this document will consist of single A4 pages which need to be bound together. This can be achieved by the document being sewn with green ribbon, either in the corner or down one side, or by binding in a machine. These machines operate a method of heat binding, the efficacy of which can wear off over the years, especially if the document is handled frequently.

Check the engrossment then to ensure that all the pages are included in the right order, and check especially any exhibits or appendices or enclosures. Plans in leases also need to be incorporated into the engrossment. Make sure these are appropriately coloured before binding or sewing. Then ensure that the plan, if larger than A4 size, is folded properly so it can be opened and examined and not obscured by the binding.

Many transactions require engrossments to be completed in duplicate. You should also ask for a file draft copy of the unsigned engrossment to keep on your file, which should be dated as with all the other drafts, save that this should mirror the engrossment in every way by inclusion of all appendices, plans or enclosures.

Signature may take place in a meeting of all parties, or separately by one party, before transmission of the documents to the other. This latter may be achieved by the client signing in the presence of the solicitor or by the latter sending the document by post to the client.

If the signing takes place at a completion meeting, you should go through the final document with your client to make sure that it corresponds with instructions, that the client understands the rights and obligations created by the document, and that the client is satisfied. If the document is not prepared for the completion meeting by yourself you should read through the final version carefully to check, from your marked-up copy, that it conforms with your understanding of the negotiated draft document and that no subsequent amendments or clauses have been 'sneaked' in by the other side. Many a (no doubt apocryphal) story is told of the completion meeting taking place long into the night where the lawyers were drafting in one room and a secretary typing up the draft in another, and so as not to break matters up the client put himself up as go-between, and once out of the room persuaded the secretary to make amendments of his own volition unbeknown to the lawyers or the other party. This subterfuge, so the story runs, is then only discovered by the diligent lawyer, having worked through the night, taking the trouble to recheck the whole document before allowing signature.

If the documents are signed separately, make sure they are not delivered or dated until they are finally agreed and properly executed. It is always preferable that signature occurs with the lawyer present, but this may not always be possible, especially when companies execute documents. You should then explain carefully the formal requirements for signing and, if necessary, the requirements for provision of witnesses, and any instructions for dating the document. It is especially important that a will is executed correctly.

If there are any last-minute alterations, these should be clearly marked on the engrossment by hand and the parties should initial the alterations in the margin.

The document will then come into existence once it has been completely executed and dated. You should keep a photocopy on your file for record or make up your engrossment file copy by filling in the date and details of the signatory. A copy should also be sent to the client, especially if the original is to be held elsewhere than by the client.

Do not omit to deal with any post-completion matters promptly once the document has been completed. These are more properly considered as part of the appropriate topics such as conveyancing, but include such matters as payment of stamp duty, registration with the appropriate registry, or filing at court.

(a)   Carefully proofread the final draft before engrossing.
(b)   Ensure that the document is appropriately engrossed and bound.
(c)   Be clear about who signs the document when and where.
(d)   Keep a copy of the completed document.
(e)   Just because the document is signed does not mean that the transaction is necessarily at an end.

17.2   Construction of Documents

The aim of the drafter is to prepare documentation which covers all the requirements of the legal relationship between the parties, and with such clarity that all dispute can be resolved by reference to the final agreement. But this aim goes awry on frequent occasions as testified by the law reports. So it is worth bearing in mind when drafting some of the important rules of construction which the courts use to interpret agreements:

(a)   The primary consideration in construction is what was the intention of the parties. Donaldson J said in *Segovia Compagnia Naviera SA* v *R. Pagnan & Fratelli* [1975] 2 Lloyd's Rep 216:

The duty of the court is to ascertain the presumed common intention of the parties, to be deduced from the words used and the background to the transaction. Their actual, but uncommunicated, intentions are irrelevant.

(b)   If there is a conflict between the printed or typed word and the written word the latter is to be preferred to the former.

(c) Any ambiguous term is to be construed most strongly against the party for whose benefit it is intended, known as the *contra proferentem* rule. See, for example, *Burton and Co. v English and Co.* (1883) 12 QBD 218.

(d) Under the *eiusdem generis* rule, specific words limit the meaning of general words following to the class of the specific. But if the general words lead to the specific, no such limitation applies. See, for example, *SS Knutsford Ltd v Tillmanns and Co.* [1908] AC 406.

(e) The document must be looked at as a whole. This is an extension of the rule concerning the parties' intentions. See, for example, *Nereide SpA di Navigazione v Bulk Oil International Ltd* [1981] 3 All ER 737.

(f) The document should be given its grammatical construction unless there is an expressed contrary intention.

(g) Words will be given their ordinary dictionary meaning, but technical words will be given their technical meaning. However, the meaning must be limited by the context in which the words are placed. If there is an obvious error the court can correct the error in the way a reasonable man would expect.

(h) Where words are capable of bearing two constructions, the reasonable construction is preferable.

(i) Words repeated in the same document will be given the same meaning throughout.

(j) An express term will override an inconsistent implied term.

Summary

Bear in mind the court's interpretive rules when drafting.

17.3   Conclusion

Happily in *The Pirates of Penzance* Frederick's contract was brought to an end, whether by *force majeure* or frustration we are not told, but like the pirates he can now take his place as husband to the lovely Mabel at the age of 21 and not at 84.

So you now should be able to set out to chart a course amongst the rocks and eddies which beset the legal drafter.

As stated by Philip Thomas in 'Legal skills and the use of ambiguity' (1991) NILQ 14: 'The aim of the legal document is the use of such words and grammar as are necessary to achieve a stated, preconceived goal: to capture the common intention of the parties in a manner enforceable through law.' This is the essence of your task as a skilled drafter and in striving for clarity or plain English, understanding or originality, style or form you must not lose sight of the ultimate objective.

Just as with any lawyerly skill, you will profit from experience, gain confidence and find a style and rhythm of your own. However, it is hoped that you may profit from a consideration of some of the points in this Chapter.

INTERVIEWING

EIGHTEEN

INTERVIEWING AND ADVISING

18.1   Introduction

The interview provides a basic form of communication between lawyers and clients. First interviews provide a basis for finding facts and other legally relevant information. They also provide a basis for establishing an appropriate professional and business relationship between the lawyer and the client. Later, interviews with witnesses, experts and other professionals may prove to be crucial in laying the foundation for action, while subsequent interviews with the client may mark turning-points in the development of a matter.

Getting interviews right is of considerable importance. If the facts of the matter, the concerns of the client, and the options available to the client are explored at the outset, then time and expense will be saved in handling the matter. If the interview is conducted skilfully and the client's trust secured, then the foundations of a successful, and hopefully continuing, relationship will have been secured.

Interviewing is, moreover, a core skill. Success in interviewing flows from the use of a range of skills: questioning, listening, probing, attending to the other person's concerns, gathering information, exploring alternative possibilities and evaluating courses of action. Careful use of each of these skills can assist the interviewer and interviewee to analyse a problem together and attempt to find mutually acceptable solutions. It can motivate the interviewee and lead to the generation of new ideas and the development of a wide range of solutions. These skills, in turn, provide the foundation for the development of the skills that underpin negotiation and advocacy.

Getting interviews right has, in the past, been a bit of a hit or miss affair. Interviewing, it is often argued, is an art not a science. It cannot be taught, only learnt from experience. It is probably true that the best interviewers are born, not made. They work intuitively, achieving success while breaking many of the technical prescriptions. Interviewing, moreover, is best learnt from practice. But practice on its own does not always make perfect. Perfect practice makes perfect, but imperfect practice can lead to disaster, at the client's expense. Experience is a valuable aid, but you have to be able to learn from experience. If you cannot, 10 years of experience may simply end up as one year of bad experiences repeated 10 times.

Until recently lawyers were rarely given formal interview training. They could either do it, or they could not. Research carried out by the Royal Commission on Legal Services suggested that many of them could not. Poor communication was cited as the largest reason for dissatisfaction with solicitors and good communication one of the most important reasons for satisfaction. Many of the complaints received by the Law Society reflect a similar concern.

Many firms have responded to this concern by providing training in interviewing and other communication skills. The Law Society has responded in turn. It requires all firms to institute client care procedures which should ensure that the client is kept up to date with the progress of any matter. The Professional Skills Course, which you will take during your training contract, provides instruction in many of the communication skills that underpin good client care procedures. Both the Legal Practice Course and your training contract require you to demonstrate basic competence in interviewing and advising.

Each of us is capable of developing these skills because an interview is, at one level, no more than a special form of a conversation, a 'conversation with a purpose'. Given that we have already experienced many conversations we all have experience that we can draw upon. But the interview is not just a conversation. It has certain special features. Its context and purpose, its importance – both for the client and the lawyer – create a setting that is, and should be, formal and businesslike. In this setting it is easy to lose sight of our existing everyday skills and move into a formal routine. The interview then becomes a stilted parody of everyday conversation. It moves rapidly through a series of highly specific questions – to determine the relevant law and facts – and only at the end is the client asked if he or she has anything to add.

Precisely because of this danger, and because interviewing is a form of conversation, it can be useful to consider the relationship between a conversation and an interview in a little more depth.

18.2 The Conversation

Conversations are a form of communication between two people. Ideas, attitudes and feelings are exchanged, through verbal and non-verbal forms of communication. Tones of voice, changes of expression and shifts in posture are all as important as the telling phrase. Both parties influence and respond to each other. Direct questions are rare, but information is frequently exchanged in the form of statements as themes are elaborated and points expanded.

Conversations tend to be diffuse, they wander around themes and across topics. There are no clear boundaries, no definitions of what is relevant and what irrelevant. Topics shift as associations bring topics to mind. A conversation is steered by both the participants. It tends to be spontaneous and unplanned.

The participants in a conversation act as equals, each raising topics, each feeling free to initiate new subjects. Conversations are engaged in because they provide mutual pleasure. They are used to explore common ground between those who have similar backgrounds, experiences and lifestyles. In a conversation the parties choose each other. When delicate issues arise conversational norms protect the participants.

18.3 The Interview

An interview, as we have seen, is a conversation that is designed to achieve a purpose. In an initial client interview it will be to identify a problem with many of its salient features. The client will identify his or her concerns, the lawyer will probe for details. The client will give instructions. In subsequent interviews, and in witness interviews, the interview may have a clear agenda and determinate structure. The lawyer may identify alternative options for action and explore these with the client. The interview has a business dimension in which the lawyer and client determine the nature of their relationship.

These features provide the interview with a formal structure, a clearly defined allocation of roles, and a different set of expectations regulating the communication.

In an interview the content is selected to achieve its purpose. Because the interview has a purpose the content is likely to have a unity, a progression and a thematic continuity. There are limits to what is said, what is noticed, and what is included.

One person plays a dominant role in structuring the interview, the interviewer. The interviewer needs to know something about the topic of the interview, to determine what is relevant, but she/he also needs to know how to structure the interview to elicit all that is relevant. The interview is not based on a relationship of reciprocity. It is designed to help the client work with the interviewer to determine the client's interests and further the client's goals. To do this the actions of the interviewer must be planned and deliberate. The interview itself is in a formal setting, it has a predetermined time, and a specific duration.

Interviews may take place between people of equal status, but they may also take place between people who differ in background, experience and lifestyles. In an interview you have to converse with people you do not like, who have acted foolishly, and who may have acted criminally. You may have to explore the unstated, make explicit that which has been left implicit, and probe personal issues. In this the formality of the interview is an aid. It provides conditions of respect and confidentiality, it can take some of the emotional edge off that which is most personal.

The interview then is a highly formalised conversation. It has a purpose and it is this purpose which provides its content and its structure. There are limits to what can and should be said. In an interview the interviewer is providing a service for the client. It is an unequal relationship in which the interviewer puts questions and the client answers. It is a relationship in which the interviewer listens intensely and focuses exclusively on the client's concerns. In an interview the time allocated is designed to give the interviewee space, it is a time in which the interviewee should do most of the talking.

Although the interview should be structured it should not be rigid. Interviewers need to retain and develop their conversational skills if the interview is to function as a form of communication. This last point is crucial. If the interview is to work effectively it needs to retain many of the features of a conversation. It needs to flow from topic to topic. Associations should spark deeper explorations, and provide bridges between themes. It should ebb and flow, it should feel comfortable. It should be positive. It should not be marked by a series of highly specific questions. But it should be controlled, it should be structured, and it should be conducted for a purpose.

The next four Chapters retain this emphasis as they introduce you to the skills involved in interviewing. **Chapter 19** seeks to identify the factors that both hinder and facilitate communication within an interview. It is essential that you understand these. Some clients will talk incessantly, some will ramble, some will be quite precise, but they may not be to the point, others will find it difficult to move beyond that which is immediately relevant. You need to understand which factors impede communication and which factors assist. One factor which facilitates communication is a well-structured interview which provides signposts and markers. **Chapter 20** introduces you to the structure of the interview. **Chapters 21 and 22** then move on to a consideration of skills and techniques involved in interviewing and advising.

18.4   Further Reading

Texts on legal interviewing

Bastress, R. M. and Harbaugh, J. D., *Interviewing, Counseling and Negotiation* (Boston Mass: Little Brown, 1990).
Binder, D., and Price, S. C., *Legal Interviewing and Counseling* (St Paul Minn: West Publishing, 1977).
Inns of Court School of Law, *Advocacy, Negotiation and Conference Skills* (London: Blackstone Press, 1993–94).

Sherr, A., *Client Interviewing for Lawyers* (London: Sweet & Maxwell, 1986).
Twist, H., *Effective Interviewing* (London: Blacktone Press, 1992).

Other texts on interviewing

Benjamin, A., *The Helping Interview*, 3rd ed. (Boston Mass: Houghton-Miffin, 1987).
Egan, G., *The Skilled Helper*, 4th ed. (Pacific Grove Calif: Brooks/Cole, 1990).
Gorden, R. L., *Interviewing Strategy, Techniques and Tactics*, rev. ed. (Homewood Ill: Dorsey Press, 1975).
Kadushin, A., *The Social Work Interview* (New York: Columbia University Press, 1990).
Middleman, R., and Wood, G., *Skills for Direct Practice in Social Work* (New York: Columbia University Press, 1990).
Millar, R., Crute, V., and Hargie, O., *Professional Interviewing* (London: Routledge, 1992).

Texts on questioning

Dillon, J. T., *The Practice of Questioning* (London: Routledge, 1990).
Morgan, N., and Saxton, J., *Teaching, Questioning and Learning* (London: Routledge, 1991).

NINETEEN

COMMUNICATION IN THE INTERVIEW

19.1   Introduction

It is not always clear, to novice interviewers, why a particular range of skills have to be developed to communicate with a client. After all, most clients approach an interview wanting to talk. They have a problem, a set of issues and concerns that trouble them. They are not always sure what it is that they want; they may have immediate needs but deeper longer-term goals. They may be unsure of their rights and obligations. Although they may want to talk, and sometimes do irrepressibly, they may not always be able to communicate. This Chapter considers the factors that may block communication in an interview, and the factors that facilitate communication in an interview.

19.2   Factors that Inhibit Communication in the Interview

It is possible to identify six factors that tend to inhibit free communication: threats to self-esteem or 'ego', a feeling that full revelation may threaten the case, expectations about the lawyer's role, perceptions of relevance and irrelevance, and memory failure (for a further discussion see Binder and Price, *Legal Interviewing and Counseling*).

19.2.1   THREATS TO SELF-ESTEEM, OR 'EGO' THREAT

A client being interviewed may have a feeling of being judged, or may feel embarrassment, fear, shame or guilt. These feelings can arise when the subject of discussion threatens the interviewee's self-esteem, sense of self, or ego. A client in a matrimonial case, for example, may wish to deny using excessive violence, while an accident victim may wish to deny that the accident occurred while he was participating in an affair. When the client's self-esteem, or ego, is threatened the client may be slow to respond for fear of being judged. Where self-esteem is really threatened a client can quite literally 'forget' key features in the case. This happened to a client in a redundancy case who only remembered the identity of Sam, the person who was to replace him in his job, when he was asked to draw a diagram of the people who worked in his office.

19.2.2   A FEELING THAT FULL REVELATION MAY THREATEN THE CASE, OR 'CASE THREAT'

A client being interviewed may be voluble and informative but may be reluctant to reveal information that may weaken his or her case. A client charged with stealing from a till, for example, may be reluctant to reveal that he had regularly 'borrowed' from the till and had a previous conviction for theft. A businessman who had made a bad business deal may be reluctant to admit not making a full investigation of the facts. In each case full disclosure is not made because it involves a 'case threat'. The client being interviewed tries to satisfy what he or she thinks are the lawyer's expectations. The client tells the lawyer what he or she thinks will please and holds back on the negative and contradictory facts.

19.2.3   EXPECTATIONS ABOUT THE LAWYER'S ROLE

Communication can also be affected because the client has expectations about the lawyer's role. The client has a problem, it is for the lawyer to resolve it. The client is unsure of his or her rights, the lawyer is knowledgeable – a figure of authority. In such a context communication is stilted. The lawyer's function is to ask questions, the client's role is to respond. These difficulties can be compounded by the gulfs created by sex, race and socio-economic background, never mind the 'trifling', but significant, problems caused by the uncertain demands of 'etiquette'.

19.2.4   PERCEIVED IRRELEVANCE

Barriers of class and status may not operate in all cases. In business cases clients may be of the same socio-economic background as the lawyer, or higher. They may be highly articulate and experienced in dealing with the law and lawyers, and knowledgeable. They can, though, be inhibited by their own perceptions of relevance and need. 'Perceived irrelevance' distracts the client who cannot see the connection between his or her case and your questions. The client is momentarily confused, speculates on your lack of insight, reflects on why you are probing this area. The client who thinks he has been made redundant, for example, does not see the relevance of questions about office personnel; he is not aware of the distinction between redundancy and unfair dismissal. The distraction experienced by the client can be compounded by impatience, even anger. The client has a need for urgent action and regards the lawyer's questions as off the point.

19.2.5   MEMORY FAILURE

Memory failure is a further obstacle to communication. Failure of memory can be acute where there has been a traumatic shock. But it can also be a problem when clients are unable to maintain accurate and complete recall. Images may remain but facts are recalled only in bits and pieces. It can be particularly difficult, as time fades, to be accurate about the order of events, to remember the chronological order in which they happened. It can be even more difficult to remember the things that you do habitually and the things that you take for granted.

19.3   Factors that Facilitate Communication

Lawyers who are able to identify the negative influences that inhibit communication have reached the first step in creating a climate that facilitates communication. The next step involves taking measures to create the emotional climate that facilitates communication.

This point needs emphasising. Most of the literature on interviewing, and other forms of interpersonal communication, focuses on the skills involved in interviewing – attending behaviour, paraphrasing, interpreting, confronting and summarising. These skills are at the heart of the interview process and are quite properly emphasised – they will be considered in **Chapter 21**.

There is, though, another dimension to interviewing which is concerned with the emotional climate within which interviewing takes place and with the expression of attitudes which create a positive climate. A cluster of such attitudes can be identified – empathy, genuineness, uncondi-tional positive regard, nonjudgmental acceptance, warmth – which provide the 'core' conditions of communication. The adoption of these attitudes has been found to establish an atmosphere which facilitates the development of a positive communication between the interview participants (see Bastress and Harbaugh, *Interviewing, Counseling and Negotiation*).

19.3.1 NONJUDGMENTAL ACCEPTANCE OF THE CLIENT

Nonjudgmental acceptance of what the client has done, and who the client is, is fundamental. It is clearly difficult for a client to articulate his or her concerns if you are dismissive of the behaviour that led to those concerns. Dismissal, whether conveyed through a gesture or an expression, can be damning. The client is stopped and finds it difficult to continue. A nonjudgmental attitude is one which suggests that the interview is not concerned to praise or blame but simply with understanding what has happened. It is an attitude which allows the client to express both the good and the bad in him or herself.

19.3.2 EMPATHY

Empathy involves understanding the nature of the client's experience and the meaning this has for the client. Empathy is a difficult concept. It is not the same as compassion, reassurance or denial. It involves two elements: 'seeing' the action from the client's point of view, and 'feeling' it from the client's point of view. In 'seeing' the matter from the client's point of view the lawyer understands the client's frame of reference, perspective, and own pattern of thinking. In 'feeling' the matter from the client's point of view the lawyer goes a stage further. Not only does the lawyer understand the client but also feels what it is like to be that client.

Empathy needs to be communicated back to the client. To respond empathetically you need to listen carefully. This involves letting the client finish speaking and observing the client's non-verbal modes of communication. You need to pause after the client speaks. You need to resist the temptation to reassure: 'Don't worry, your anger will soon pass'. You need to resist overeager statements of assistance: 'Don't worry, I'm sure we can sort that out'. You then need to articulate your understanding of the client's position. It is then that the client will know that you have listened and that you understand.

19.3.3 THE CLIENT IS PROVIDED WITH FEEDBACK

Communication to the client is facilitated where the client is given feedback. Feedback can help the client by producing encouragement – for example, praising the client for providing a good description of an accident and encouraging the client to talk further about some of the details. Feedback helps the client feel confident – it can be particularly important where a client is uncertain of the relevance of an issue. But feedback needs to be tempered with caution. Feedback on the merits of the case should be held back. Early statements suggesting that the lawyer can help the client may in fact be discouraging. The client may know that there are difficulties in the case. Early positive statements can hinder the client who may feel that the difficulties the client knows about need not, or should not, be revealed.

19.3.4 LANGUAGE

Language is a crucial element in the interview. It is a primary form of communication but it is loaded with difficulties. Lawyers need to be able to step outside of their own jargon and understand the language of the client. Jargon is the language we use within our own community – it is a shared language which is full of familiar terms and common expressions. This helps communication within our own community, the firm, and it provides a tight social bond. Clients will have their own private language, their own forms of expression that operate within their own shared community. You need to find a way of speaking plainly, avoiding legal shorthand, and explaining legal terms where their use is unavoidable. You also need to find a way of working with the language of the client – asking for clarification where necessary, but be sensitive to its use and value.

19.3.5 CLARIFYING EXPECTATIONS

Communication is facilitated where expectations about the nature of the interview are articulated. You need to agree a structure and an agenda for the session. This sets a framework and provides an opportunity to explain your own role. If you believe that clients should be involved in both the fact-finding and decision-making processes then you need to make this clear at the outset. You need to define your joint responsibilities and clarify your expectations. You need to do this throughout the interview. When you are following a line of inquiry that isn't immediately obvious it can help if you explain what you are doing. If you ask a question that confuses the client, give it a context. If you shift topics try to lead naturally through or explain the move. If the client looks disconcerted as you start to probe a delicate area, or if you encounter resistance, explain why you are pushing in this direction.

TWENTY

ELEMENTS OF THE INTERVIEW: ANATOMY AND STRUCTURE

20.1 Introduction

All good interviews have a sound structure and a coherent shape. The structure provides the interview with a series of stages each invested with their own purpose, each emphasising different methods and activities and each with its own tempo. The structure provides the space for interaction between lawyer and client: it is this interaction which provides the interview with its shape, its characteristic turns, and its mood.

The interview can be structured around six different but related stages (different accounts of the stages of an interview can be found in Sherr, *Client Interviewing for Lawyers*, and Binder and Price *Legal Interviewing and Counseling*):

(a) Interview preparation.
(b) 'Ice-breaking'.
(c) Identify the issues.
(d) Elucidating details.
(e) Determination of client goals.
(f) Closing.

This section provides a description of these stages, their function and the activities that take place within them. It considers, in outline, the related processes involved in analysis and advice, and it considers, in addition, the practical dimensions of the interview process.

20.2 Interview Preparation

Preparing for the interview helps you plan and structure the meeting. If it is an on-going matter you need to review the files and check progress. Where it is a new client you need to consider who the client is. You can check with your colleagues, especially where the client has been referred by one of them. If you or your colleagues know the client's company you can do some initial research. If you know the general area of concern you could review a checklist.

Where possible you should determine the purpose of the meeting, work out the structure of the meeting, determine the structure of your approach and plan an agenda.

Prepare the physical setting. A physical setting that is informal, friendly and private will help make the client feel relaxed and comfortable. Seating will make a difference too. It is not a good idea to seat a client in a low soft armchair across a large desk from a lawyer in a firm high chair. The desk and the chair provide crutches for the lawyer's authority and put the client at a disadvantage. A desk covered in files and papers, and an ever-ringing telephone, can create an impression of 'business' – or panic. Use the desk if you have to, to write notes and provide a place for the client to put documents, but try to sit across a corner or alongside the desk. Strive for a degree of informality that is compatible with the formality of the occasion. Provide coffee and other drinks. Avoid interruptions. Time the interview so that you can accomplish what you have planned.

Prepare yourself for the interview. This may involve little more than bringing work to an end prior to the interview, clearing your desk and clearing your mind of pressing concerns.

20.3 'Ice-breaking': Setting the Scene for Effective Communication

The opening of the interview provides a bridge between the outside world of conversation and the professional setting of the interview. Greet the client, make him comfortable in your office, offer him coffee or soft drinks. Spend a little time breaking the ice with small talk – about traffic, the weather, difficulties in parking etc. Then spend a few moments learning about the client. This shows that you value him as a person, not just another case.

Meeting and greeting the client, 'ice-breaking', are not just optional extras. They put the client at ease and provide a moment during which both the client and the lawyer can size each other up. 'Small talk' can ease the conversation into more formal concerns while providing the lawyer with an opportunity to assess the client. It is through 'small talk' that the lawyer can determine how the client communicates, whether the client is tense or relaxed, aggressive or withdrawn, sophisticated or unsophisticated. While exploring the client's background you may begin to move into the substantive stages of the interview. In a criminal case before you have received the charge sheet you may want to explore only the client's background. In a legal aid case you may need to explore eligibility.

Careful attention, while engaging in 'small talk', provides leads which will move you into the more formal business of the interview. It is at this point that you can agree a structure and an agenda for the session. This need not be too detailed, just a sketchy outline of the structure will do: 'In the first part I want you to describe in your own words . . . then I shall pursue some of the matters in more detail . . . finally, we can consider what we're going to do'. This helps to structure the session. It can also be used to introduce the topic of fees, to indicate when they will be discussed, to discuss note-taking, and to provide the reassurance of confidentiality. Pausing at this point provides a space for the client to settle his or her thoughts and put them in order.

20.4 Identify the Issues

As you move into the next phase of the interview you need to gain a preliminary understanding of the client's concerns. You will usually have a general idea, from when the client made the appointment, that you are being consulted about a 'car accident', a 'contract problem', or the making of a will.

You can then use open questions to start the client off: 'I know you were involved in an accident. Why don't you tell me what happened in your own words?' Then allow the client to tell his or her story, without interruptions, in his or her own way. The client should do most of the talking but may be guided by the use of open questions, reflective statements and non-verbal reinforcers. In this way the account will be from the client's own perspective and talking freely will help to relieve the client from the worry of the problem.

While the client tells the story, listen not only to what the client says but also note the things that are omitted, things that would usually be mentioned. When the client has finished you can summarise or paraphrase what he or she has said. This provides a check for accuracy and shows the client that you have been listening actively.

You may form a tentative hypothesis at this stage and give a preliminary explanation. But you should hold back on advice. You still do not have the full facts and a confident declaration of intent may be off-putting. The client may want to explore a range of options. The client may have been holding certain things back. Premature advice can easily hinder full communication.

20.5   Elucidating Details

Now you move to a more detailed account of the issues the client seeks to resolve. By this stage you will have formed a vision of what options are open to the client and you will want to verify the issues through closer questioning. You will want a more detailed account of the events that have caused your client concern and you will want other background facts.

In describing his or her concerns the client may have failed to cover a number of points and it is at this stage that you should seek to obtain a more detailed account of the issues that the client seeks to resolve. A client naturally wishes to make a good impression and convince the lawyer that the case is a good one. You will be given the client's version of what will be disputed facts, and unfavourable aspects will be omitted. It is now time to use more focused questions and seek elaboration and clarification through the use of 'probing' questions or 'probes'.

You need to look for information that might adversely affect the client's position. Are there problems in the client's background? What details has the client omitted in his or her presentation of the account? It is here that you need to be 'soft on the person, but hard on the problem'. Remind the client that you need to get all of the facts, good or bad, to assess the position accurately. Ask the client, and yourself, what is probably going to be told to the other side's lawyer. Think the case through from the position of the other side.

Although you will direct the account the client should still do most of the talking. Keep a conversational style, identify topics, provide prompts and structure the account.

Up to this point you will probably not have taken any notes. Notes are an effective aid to concentration and are a stimulus to active listening. But they can also interfere and intrude. It may not be necessary to take notes in the early part of the interview. Notes should not be comprehensive – taking full notes would block concentration. Notes should focus on keywords and key phrases. The key phrases should, where possible, be in the client's own words. If ideas need further elaboration or clarification then the key phrase can be underlined or circled. Spaces should be left to add comments or fill in with detail later. Diagrams might be useful to describe relationships – as in the 'redundancy' case referred to in **19.2.1** – or to provide a structure to the account.

An outline, or a checklist, may provide a structure for this stage. It will identify the key points and issues and highlight the information that needs to be recorded, and is a useful aid in planning the interview. But the checklist should, as far as possible, be held in the head. It should not be used as a questionnaire – because that would lead to a routine approach to interviewing in which the lawyer starts at the top of the list and moves through to the bottom. In the light of the specific facts of the case the order may be illogical. It may not coincide with the client's sense of what is important. It can exaggerate the lawyer's natural tendency to pursue an interview through a series of very focused questions.

20.6   Determination of the Client's Goals

What does the client really want? The answer may often be simple. It may have been stated immediately by the client; it may have emerged in the course of the small talk at the beginning of the interview. The client may have been injured and want monetary damages. The client may have been excluded from the matrimonial home and want a divorce. The client has a number of properties and wants to make a will.

Even where the client states immediate concerns it is important to probe deeper. What are the client's underlying concerns? What would the client view as a favourable outcome? Does the client want the case to go to trial, is he or she willing to settle? Is the client angry and hurt and looking for financial remuneration to make amends? Is the dispute with another business with which the client has an on-going relationship? Is that long-term relationship more important than the short-term breach? In the case of a will, has the client considered all the potential beneficiaries. Is he or she aware of the tax effects of different forms of disposal? What does the client really want? Now is the time to find out what the client wants and begin to assess whether those expectations are realistic or need to be modified.

20.7   Closing

The purpose of this stage is to determine the relationship between the lawyer and the client and to provide the client with an indication of what will happen next. It provides an opportunity to determine whether the client has instructed the lawyer. The lawyer should explain and discuss what will happen next, determine the lawyer and client's responsibilities, discuss fees and billing arrangements, and provide an idea of the time-scale for further action. If appropriate, it is at this stage that the lawyer may determine that he or she is not competent to handle the matter and refer the client to another source of assistance.

No interview should be terminated without attending to the procedures needed to close the interview. You need to know that you are acting according to the client's instructions and the client needs to know what will happen next. Many clients may be uncertain after the interview. They may be unsure about how to proceed; they may not know exactly what is going to be done or who is going to do it. They may not know how long it will take, how much it will cost and when or whether they need to return. The client needs to know what he or she is expected to do, how fees will be determined, and what the time-scale for future action is likely to be. The client also needs to know who will be handling the case and if problems arise how complaints will be dealt with.

The client will need to be told what he or she should do next: collect documents, records or paperwork of any kind. The client should be given a plan or chronology describing the progress of the matter and this should provide an indication of critical dates. Regular communication should be maintained with the client. Copies of relevant documentation should be sent when appropriate. You should write regularly to let the client know what is happening in the matter and why. If nothing is happening, let the client know and explain why. A well-informed client is likely to be cooperative and satisfied, and is also less likely to trouble you.

The cost of the action is a critical matter for the client and a major cause of mistrust. An indication of when costs will be discussed should be provided at the first opportunity. It will often be raised by the client or emerge naturally in the course of the interview, but where it is not the lawyer should take the initiative. The solicitors' written professional standards require every solicitor to provide clear and unambiguous information on the basis for charging and where possible the likely cost of every matter.

After the interview a full note should be taken. The note should be typed. It is at this stage that a checklist can be used which provides a basis for recording all essential factual details: names, addresses and telephone numbers. Checklists can also be used as a device for structuring the factual information recorded during the interview. The file note should record preliminary opinion of the matter and your view of the alternatives available to the client. Work that is still to be done, and a plan of action for completing the work, should also be recorded. You may also want to record your impressions of the client. This can be useful in subsequent interviews. It may provide a basis for introducing small talk at your next meeting, it may affect the manner in which you tender your advice.

It is good practice to confirm in writing the advice given to a client and to confirm any instructions received. This will reduce the risk of misapprehension by the client about the services that will be given, and it will serve as a reminder of what the client needs to do as a consequence of the interview. It will also provide a clear written record of action taken should any complaint be made at a later date.

There are two further components of the interview process: analysis and advice. These may or may not form part of the initial interview.

20.8 Analysis

The purpose of this stage is to identify the legal and non-legal elements that underpin the client's concerns. You should already have formed a tentative diagnosis of the issues and this will have informed questioning at the previous stage. You may form tentative hypotheses and may explore preliminary options with the client during the first interview. You should check the analysis with the client. In many cases you will need to gather more factual information and engage in research before available remedies can be explored. More interviews may be needed with the client to complete the process of information gathering and this itself may lead to a further analysis of the client's concerns.

20.9 Advice

The purpose of this stage is to identify and evaluate the possible options open to the client and to assist the client to decide which option to pursue. In the previous stages of the interview the client should have done most of the talking. You will have listened and attended to the client's concerns and questioned and probed for further details. At this stage listening and questioning skills are still crucial. You will have to watch the client's reactions and evaluate the response to the options presented. In addition you will have to use presentation skills to provide the client with a clear picture of the options available and their consequences.

TWENTY ONE

THE SKILLS INVOLVED IN INTERVIEWING

21.1 Introduction

At the heart of the interviewing process are a series of skills and techniques: attending behaviour, minimal encouragements, question formulation, reflecting, paraphrasing, interpreting, confronting, summarising and listening. An interview is a dynamic process using the same techniques that characterise a conversation: it should be fluid, ebbing and flowing, bridging from one topic to another. Following a course it is punctuated by pauses and momentary silence: gaps as thoughts are collected and concentration gathered.

These skills and techniques are considered in this Chapter. The skills are used for different purposes and will be considered in four sections:

(a) Listening.
(b) Range: exploring all aspects of a client's problem.
(c) Depth: using questions effectively.
(d) Depth: moving beyond questions.

21.2 Listening

Listening is both a fundamental skill and a foundation for other skills. It is fundamental for the child, who learns to listen before learning to speak. It is fundamental, too, for adults, but they tend to do the opposite. They typically speak before they listen; they talk across each other, fill in gaps, and interrupt. In the interview this setting may be compounded as the interviewer talks too much and fires off a mass of questions.

The problem is that listening is actually quite hard. Listening is distinct from hearing. Hearing is the physical phenomenon that takes place in the ears. Listening is the mental processing of what you have heard – it takes place between the ears. The problem is compounded because the mental work depends not just upon the ears, but the eyes and other senses. To listen effectively you need to attend both to the verbal messages given out by the speaker and the non-verbal cues that accompany them. Good listening requires you to focus both on what is said and what is not said. It involves following both the overt-messages, those which are spoken, and the latent undertones.

The nature of speech itself produces special problems. The average rate of speech is between 125 and 175 words per minute, while the average 'thought' rate, at which information is processed, is between 400 and 800 words per minute. This differential between the speech rate and the thought rate provides the listener with an opportunity to assimilate thoughts, organise them and respond to the speaker. It also provides the listener with a space which can be filled with other unrelated mental processes: stereotypes, mental sets and preconceptions, which can all lead to a subtle distortion of what is heard.

In the course of normal conversation we use a range of verbal and non-verbal techniques to demonstrate we are listening and to provide feedback to speakers. It is easy in the formality of the interview to forget these techniques.

Non-verbal behaviours, changes of posture, eye gazes and gestures are a crucial element in communication. They are used to signal attention, provide feedback, signal disapproval, and mark changes in communication. Clear non-verbal signals are usually used to signal the move from listening to speaking, or to block a speaker in mid-flow.

Head nods, forward leaning posture, visual attention, smiles and eyebrow raises are all seen to express an eagerness to hear. When listening it is important to look at the speaker, though it is normal for speakers to look into the middle distance. Nods of the head indicate readiness to listen. A forward or sideways lean in the chair is seen as the sign of an attentive posture, so, too, is a sideways tilt of the head.

Doodling, fidgeting or looking at your watch are distracting mannerisms which may, correctly or incorrectly, convey that you are bored or irritated and wish to move on with the interview.

Listeners need to be mentally prepared to listen. You need to remove all other thoughts from your mind and concentrate fully on the speaker. You need to be aware of your own biases and avoid preconceptions. Listeners can talk to themselves to heighten receptivity. This may involve asking covert questions ('Why am I being told this now?'), the use of covert coaching ('I'm not paying enough attention. Listen carefully.'), or self-reinforcement ('Good, I've got that and I've got that, let's pursue this.').

You can use the time made available through the slowness of speech positively. Move through what the client is saying, connect ideas, ask yourself questions: 'How did that happen? What happened next? Will that stand up?' But do not formulate these as questions. Watch for the answers, look for gaps, identify the emerging message. Develop a system of mental 'banking', where the ideas you wish to pursue are 'deposited' and withdrawn later. Pay attention to dominant themes, but let the themes develop over the course of the interview. Resist the temptation to analyse and advise too early in the interview. Making up your mind too soon provides yet another filter. Listen tentatively and be prepared to recast your understanding. Remember, throughout, that listening is hard work. It takes energy to listen actively and it demands a firm commitment to the client.

21.3 The Broad Pattern: Exploring all Aspects of a Client's Problem

In the early stages of the interview it is best to get an account of the client's concerns in the client's own words. As the interview moves on you should ask the client to elaborate, to enrich the account. In these stages you are still not pushed for detail: you want to get a broad outline of the factual context which may have stimulated the client to take action.

In litigation cases you may ask the client to elaborate the account through a chronological story-telling approach. Most people think chronologically and this can provide an approach which enables them to cover the ground. You will need to start the client off using 'open' questions (see 21.4.1) but your client may need to be 'nudged' while talking.

A variety of techniques may be used to encourage the client and maintain the flow of conversation:

(a) Attending behaviour and minimal encouragements.
(b) Paraphrasing.
(c) Summaries and recapitulation.
(d) Reflection.
(e) Bridging and transitions.

21.3.1 ATTENDING BEHAVIOUR AND MINIMAL ENCOURAGEMENTS

A first requirement of a good interview is that attention is focused upon the client and what he is communicating. Attending behaviours indicate that the lawyer is interested and paying attention. The skills used in attending can be expressed in the acronym S-O-L-E-R. Face the client *squarely*, adopting a posture that indicates involvement. Adopt an *open* posture, one which suggests that you are receptive to the client. *Lean* slightly forward, not aggressively forward but enough to show that you are interested in the client. Maintain *eye* contact. Initiate and maintain eye contact but do not stare. Use your eyes to convey interest, but vary your eye contact in response to the flow of the conversation. Stay *relaxed*. Do not fidget, be natural in your expressions.

Minimum encouragement can be provided through the use of verbal reinforcers. Expressions such as 'mm hmm', 'yes', 'I see' indicate that the interviewer is attending to the client but they do not constitute interruptions. Statements which praise, encourage or support the client – 'That's a helpful description' – provide further reinforcement and promote further communication. Expressions of encouragement show that you are listening and indicate that the client should proceed. They indicate that you accept what has been said and wish the client to continue without specifying what the client should say.

Verbal following provides further evidence of attention and involvement. By following on from what the client has just said you demonstrate concentration and a focus on what the client perceives as relevant. This keeps the interview moving smoothly and naturally from point to point. Where the interviewer does not 'follow on' it is usual to mark this consciously: 'Can I take you back to an earlier point?', 'Before I forget can I ask?'

Silence is a form of attending behaviour. It can be used after the client has apparently finished or in the form of a pause before you formulate a question. Silence makes no effort to steer the client in any direction. It neither designates the area of discussion nor does it structure the answer in any way. By using silence you slow down the interview's pace and allow the client to gather his or her thoughts. Silence is hard to deal with. To start with, all pauses feel too long. Counting slowly to 10 can help. But you need to be careful. It is only too easy to shift from the 'permissive pause' to the 'embarrassing silence'. You need to watch and see how the client is responding to the pause. Then relax, listen and observe before proceeding.

Many of these responses are delaying tactics. They keep the client talking and give the interviewer an opportunity to build up a picture of the situation. The responses provide a space for the interviewer to think and work out what is going on yet suggest to the client that the interviewer is with the client.

21.3.2 PARAPHRASING

Through paraphrasing you provide a selective restatement of the main idea in phrasing which resembles, but which is not the same as, that used by the client.

When paraphrasing it can help if you lead in with a short phrase: 'If I've got this right . . .', 'It seems to me . . .', 'So, the car seemed to swerve across the road'. To paraphrase effectively you need to listen carefully and understand what is being said. A paraphrase highlights significant aspects of a client's statement, it makes them visible and pertinent. It shows that you are interested, that you are following the client and urging the client to continue.

21.3.3   SUMMARIES OR RECAPITULATIONS

Partial or detailed summaries and recapitulations help to extend the range of communication. You briefly review what has been said and give the interview its direction.

In moving to a summary or a recapitulation you might say: 'Let's make sure I understood you...', 'Okay, well we've identified five or so issues...', 'Okay, this gives me a little idea of your situation. Before moving on, let's see if I've got this right...', 'You describe – I think I've got it, and you correct me if I'm wrong – a situation in which...'.

Recapitulation provides you with an opportunity to give the interview some structure. A summary provides a form of recapitulation. It combines selected elements from the interview and summarises them for the client. No question is put and the client is free to respond. Recapitulations and summaries give the client the opportunity to reflect on what they've said and to think further as you summarise points. It allows the client to correct misunderstandings and develop themes that you have summarised. When the client uses a narrative structure the re-presentation of that story can stimulate fresh points and provide greater detail. It is a relatively open form of intervention and it can reduce the need for interruptions to seek greater detail.

Recapitulation provides you with a similar opportunity. As you verbally scan the narrative you can see issues that need to be pursued in further depth. It is a particularly effective device for moving on from bottlenecks as a vein of questioning runs dry. It provides a space for further open questions and allows the client to resume the narrative along a different theme.

21.3.4   REFLECTION

Reflection takes the conversation further by repeating the essence of the client's statements. Reflection is used in counselling as a means of affirming the client's feelings and to confirm to the client that the interviewer is interested in the client. It is the main form used for expressing empathy. Reflection has to be used with care.

A reflection which simply 'echoes' or repeats what the client has just said, suggests that the interviewer is simply following a mechanical routine.

Reflections which attempt to reflect the *meaning* or *feeling* behind the words used by the client can be more effective. The response needs to be succinct, yet fully capture the essence of the client's experience. The reflection must show that you understand precisely how the client feels. It is no good reflecting a couple's sadness at their daughter's death, if they are really expressing anger at the careless driving that led to it.

21.3.5   BRIDGING AND TRANSITION

At times during the interview the interviewer may decide that a change should be made in the material being discussed. Transitions help extend the range of the interview by moving from the discussion of one topic to another. Transitions can be effected by using an introduction which allows the client to take the lead in moving into the new topic. The introduction affirms the direction of the interview and opens the way to further elaboration: 'The information that you've given me on the accident is very helpful. You mentioned earlier that you had a problem with the car. Can you tell me more about that?'

Before using a bridge you need to make sure that you've adequately covered the topic. Ineffective interviewers tend to move too quickly from topic to topic. Pause before using a bridge to check that the client has finished the current train of thoughts.

At times a transition can take the form of an interruption. If the client has embarked on a prolonged digression, is rambling or repetitious then an interruption may be necessary. A 'bridge' can provide an effective form of interruption: 'Okay, I think we've explored our consideration of that, let's move back to what you were saying earlier. What happened after . . .?'

21.4 Depth: Using Questions Effectively

In an interview the major type of communication from lawyer to client takes the form of questions – who, what, where, why? This is hardly surprising. Questioning is one of the most obvious ways of obtaining information, and it is a social skill that we all acquire at the earliest age. Questions can be used to extend the range of the interview, to make transitions, and to explore situations in depth. Good questioning helps the client organise their presentation and ensures that all the relevant material will be included. Questions can be used to help the client think about his or her problem situation in an explicit, systematic manner. They can clarify the situation for the lawyer and provide clarification to the client at the same time. Questioning is, though, a deceptively complex process. The badly phrased question can confuse the client; the badly timed question interrupts the client; the badly structured question cannot be answered. Part of the skill in interviewing is knowing what kind of question to use and when. Part of the skill lies in knowing when to use silence, pauses and non-verbal sounds of encouragement which can be just as effective as questions.

A variety of different question forms can be used at different times during an interview. Questions vary according to the degree of control they exert over the interviewee. Open questions place the least restrictions on the topic and provide considerable freedom in response. Narrow or closed questions limit the topic but permit a limited range of possible responses. Leading questions are even more restrictive – they virtually suggest the answer. Probing questions, on the other hand, encourage the client to pursue a line and give the client freedom to continue a response.

21.4.1 OPEN QUESTIONS

Open questions are questions which can be answered in a number of ways, the response being left open to the client. Open questions allow the client to select the subject-matter for discussion or the information related to the general subject which the client believes is pertinent and relevant.

In interviewing a client involved in a car accident the use of an open question, 'Tell me about your accident', identifies the topic generally but does not impose a structure or emphasis. Open follow-ups might ask the client 'What happened next?' or 'Tell me more about . . .'.

Open questions are useful where the facts lend themselves to narrative or chronological development. They allow clients to develop their own themes. The client's emphasis will structure the account and provide you with a sense of what the client sees as relevant. Open questions can help the client deal with sensitive or threatening subjects. Open questions can be more effective in helping the client disclose personal information. They also produce more accurate information. The client is not prompted along lines suggested by the interviewer, or encouraged to structure the account to suit the interviewer's emphasis.

Open questions provide an overview but they do not tend to produce sufficient data. They can encourage the client to ramble with little sense of relevancy. They provide very little structure to the account and they can be unsettling for the client who is reluctant to talk – they provide no prompts and no stimulus to move forward.

21.4.2 NARROW OR CLOSED QUESTIONS

Narrow questions seek specific information and ask for only short responses. Most people find narrow questions easy to answer. They provide direction and a stimulus. Narrow questions can be employed to gain very specific information. They can be prepared in advance and they provide the interviewer with a high degree of control over the content of the interview.

In an accident case you might use narrow questions to ask: 'How fast were you going?', 'Was it raining?', 'Who was in the car?', 'How far from the kerb were you?'

Narrow questions are useful when your goals are very specific, where you need to get at particular facts or where your client's goals require specific information. In an interview on the drafting of a contract, for example, you need to know what provisions, other than the standard terms, you need to draft to further the client's interests. In will interviews you may need to put specific questions to determine the taxation implications of the disposition of sizeable property holdings.

Narrow questions can also be used where the client lacks confidence. The lawyer who senses that the client is avoiding a sensitive topic can use narrow questions to nudge the client through a difficult moment.

Narrow questions have to be used judiciously. They can be used to elicit detail when the client has already been given the opportunity to explain concerns in his or her own words. Narrow questions may be misused if detailed probing begins before the client is ready. Narrow questions can damage rapport and lead to a stilted exchange. Interviews conducted through a series of highly specific questions put the client into a passive position. It becomes the client's job to tell the lawyer the problem and the lawyers' job to tell the client the solution. The opportunity to open up the broader dimensions of a problem may, as a consequence, be lost.

21.4.3   LEADING QUESTIONS

Leading questions are a particular form of narrow question. They are questions which, by the way they are worded, lead the client towards an expected response. They typically require a yes or no answer and suggest what the appropriate choice is.

Leading questions are frequently used in everyday conversation: 'Isn't this meal really delicious?' They function then to ease conversation, to start from an accepted position – they serve to solicit mutual support.

Leading questions are also used, notoriously, by lawyers in cross-examination: 'Isn't it true that you had drunk six beers before you left to drive home?' They should be used sparingly in an interview. They tend to dramatise the authority and aggressiveness of the lawyer and confine the client, who may feel threatened and defensive, to a narrow line of response.

Leading questions can, though, be used to express empathy: 'You're feeling dejected because you worked so hard and now you could loose your business?' They can also be used to seek confirmation of particular facts – and to lead the client to push forward in the account: 'So you left the ring road by Moorfoot?'.

Leading questions can also be used where a client reveals a bit of information but is reluctant to reveal more: 'So you've had trouble with the police before?'.

The use of a leading question can convey acceptance by the interviewer of the client's behaviour. Kinsey used leading questions as a device to obtain data about sexual behaviour for precisely this reason. Leading questions like 'When did you have your first homosexual experience?' take the behaviour for granted, leaving the interviewee to confirm the interviewer's expectations. Again, the dangers in a legal context should be obvious. The client can give an affirmative nod to the question rather than actively agreeing, or disagreeing.

21.4.4   MULTIPLE QUESTIONS

A multiple question is a question that is made up of two or more questions phrased as one. Multiple questions may contain a number of questions of the same type. They may also mix questions of different types. An open question, for example, may be used with the intention of exploring a general topic, but it is followed by a closed question which narrows the focus: 'Have you had a problem with the car before, what was wrong with the brakes?' Such questions can confuse both the client, who is not sure how to reply, and the interviewer, who may not know which question has been answered.

21.4.5   TACTICS: THE USE OF QUESTIONS THROUGHOUT THE INTERVIEW

A skilled interviewer will vary the format of questioning so that no one pattern characterises each interview. Sometimes open questions may have a few closed questions tucked in, and questions may be varied with comments, remarks and statements. To gather information in an interview it is necessary to use the full range of skills – listening, attending, and questions. Putting these together is a central part of the skill of interviewing. Part of this skill can only be acquired and demonstrated in the course of the interview itself. But there are some general principles.

It is best to use a consistent sequence or pattern of questions: from open to closed, or from closed to open is best. An erratic sequence of open and closed questions can confuse the interviewee and reduce the level of participation. Advocates commonly recommend the use of erratic questions with a quick change of focus which is designed to catch the witness off-balance. An erratic sequence is used in interrogation too – to confuse the suspect who will not know what type of question to expect next.

Three forms of sequence are usually recommended: the chronological sequence, the funnel and the inverted funnel.

21.4.6   THE CHRONOLOGICAL SEQUENCE

A chronological sequence provides a simple means of structuring the interview. To be effective the subject of the interview needs to lend itself to a narrative structure. In a tort case or a breach of contract case, for example, the facts can usually be structured chronologically. The format provides the client, or witness, with a simple structure while assisting your understanding.

The lawyer's role in chronologically structured interviews is simple. You start with an open question with the structure implicit: 'Please start at the beginning and tell me all about it'. Then you can probe where elaboration is needed: 'What happened after that?' or 'Then what?' or 'Tell me what happened next?' The interview can be rounded out with probes for clarification and recapitulation.

21.4.7   THE FUNNEL SEQUENCE

The funnel sequence begins with the broadest form of question available and gradually narrows to the specific. This approach is common in counselling interviews, where the helper does not want to impose on the person being helped any restrictions about what is to be discussed. In legal interviews it is effective in cases that lend themselves to topical breakdowns or when the interviewee's perspectives and priorities are important – in the initial client interview, for example.

The funnel explores a topic by employing a series of open-ended questions at the beginning. These questions are used to get at the facts the client recalls. When these questions are no longer productive, you employ a series of narrow questions. The narrow questions are used to focus on the possibilities you have thought of but which are not mentioned in response to the open-ended questions.

The funnel sequence combines the advantages of both the open and the narrow question. The open question allows the client to follow his or her own associations and produce a personal narrative. Narrow questions can disrupt the associations by moving from subject to subject. But narrow questions may be useful in focusing on specific facts and probing for further detail. It is then that narrow questions can be brought to bear.

The funnel sequence should be repeated throughout the interview. Once the client has related his or her story it will be necessary to move through the account in more detail. Open questions can be used to start the funnelling process in one area, but they then need to be used again to reopen the funnel to move into the next area of investigation. Starting the general inquiry again by opening another funnel with another open question is in fact quite difficult. It is easy to get pushed into a narrow line of questioning and to become constricted by the first funnel. When this begins to happen it is time to use silence, to pause, to look down the outline notes that you have made, perhaps to summarise what the client has said earlier. Summarising is particularly useful because it provides an opportunity to scan the narrative for elements that need to be pursued more precisely.

21.4.8   THE INVERTED FUNNEL

In the inverted funnel the sequencing of questions begins with very closed questions and gradually opens out to embrace wider issues. This approach is often used in careers guidance interviews in which the interviewer may want to build up a picture of the client (e.g., academic achievements, family background, interests etc.) before progressing to possible choice of career and the reasons for this choice. By using closed questions initially to obtain information about the client, the careers interviewer may be in a better position to help the client evaluate possible career options.

The inverted funnel may be useful in advising a client to decide on action to be taken. You begin by exploring the key issues first and build up the broad picture from the mass of detail. Once you have a clear picture of the facts – the estate of a client in a will case, for example – it may then be appropriate to consider the options that the client has in mind.

The inverted funnel is also useful when you are interviewing individuals who are reluctant to talk – a witness, for example. By beginning with narrow questions you are more likely to get at least some answers. The inverted funnel can also be used to probe sensitive subjects.

It is common, of course, to combine each of these sequences. The chronological account may be triggered with a series of open questions. As the client moves through the narrative you use open or narrow probes to capture some detailed points and then you progressively move back towards more open-ended questions and encourage the client to resume the narrative.

21.4.9   THE SKILLS OF QUESTIONING

The skill of questioning is often used ineffectively in interviewing – partly because interviews are dominated by narrow specific questions that require only a limited response, partly because interviewers are unaware of the range of strategies, including questioning, that are available. The best questions are those that arise organically and almost spontaneously from what the interviewee says. Questions should be used as they are in conversation, opening lines of inquiry, broadening the range of inquiry, and probing for details. But as in conversation they should be used sparingly.

A well-formulated question is clearly focused, it is short, precise and clearly phrased. Questions should avoid jargon, they should be tuned to the client's vocabulary, they should operate within the client's frame of reference. Prefaces, lead-ins or contextualising statements can help the client. They locate the questions and define their content.

All interviewers need to treat questions with care. Relentless consistency in the use of any particular style of question is likely to be counter-productive. Relentless use of questions on their own can be wearing. It can be better to use alternatives that are less interrogative in form. If you consider a conversation you will be surprised to see only a few questions but a variety of other techniques. In an interview these techniques can be used to open up the problem, to move a little deeper, to probe for details, to check out inferences and make connections.

21.5   Depth: Moving beyond Questions

Interviewers who are not skilled at using the full range of interviewing techniques can finish an interview with a mass of superficial information or information that is only half complete. They fail to follow up client responses, they accept vague and indeterminate answers to open questions, they stumble at the end of a long line of very specific narrow questions when the client dries up.

Probing by the interviewer ensures that significant statements by the client are not accepted at face value. Probing questions are designed to encourage the client to expand upon initial responses. Probe questions seek additional, more specific information which may be necessary because the initial answer is insufficient, irrelevant, unclear, or inconsistent with some previously offered information. Probe questions direct the client to a response (an excellent treatment of probe questions can be found in Helena Twist's *Effective Interviewing*).

Probes, though, are only one way of moving beyond questioning to a more problem-solving orientation. This section considers a variety of such techniques:

(a)   Completion.
(b)   Elaboration.
(c)   Clarification.
(d)   Interpretation.
(e)   Drawing inferences.
(f)   Recasting problems.
(g)   Confronting.

21.5.1   COMPLETION

Completion probes are directed towards neglected or inadequately covered content and call upon the client to elaborate and amplify details and to fill in omissions. They include such questions as: 'And then?', 'Does anything else come to mind?', 'What happened then?', 'You said you swerved to the right, what happened next?'

21.5.2   ELABORATION

Requests for elaboration suggest that you approve of what the client is saying but would like the client to say more. The probe pushes the client on, rather than changing the subject or focusing on a particular point. The interviewer can encourage the client to elaborate by saying 'And then?', 'Then what happened?' or 'What happened next?'. This encourages the client to continue the narrative.

The interviewer can also probe the client to say more about the topic at hand by saying: 'Tell me more about that', 'Would you like to tell me more about that?', 'Could you spell that out a little more?'

Probes can also be used to refer back to something previously said in the interview: 'Earlier you indicated that you'd been having a problem with the car. Can you tell me about that?' Here you are changing the topic, moving back to an earlier part of the interview, but asking the client to structure and develop the response.

The use of probes which encourage the client or call for elaboration tell the client you are listening and that you want to hear more. They are useful in following up broad open questions that you have used to initiate the interview.

21.5.3   CLARIFICATION

You seek clarification when you want to check out your understanding of what the client is saying. Requests for clarification enlist the client in a cooperative problem-solving mode. A call for clarification not only seeks more information, it specifies the kind of information needed, and calls upon the client to assist the lawyer find it. Probes can be used to seek additional information about specific parts of preceding answers. They mark a move to more narrow courses of questioning. A clarification probe not only asks for more information but it also specifies the kind of additional information that is needed.

You might ask for a more detailed sequence of events: 'What exactly happened as the car went off the road?', or to seek more detailed information: 'What exactly was wrong with the brakes?' They can also be used to reduce ambiguities and conflicts in details: 'What do you mean by fast, how fast?', 'I don't understand that, how did the car swerve?'

Some clarification probes permit further specification of responses so that the client defines his or her situation more clearly. Vague or inconsistent responses to an open-ended question may lead to probes asking for greater clarification.

Probes can also be used to switch back to a topic raised earlier in the interview: 'You said earlier that you've had problems with the car before – what was the problem then?'

21.5.4   INTERPRETATION

Interpretation goes a stage beyond clarification, paraphrasing or reflection. While a request for clarification stays close to the client's account and encourages additions to it, interpretation moves beyond the client's frame of reference. It takes off from the client's account and adds to it your perspective. It is what is heard plus what is inferred. A speculative probe is a useful device for prodding the client. It can be used to articulate a point that is implicit in what a client has said: 'I'm just thinking ahead, but maybe . . .', 'Perhaps another way of looking at that is . . .'.

21.5.5   DRAWING INFERENCES

Sometimes clients protect themselves by not saying all that they mean or wish to say. They may be unsure themselves of what really happened or how significant an event is. They may not catch the implication of what has happened because they are so busy experiencing it. When this happens you need to fill in the missing pieces and draw inferences.

An inference is a statement that needs to be confirmed or denied. It is incumbent upon you to check inferences for accuracy. You can do this by stating the inference and asking the client if it is accurate. In so doing you can provide new insights and connections. You may also have to confront the client's perception of events. In the case of the 'redundant' worker (see **19.2.1**), the lawyer asked him to draw a diagram because she had inferred from his account that something was wrong – his account did not add up. When he drew Sam, who was to replace him, she had to confront him and his understanding of the event. She had to consider the possibility of a claim for unfair dismissal, and in doing this, she had to explore his own behaviour and consider possible justifications.

21.5.6   RECASTING PROBLEMS

The diagram in the redundancy case (see **21.5.5**) provided a new perspective on a set of events. It provided a different vantage point for thinking about a troubling issue, thereby shifting and/or increasing the range of alternative actions considered appropriate for dealing with them. This skill could be used wherever the client seems stuck with one definition of the problem under discussion, where the client's own definition is not the only way to frame the problem, and where the client's definition of the situation hinders potential problem definition.

Recasting can be done by linking patterns of behaviour, showing how the current situation could be seen to be a recurrence of earlier behaviour. It can be done by pointing out the possible consequences of particular action and then reflecting back to the original accident. Or you can run out alternative courses of action for the other person to consider.

These strategies may be essential in litigation where you have inferred that the client has contributed to the accident. By listing possible courses of action, which may include settlement, you first explore the options open to the client. In so doing you then link the reason for choosing settlement to different ways of considering the earlier accident.

21.5.7   CONFRONTING

It may be necessary to move one stage further and confront the client. This may be necessary where the client's account is contradictory, partial, skewed or otherwise inaccurate. Clients sometimes filter the information they provide through wishful thinking, fear of exposure, and because they wish to solicit your support. They can strongly believe their own account, despite the contradictions that may be apparent in it.

This can be particularly difficult in matrimonial cases. The client may admit to violence but still not accept an agreement to end violence: 'I just slapped her around a little, this is going right over the top'. The solicitor may need to challenge this: 'No, that's not true. You gave her a black eye and dislocated her jaw.'

TWENTY TWO

ADVISING THE CLIENT

22.1   Introduction

Advising is a highly complex and challenging process. It draws upon many of the skills involved in interviewing, while adding more advanced skills. In interviewing you build rapport with the client and gather facts. To do this you use the skills involved in listening, attending, questioning and probing. In advising you need to analyse the client's problems, formulate alternative courses of action, and help the client to reach decisions and select action. To do this you need to present your advice to the client clearly and effectively. Advising builds upon the listening and questioning skills demonstrated in interviewing and adds to them the skills involved in fact and legal analysis, cooperative decision-making and the skills involved in clear speaking and presentation.

Although advice is frequently treated as part of the interview process it is, in fact, relatively distinct. It will often be separated in time because, although tentative advice may have been given to the client at the first interview, fuller advice is often deferred. Often the fact-gathering process will have to take place over more than one interview and you may have to obtain information from sources other than the client. You may also have to engage in a detailed analysis of the courses of action open to the client. Advice, moreover, is not a simple process in which you listen to the client and then suggest one particular course of action which you consider best for the client. It is a more complex process in which you present a number of options for the client and then help the client to go thoroughly through those options while allowing the client to make the final choice. (In the American literature this complex process is usually termed 'counselling'. In England the term 'advising' is used to include both forms of giving advice because the term 'counselling' has misleading therapeutic connotations.)

22.2   Analysing the Courses of Action Open to the Client

The analysis of courses of action open to the client will draw upon some of the skills already developed during the course of an undergraduate legal education but its success will draw upon more advanced skills of reasoning. As a student you will have had experience of applying the law to a given set of facts and will know how to determine legal liabilities and identify courses of action (for example, whether to form a partnership or incorporate a company). Different courses of action provide different kinds of benefit and incur different kinds of cost. Some are quick, some take a considerable time and require decisions to be made about intermediate steps. Some will cause other parties to react in ways that will inflame the situation. Some might lead other parties to settle but at a lower cost than is initially anticipated. Some courses of action produce immediate tax benefits but provide a structure that may be less beneficial in the case of insolvency.

Advising a client on the courses of action open requires an analysis of the different benefits or costs of adopting one set of action as against another. It will require an assessment of the time needed to complete a form of action. It will require the ability to predict the effects of adopting a form of action on other parties. Clients may also like to know what non-legal consequence may follow from the adoption of a particular course of action. They may, in addition, be advised that in the long run it might be wise to take non-legal, practical courses of action.

Advising the client, or 'counselling', refers to this process in which potential solutions with their positive and negative consequences are identified and then weighed in order to decide which alternative is most appropriate. A plaintiff in a personal injury action may, for example, when faced with the offer of a settlement, have to determine whether to proceed to trial, accept the offered settlement, push for a higher offer before trial, apply for pre-emptive relief to increase the pressure on the defence, or abandon the case because the emotional and economic costs of pursuing the action are too high. A defendant may have to consider defending the action, asserting a counterclaim, effecting settlement or forgoing litigation by allowing a default judgment to be entered.

By the end of the first interview, or, in any case, prior to formulating advice, you need to determine the client's objectives and desired relief. To assist the client decide on a course of action you need:

(a) to determine the legal alternatives and their consequences;
(b) to determine the non-legal alternatives and their consequences;
(c) to assess the consequences of adopting the alternatives.

22.2.1 LEGAL ALTERNATIVES

In civil litigation you would need to consider:

(a) how the court is likely to resolve issues of disputed fact;
(b) how the court is likely to rule on the issues of law;
(c) how the court is likely to exercise its discretion on any issue;
(d) any financial consequence of the legal proceedings (i.e., costs) as a direct result of the decision;
(e) further litigation as a result of commencing legal proceedings or the prospect of matters going to a higher court;
(f) the time factor, and any potential delays in the resolution of the matter;
(g) whether a negotiated settlement is possible;
(h) the effect of legal action taken on the prospect of a settlement;
(i) abandonment of the claim.

22.2.2 NON-LEGAL ALTERNATIVES

The lawyer may need to consider the following factors:

(a) Economic: e.g., the realistic effect of a divorce in relation to the parties being able to rehouse themselves, or the employment prospects of a person convicted of theft.

(b) Social: e.g., the effect on any children who may have to move schools as a result of a divorce, or the way the neighbours will regard a conviction for shoplifting.

(c) Psychological: e.g., the emotional feelings of someone, following an accident, who is forced to take employment which may be regarded as inferior to a position previously held; or emotional damage to children who are obliged to live in undesirable circumstances following the breakdown of their parents' relationship.

(d) Involvement of any non-legal agency to resolve the dispute: e.g., enrolment in a voluntary programme of family therapy where there is some evidence of child abuse, or agreement by one party to seek counselling for alcoholism where it is clear that drink is creating the underlying problem (these examples are taken from *Advocacy, Negotiation and Conference Skills* (London: Blackstone Press, 1993–94)).

In preparing alternative courses of action it is necessary to bear in mind that you will be better at predicting the legal courses of action and their consequences. Clients, on the other hand, may be better at predicting the non-legal alternatives or the non-legal consequences of legal courses of action. A businessperson, for example, would normally be better informed than the lawyer in evaluating the commercial impact of alternative contract provisions, though the lawyer may have to push the client to analyse that impact. Clients, typically, are the experts on their own feelings and needs.

22.2.3 ANALYSING THE CONSEQUENCES

Analysing the alternatives and weighing their consequences involves a process of prediction. In some cases the prediction will be quite straightforward. If a defendant in a civil action fails to file an answer within the time-limits then it is possible to predict that a default judgment will be entered against the defendant. Usually prediction can only be based on what will probably happen. Experienced lawyers will be able to draw upon their experience of prior cases to determine what is likely to happen. Inexperienced lawyers can only draw upon legal principles and the results of decided cases – or they can ask colleagues for advice.

Once the various alternatives have been identified they can be presented in a chart. This need not be complicated. It can simply represent the advantages and disadvantages of opting for a particular course of action.

Assume a simple action with two alternatives, settling for £3,500 or proceeding to trial. The most probable result at trial is a judgment for £12,000 and the lawyer predicts there is a good chance of obtaining such a judgment. The chart might look something like table 22.1.

In presenting the alternatives to the client the chart can be presented in this form. But in analysing the alternative the advantages and disadvantages can be sketched out and preliminary probing questions can then be formed for the client (see tables 22.2 and 22.3).

The example used here is from the field of litigation but similar charts can be constructed where the client needs to know whether a partnership, joint venture, or a corporation are most likely to offer the most advantageous tax benefits.

Table 22.1

Trial	*Settlement*
Very good chance of £12,000	£3,500
Advantages	*Advantages*
Disadvantages	*Disadvantages*

Table 22.2

Trial	Settlement
Very good chance of £12,000	£3,500
Advantages 90 per cent chance of some success. 60 per cent chance for some damages to offset costs. Feel vindicated in taking stand.	*Advantages* Time (less than litigation). Money for lawyer's fees (less than litigation). Probability of meaningful success.
Disadvantages Time and effort of going to court. Money to pay for fees and expenses Exposure to trial examination. Need to take public stance.	*Disadvantages* Relief far less. Negotiated settlement will adversely affect ability to seek total relief from court at a later date.

Table 22.3 Preliminary probing questions

Trial	Settlement
How does the client feel about litigation? about being out front as a plaintiff? about being cross-examined? How much time and money will the client commit to seeking relief? How important are damages?	How important is it to the client to get full relief? How cooperative is the client prepared to be? How cooperative is the other side likely to be? What sort of conditions would the client want in the negotiated settlement?

22.3 Presenting the Advice and Helping the Client Reach a Decision

In advising the client, which is taken to mean helping the client reach a decision, the lawyer needs to plan the session carefully. This can best be done by structuring the advice around four elements listed below.

22.3.1 REVIEW THE RESEARCH AND PREPARE THE ALTERNATIVE COURSES OF ACTION AVAILABLE

Before the session with the client it is necessary to review the research completed and prepare the alternative courses of action open to the client. In preparing the alternative courses of action available to the client you need to develop a language of prediction. You can use adjectives along a continuum; for example, the range could include 'certain', 'excellent', 'very good', 'good' 'fair', 'poor', 'very poor', 'impossible'. Alternatively you could use percentage descriptions (70 per cent) or mathematical odds (50–50, 10–1 etc.). Numerical indicators appear to provide clarity but may also convey a misleading sense of mathematical certainty.

In litigation cases Binder and Price advise presenting the alternatives in the form of a continuum that ranges from: (a) the best possible result, (b) the best likely result, (c) the most probable, (d) the worst likely, (e) the worst possible. This may not be appropriate in non-litigation cases and the full range may not always be used.

22.3.2 DETERMINE GOALS FOR THE SESSION

Wherever possible you should formulate goals for each session with a client, but this is particularly important when planning a session in which you need to move through a range of options with the client. You need to determine what needs to be accomplished. What decisions need to be made? What does the client need to do next? What do you need to do next? When do you next need to meet?

During the session you will need to accomplish three related objectives: (a) clarify the client's priorities, (b) ascertain the client's reactions to the possible consequences of the identified alternatives, and (c) cure informational gaps and ambiguities. Each of these tasks requires forethought about the specific topics to be probed.

22.3.3 PLAN THE FORMAT OF THE SESSION

You must plan the order in which you want to treat the alternatives, the consequences and the probing areas.

Binder and Price recommend that the lawyer first sets out all the available alternatives and then goes back with the client to identify and predict the positive and negative consequences related to each alternative. Once the lawyer has done this the lawyer should then check to see if the client can identify other options. The advantage of this structure is that it eases the client's curiosity at the outset while clarifying the issues for the client.

22.3.4 PLAN THE PRESENTATION

The presentation of alternatives can be eased by careful planning of the session.

As with the initial interview it can be useful to provide a brief introduction to the session. The introduction can include a description of what the session will involve, and emphasise that the final decision will be left to the client.

The presentation may be facilitated by the use of verbal and non-verbal markers to provide emphasis and to switch from topic to topic. A numerical breakdown of the options available can help: 'There are four options available to you, one . . ., two . . .. Let's now turn to the first, ... Remember, I said there were four options, so now let's turn to the second . . .'. You can then provide further verbal markers to highlight elements in the presentation: 'It is important to note . . .', 'One of the main features . . .'. Tonal variation, changes of expression and posture can be used to provide non-verbal markers.

A summary at the conclusion of the presentation, or a synthesis of the different elements, will serve as a reminder to the client and enable you to check for understanding.

It is important that you think carefully about the use of legal jargon. At times you will need to use legal phrases and terms, but it is important that you explain these to the client. It is also important to hold back on the lengthy explanation of legal analysis. This may inform your identification of alternatives and recommendations but it may confuse the presentation, and may not be of too much interest to the client. The client will want to know what can be done, and may not be too interested in the legal reasons that allow it to be done.

NEGOTIATING

TWENTY THREE

NEGOTIATION

23.1   Introduction

Negotiation is a central feature of a lawyer's life. For the most part lawyers negotiate with other lawyers, who represent other clients. Many lawyers will negotiate settlements in disputes; most disputes are settled out of court, and many are settled before negotiations begin. Many more lawyers will negotiate agreements in transactions; processes in which clients seek legal assistance in purchasing a house, constructing a business deal, or establishing a joint venture. Lawyers also negotiate with their professional colleagues, with partners and associates, with their trainees and secretaries, and with their clients. Lawyers, like other people, will have to negotiate in their everyday lives, with their parents, friends and acquaintances. As a student you, too, will have had to negotiate; with lecturers over deadlines on course work, with landlords about the conditions under which you live, in everyday transactions.

The skills involved in negotiation are taught in most vocational courses across the Commonwealth; they are taught in the Bar course at the Inns of Court School of Law. The skills are taught to prepare you for both the formal negotiations you will conduct as a lawyer and for the less formal negotiations that will be required as you work in an office. Negotiation is, though, taught for other reasons. It requires you to develop the critical analytical skills that you acquired in your academic education. It requires, in addition, creativity and insight, as you seek to develop proposals and consider the position adopted by the other side. It also requires you to engage in complex forms of interaction with another person. This will refine the skills you have learnt in interviewing, and lay the ground for the skills that you will develop as an advocate.

23.2   The Meaning of Negotiation

Popular accounts of negotiation sometimes present it as a sophisticated form of haggling, a ritualised form of warfare conducted by words. It is a game of subterfuge in which each party seeks to browbeat the other, conceal information from the other, and engage in a stylised minuet of demands, offers and responses. At times some negotiations, at certain points in the negotiation, feel like this.

Negotiation should, though, be considered as a subtle form of interchange. It has a variety of elements which require, in their turn, a particular combination of quite complex skills. Alan Fowler, writing on negotiation in the management context, suggests the following seven principles as common to all forms of negotiation:

   (a)   Negotiation involves two or more parties who need – or think they need – each other's involvement in achieving some desired outcome. There must be some common interest which puts or keeps the parties in contact.

(b)   While sharing a degree of interest, the parties start with different objectives, and these differences initially prevent the achievement of an outcome.

(c)   At least initially, the parties consider that negotiation is a more satisfactory way of trying to resolve their differences than alternatives such as litigation or arbitration.

(d)   Each party considers that there is some possibility of persuading the other to modify their original position.

(e)   Even when their ideal outcomes prove unattainable both parties retain some hope of an acceptable final agreement.

(f)   Each party has some influence or power – real or assumed – over the other's ability to act. The power or influence may, however, be indirect and bear on issues other than those which are the direct subject of the negotiation.

(g)   The negotiating process itself is one of interaction between people – in most cases by direct, verbal interchange. The progress of all types of negotiation is strongly influenced by emotion and attitudes, not just by the facts or logic of each party's arguments.

Putting all these principles together gives a definition which provides a summary and a starting-point for a detailed examination of the various parts of the process, and the strategies and skills involved:

> Negotiation is a process of interaction by which two or more parties who consider they need to be jointly involved in an outcome, but who initially have different objectives, seek by the use of argument and persuasion to resolve their differences in order to achieve a mutually acceptable solution (Alan Fowler, *Negotiation: Skills and Strategies* (IPM, 1990)).

This definition of negotiation is very wide but it captures its salient features. Usually there is some underlying common interest, an interest in setting up a commercial concern, but differences about how best to do it. Sometimes, as when negotiation is a stage in the litigation process, there can be fundamentally opposed interests. Sometimes it is about a single issue, like the price to be paid for an item, but this is unusual. Most negotiations revolve around a number of issues, even where they have been translated into a monetary equivalent. In some cases the power of one party will be expressed in a clear alternative, going to court. In other cases one party's power may be expressed in its ability to go elsewhere to construct a deal. But a key characteristic of negotiation is the fact that it represents an attempt by the parties to reach a joint decision. This key characteristic is apparent from a consideration of the relationship between negotiation and adjudication.

23.3   Negotiation and Adjudication

23.3.1   IN COURT THE JUDGE DECIDES

In a court the judge decides the issues and the judge's decision is binding on both the parties. In a court the judge is the focus of attention. Information and arguments are presented to the judge by each party in an attempt to persuade the judge to decide in favour of that party. The judge may be open to persuasion on questions of fact, interpretations of law and fact, applications of the law, recognition of extenuating circumstances, and so on. But the judge can disregard parts of either party's presentation.

In a court, rules of procedure, and decisions made by the judge, lead to decisions about such things as the time and place of proceedings, the compilation of the agenda, the selection of issues, whether evidence is admissible, and when to adjourn. The parties may make representations on many of these issues, but, in the final analysis, the judge decides how the proceedings will be organised.

23.3.2   IN NEGOTIATIONS THE PARTIES MAKE A JOINT DECISION

By contrast, in a negotiation, the parties make a joint decision. Each party can only obtain what the other is, in the end, prepared to allow. As the parties begin with differences between them, the process of decision-making must involve a coming together. This may occur as a result of a compromise. It may follow as one party is encouraged to adopt the other party's point of view. It may arise as a result of the joint creation of something new which is to the benefit of both parties. In either case it is a joint decision.

In the process of making this joint decision the parties' primary concern is to influence or coerce the other. Negotiation, therefore, involves the exchange of information. The parties allege facts and try to interpret them; they appeal to values, they present arguments, they make threats, promises, demands, offers, counter offers and so on.

Through this process the parties learn about each other's position and interests. What each party learns affects its position. If the negotiation is successful, both parties work together to reach a joint decision.

In a negotiation, then, there is no figure like a judge, to reach a decision. Only the parties can make decisions. The only outcome is one to which they both agree.

In a negotiation, the parties acting together have to make all the decisions on procedure. No one else can impose an agenda, identify issues, set timetables. These decisions may be made consciously by the parties, acting in agreement. Or they may be made implicitly, by the manner in which the parties proceed.

23.3.3   THE IMPLICATIONS

The absence of a judge is extremely important. It means that there are no limits to what the parties may say, how they argue and how they behave. The limits are voluntary. This can be difficult for the lawyer who views negotiation as a fight, who views argument as a form of battle. Insofar as there are limits on argument, they are self-imposed. Each party has to exercise restraint. It is best not to abuse a person you want to persuade. If emotions run high and you get angry or make threats, then the negotiations may break down.

The absence of a judge means that in addition to addressing matters of substance, the parties also have to address questions of process. It is up to the parties to define the agenda; it is up to the parties to determine the procedure. This can be difficult. It requires some hard decisions. It requires thinking along two fronts. It requires sensitivity to the changing demands of particular elements in the negotiation. It puts responsibilities into the hands of the parties, but it also gives them the power to manage the process in their own joint interest.

23.4   The Skills Involved in Negotiation

Some people are quite definitely better at negotiating than others. They have a natural flair, it is intuitive and flows from their personality. This does not mean that they cannot improve, nor does it mean that other people cannot develop the skills involved in negotiation. Negotiating skills can be acquired and developed by planning, practising and reflecting upon negotiation.

Negotiation is a process which draws upon several different elements:

   (a) Knowledge:

      (i)   of applicable principles,
     (ii)   of the context of a particular negotiation,
   (iii)   of the detailed subject matter involved.

    (b) Skills:

        (i)   in analysing the issues,
        (ii)   in personal interaction,
        (iii) in communicating.

    (c) Attitudes:

        (i)   towards the negotiating process,
        (ii)   towards the specifics of each negotiation,
        (iii) towards one's own role.

23.4.1 KNOWLEDGE

To negotiate effectively you need to have a broad understanding of the context in which the negotiation occurs. The context of each negotiation differs, if only subtly. You need to be able to 'read' the negotiation context to determine how you should play in a particular arena.

23.4.1.1 Knowledge of the setting

The law shapes and structures a negotiation – the parties, quite literally, bargain in the 'shadow of the law'. You need a thorough understanding of the operative substantive law but you also need an understanding of the specific legal and quasi-legal factors that impinge on a dispute.

In a personal injury case, for example, the defendants will act differently depending on how the plaintiff is funded – they will be aware of the constraints operating upon a privately funded litigant, they will be aware of the differing constraints and possibilities affecting a litigant funded by legal aid, and they will be aware that a litigant funded by a trade union will have few worries about costs. These factors will affect both the plaintiff and the defendant and will determine the manner in which they conduct negotiation.

Different but similar considerations apply in a commercial case. You need to know which warranties should be included in a contract, what measure of damages will apply if warranties are broken, what the bases for liability will be, and what the likely measure of damages will be if the matter goes to court.

23.4.1.2 Knowledge of the context of a specific negotiation

Effective negotiators understand the culture, conventions, constraints and opportunities surrounding each negotiating episode. They will brief themselves accordingly, asking: Who are the negotiators? What are their personal strengths and styles? What issues might influence them?

23.4.1.3 Knowledge of the subject-matter

To be effective you should have complete knowledge of the file. You need to know the history of the case, the sequence of events that created the dispute, and the sequence of events leading up to the negotiation. You need to have an in-depth knowledge of the governing law – you cannot go off to a library in the middle of a negotiation. You need to know, in addition, what kind of agreement might work and you need to be familiar with sample precedents of the kind of agreement that might be reached.

23.4.2 SKILLS

23.4.2.1 Analytical skills

Negotiations can involve consideration of a complex sequence of events in a complex series of interactions. Skill in analysing the negotiation is crucial. An effective negotiating plan will, therefore, need to look analytically at the situation and consider such questions as:

(a)   What is the central issue? What are the subsidiary issues? What are peripheral issues?

(b)   What is the central objective? What are the subsidiary aims and to what extent can these be traded in for the main objective?

(c)   What are the main barriers to achieving what we want?

(d)   What are the outside limits of an acceptable agreement?

(e)   What alternative approaches are there? What are their strengths and weaknesses?

(f)   What information do we need to support our case?

(g)   What are the arguments and information most likely to be used by the other party?

(h)   What contingency plans are there should we fail to reach an acceptable agreement?

23.4.2.2   Creativity

A negotiator needs to be flexible and creative.

Flexibility enables you to change your view of a case as you learn more about it. Flexibility is vital while the negotiation is in progress, when you will need to adapt your strategy and tactics in response to the position presented by both sides.

Creativity enables you to think of different ways of solving different aspects of the case. It enables you to look at it from different points of view and construct solutions that may satisfy both parties' interests.

23.4.2.3   Communication skills

Negotiation builds upon many of the skills that you will learn while interviewing. At the heart of a negotiation are the skills of listening and questioning. To elicit information from the other side – who may have an interest in concealing it – you will need to remain attuned to verbal signals, demonstrate active listening skills, and use a mixture of open questions and more directive probes.

To structure the interaction between the two parties you will need to be able to manage a meeting, prioritise topics, learn to take turns, and bring the other side in. You will need to put together a series of contributions – questions, answers, arguments, proposals, promises, threats, gestures and responses. You will need to prepare your own contributions and prepare to meet the contributions of the other side.

23.4.2.4   Influencing skills

Good negotiators develop an ability to sense and influence the changing moods and concerns of individuals and encourage progress towards agreement.

You can do this by being supportive and positive, not negative and undermining. It helps to focus on issues not personalities. Instead of saying, 'I do not understand how *you* could say that!', try 'That's a new point, perhaps you could explain'. You can lead conversation positively, without using debating points. Instead of saying, 'Do you realise you have just contradicted yourself?', try 'I'm not quite sure that I follow that line of thinking. Could you explain it a bit further?'

Statements should end on a positive, rather than a negative note. Instead of saying, 'We're happy with the small sum, but don't like the timing, try 'We'd like to address the issue of timing, but we are more than happy with the overall sum'.

23.4.3   ATTITUDES

Your behaviour in a negotiation will be influenced by your attitudes to negotiation. You may have personal needs for recognition or achievement – a perception of yourself as a good debater, or as someone who will push to the end; as someone who is determined and demanding. You may also be confident in your own abilities.

You will need these abilities in negotiation, but you will also need to be critical and persuasive, and you will need to maintain self-discipline. You are exercising these qualities not for yourself, but for your client.

You should try to detach yourself from the negotiation and its outcome. All negotiations should involve collaborative as well as competitive elements. It should be a process which at least tries to achieve an outcome which satisfies both of the parties, not simply an arena in which you both demonstrate your negotiating prowess.

23.5   The Elements of Negotiation: – Styles, Strategies and Stages

There is only way to learn how to negotiate – practice. Practice, in role-plays and simulated legal settings, will provide you with an insight into the processes involved. Before engaging in a role-play you will need to plan, and afterwards you should reflect. You should ask how well did the plan work? How did you contribute to the outcome? What were your strong points? How could you build upon your performance?

To aid your practice you need understanding. Negotiation is a complex process. You can negotiate in different ways, in different contexts, for different purposes, and at different stages in the negotiation process. Two sets of concepts can help your understanding of the negotiation process:

(a)   Negotiation styles and strategies.
(b)   Negotiation stages.

23.5.1   STYLES AND STRATEGIES

It should be clear from the discussion in **23.2** that there is much more to negotiation than mere haggling. Negotiation is a complex phenomenon which lends itself to different styles and methods and different strategies and orientations.

A negotiator's *style*, or set of methods, describes the manner in which that negotiator behaves in the negotiation process – how he or she asks questions, how he or she responds, how she reacts to the other side. It describes a personalised behaviour pattern, flowing from individual traits, habits and personality. It refers to the personal behaviour, skills or methods that the negotiator uses in carrying out the strategies chosen. Two personal styles are usually distinguished: the 'competitive' and the 'cooperative'.

A negotiation *strategy* directs the negotiator in planning the negotiation towards a particular conceptualisation of the negotiation process. A negotiation strategy spells out the specific goals to be achieved and the pattern of conduct that should improve the chances of achieving those goals. Two negotiating strategies are usually distinguished: the 'adversarial' and the 'problem-solving'.

Some methods will be necessary in some cases, some in others. You will need to determine which methods and strategies are appropriate, and when. The first step is to analyse the objectives of the case and evaluate its strengths and weaknesses. Then you must consider the case of the other side. Then you need to consider the stage of the negotiation. Different styles and different strategies may be appropriate at different stages in the negotiation.

23.5.2   THE STAGES OF A NEGOTIATION

Negotiations pass through a series of events, a sequence of stages. Not all of these stages will be carried out in the same order in each negotiation. Some strategies prioritise different stages. But none of the stages should be underestimated.

Many analysts divide a negotiation into seven or eight stages. It is easier to work with three:

(a) A preparation phase before the negotiation begins.

(b) The actual negotiating process – the interaction which leads to an agreement about the outcome.

(c) The agreement, and the steps required to implement the agreement.

23.5.2.1 Preparation and planning

The preparation of the negotiation is critical. When the parties meet the interaction can be difficult to manage. Preparation and planning help you to manage the process. Preparation and planning have two aspects, the preparation of the case and the planning of your strategy.

23.5.2.2 The actual negotiating process.

Negotiations are sometimes conducted entirely through correspondence or over the telephone. It is easiest, though, to think of a process when the parties engage in the negotiation discussions in the course of a single meeting. This meeting is likely to go through three phases:

(a) Initial meeting: the parties start by setting a climate, agreeing an agenda, defining the issues, and stating their initial positions.

(b) Exploring the issues: a more open phase when the issues are explored, information is exchanged, and a tentative exploration of the possible outcome takes place.

(c) Narrowing of differences and closure: firm or final proposals are made, discussed and, perhaps, modified. An agreement is defined and constructed.

23.5.2.3 Agreement and implementation

The agreement will need to be defined and agreed. It will need to comply with legal formalities. The agreement will need to be confirmed in writing and suitably drafted. You will also need to have agreed who will be doing what and by when.

23.6 Outline of this Part

The remaining Chapters in this part present an introduction to the skills involved in negotiation. **Chapter 24** focuses on the skills involved in negotiation which it considers through a discussion of the styles, methods and strategies that may be appropriate at different stages of a negotiation. **Chapter 25** focuses on preparation and planning and provides a five-step preparation and action plan. **Chapters 26** and **27** consider how to conduct two types of negotiation: a problem-solving and an adversarial negotiation.

23.7 Further Reading

Bastress, R. M., and Harbaugh, J. D., *Interviewing, Counseling and Negotiation* (Boston Mass: Little Brown, 1990).

Fisher, R., and Ury, W., *Getting to Yes: Negotiating Agreement without Giving In* (Business Books, 1989).

Fowler, A., *Negotiation: Skills & Strategies* (IPM, 1990).

Genn, H., *Hard Bargaining* (Oxford: Clarendon Press, 1987).

Gifford, D. G., *Legal Negotiation: Theory and Practice* (St Paul Minn: West Publishing, 1989).

Gulliver, P. H. *Disputes and Negotiations: A Cross-Cultural Perspective* (New York: Academic Press, 1979).

Hall, L., *Negotiation: Strategies for Mutual Gain* (London: Sage, 1993).

Halpern, A., *Negotiating Skills* (London: Blackstone Press, 1992).

Lax, D., and Sabenius, J., *The Manager as Negotiator: Bargaining for Co-operation and Competitive Gain* (Free Press).

Menkel-Meadow, C., 'Towards another view of legal negotiation: the structure of problem-solving' (1984) 31 UCLA L Rev 754.

Murray, J. S., Rau, A. S. and Sherman, E.F., *Processes of Dispute Resolution* (Westbury: Foundation Press, 1988).

Riskin, L.L., and Westbrook, J. E., *Dispute Resolution and Lawyers* (St Paul Minn: West Publishing, 1987).

Pruitt, D. G., *Negotiation Behavior* (New York: Academic Press, 1981).

Williams, G., *Legal Negotiation and Settlement* (St. Paul Minn: West Publishing, 1983).

Scott, B., *The Skills of Negotiating* (Aldershot: Gower, 1982).

TWENTY FOUR

NEGOTIATION STYLES AND STRATEGIES

24.1   Introduction

Many law students, and many lawyers, rely on intuitive knowledge and skill when negotiating. By way of contrast, the effective negotiator resists this temptation and will have reflected on his or her negotiating experience and will have developed an operating theory to guide his or her negotiating practice. A negotiation theory is not made up of abstracted concepts. It consists, instead, of a set of working assumptions, accepted principles and rules of thumb which can be used to analyse, predict and understand the nature or behaviour of a certain situation (see Murray, Rau and Sherman, *Processes of Dispute Resolution*). Theories of negotiation should not be ignored by lawyers, or law students. A good sense of theory is important in selecting the best strategy and style for use in a particular setting.

Negotiation theories usually distinguish between negotiation styles and negotiation strategies; though the two terms are not always used consistently. A negotiation *style* refers to the personalised behaviour pattern that flows from individual traits, habits and personality. It refers to the personal behaviour the negotiator uses in carrying out the strategies she/he has chosen. A negotiation *strategy* spells out the specific goals to be achieved and the pattern of conduct that should improve the chances of achieving those goals.

This Chapter distinguishes two styles, the competitive and the cooperative, and two sets of strategy, the adversarial and the cooperative. It then considers various combinations of style and strategy before going on to consider which should be used under which circumstances.

24.2   Negotiation Style: Competitives and Cooperatives

The personal style that a lawyer adopts in a negotiation is reflected in his or her interpersonal behaviour – how he or she acts towards the other side, asks questions, responds, raises issues, and moves through the agenda. A distinction between two relatively distinct styles of negotiator, the competitive and the cooperative, can be found throughout the literature on negotiation. The distinction first emerged in considerations of legal negotiation as a consequence of research conducted by Gerald Williams into negotiator effectiveness (G. Williams, *Legal Negotiation and Settlement*).

Williams found that all effective negotiators had a number of features in common: they prepared on the facts, prepared the law, observed the customs and courtesies of the Bar, took satisfaction in using their legal skills, were effective as trial advocates and were self-controlled. But he found distinct patterns of behaviour that distinguished effective competitive negotiators from effective cooperative negotiators.

24.2.1 COMPETITIVE NEGOTIATORS

Competitive negotiators tend to be perceived as ambitious, egotistical, arrogant, clever, tough, dominant, forceful, aggressive and attacking. They aim, like cooperatives, to get the best settlement for their client, but for competitors this includes a reward to self, both in the form of monetary gain and in the satisfaction gained from outdoing an opponent. They appear to take a gamesmanship approach to negotiation – they want to outdo the other side and score a clear victory. Competitives move psychologically against the other person, both in words and action. They make high opening demands, they use threats, they are willing to stretch the facts in favour of their client's position, they stick to their positions, and they are parsimonious with information about the case. Competitives are careful about the timing and sequence of their actions and have a high level of interest in tactical or strategic considerations.

Competitive tactics are designed to undermine the opposing lawyer so that he or she loses confidence in the case and will reduce expectations of what can be obtained. The opposing lawyer then accepts less than he or she otherwise would as a settlement. This may lead to a higher payoff for the client but it is a high-risk style.

The effectiveness of the competitive negotiator depends upon creating enough pressure and tension to induce an emotional reaction and a reduction in the expectations of the opposing party. But if the pressure is excessive, or is maintained too long, the strategy backfires and trial against a vindictive party results. The use of toughness is, moreover, likely to damage long-term relationships that depend upon mutual trust. Where lawyers are likely to encounter each other over the years the tension and mistrust created in one case can easily influence the dynamics and outcome of later cases.

Williams's research found that only 24 per cent of the lawyers in the sample adopted a competitive style, and only a quarter of the competitive negotiators were described as effective. 33 per cent of the competitive negotiators' cases ended in deadlock.

24.2.2 COOPERATIVE NEGOTIATORS

Cooperative negotiators tend to be perceived as courteous, personable, friendly, tactful, sincere, organising, wise, careful and facilitating. Cooperative negotiators are concerned with obtaining a maximum settlement for their client, but they tend to feel constrained in their behaviour by a standard of fairness and ethical dealing. They are seen as fair, objective, reasonable, logical and willing to move from their established positions. Effective cooperatives move psychologically toward the opposing lawyer. They seek common ground to facilitate agreement, they avoid threats, they accurately estimate the value of cases they are working on, they are sensitive to the needs of their clients and they are willing to share information with their opponents.

Cooperative negotiators seek to create a trusting atmosphere appearing to seek no special advantage for themselves or their client. The cooperative negotiator shows his or her own trust and good faith by making unilateral concessions. Making unilateral concessions is risky but cooperative negotiators believe it creates a moral obligation in the other to reciprocate. A cooperative style is believed to produce more favourable outcomes and result in fewer ultimate breakdowns in bargaining.

The major disadvantage of the cooperative style is its vulnerability to exploitation. When a cooperative negotiator attempts to establish a cooperative, trusting atmosphere in a negotiation with a tough, non-cooperative opponent, the cooperative lawyer is said to have an alarming tendency to ignore the lack of cooperation and to pursue the cooperative style. The logic of this position requires the cooperative lawyer to continue discussing the case fairly and objectively, to make concessions about the weaknesses of his or her case and to refrain from self-serving behaviour. In this situation the competitive negotiator is free to accept all of the fairness and cooperation without giving anything in return. Competitive negotiators interpret cooperation as a sign of weakness. From their point of view people who are strong, and people with strong cases, do not make concessions or admit weaknesses. When an opponent acts cooperatively with them, competitives actually increase their level of demands and their expectations about what they will be able to obtain in the case.

Williams's research found that 65 per cent of the sample of lawyers used a cooperative style and, of these, more than half were judged to be effective.

24.3 Negotiation Strategies: Adversarial and Problem Solving

While the personal style of a negotiator is reflected in the methods the negotiator uses to achieve a particular goal, the strategy depicts the overall orientation towards the negotiation process. A strategy is a particular sequence of negotiating moves designed to achieve a particular goal. Two strategies are normally distinguished: an adversarial strategy and a problem-solving strategy. The strategy adopted leads to a view of what can be achieved through negotiation, and this in turn affects the behaviour chosen, competitive or cooperative, and the solutions arrived at, narrow compromises or creative solutions (see Menkel-Meadow, 'Towards another view of legal negotiation: the structure of problem-solving').

24.3.1 THE ADVERSARIAL NEGOTIATION STRATEGY

The adversarial negotiation strategy has a simple underpinning assumption – that each party wants as much as can be got of the thing bargained for, and the more that one party receives, the less the other party receives. Negotiation is about 'winning', the winner is the party who has gained the most at the expense of the other party. Negotiation, then, takes the form of a 'zero-sum' game, in which the gains of one party equal the losses of the other party and the resulting balance sheet always equals zero.

For these assumptions to work further assumptions come into play. The first is that the issues at stake in the negotiation can be treated as equivalent to a cash sum. Where the issue at stake is not initially expressed in monetary terms – such as the pain suffered by a plaintiff in a personal injury suit, or a party's emotional distress resulting from action taken by the other party – then it will be transformed into a monetary equivalent. It is assumed, further, that the parties have equivalent goals – that they are each after the same 'monetary' resource – and that the solution to the dispute will turn upon a division of the goods.

Once negotiation issues are transformed into monetary equivalents the adversarial strategy leads to them being placed on a continuum. Negotiation leads to a process of movement along the continuum, through a process of concessions, with each party attempting to get as much movement as possible towards its side, and away from the other side. Given this linear conception of the structure of negotiation it is easy to see why the results of negotiation are perceived as 'compromises' and why solutions which 'split the difference' are favoured.

Adversarial strategies are frequently characterised by arguments and statements rather than questions and searches for new information. The adversarial negotiator refuses to reveal information and makes exaggerated demands to conceal the real state of play. This leads to a stylised ritual of offer/response, counter-offer/counter-response and a form of negotiation debate that is marked by competitive reactive dynamics.

24.3.2 THE PROBLEM-SOLVING NEGOTIATION STRATEGY

Proponents of the problem-solving or principled approach to negotiation, like Fisher and Ury, the authors of *Getting to Yes*, argue that the adversarial strategy, or positional bargaining, underpins both competitive and cooperative styles of bargaining.

Hard, competitive, bargaining is characterised by the standard minuet of individual decisions as each negotiator decides what to offer, what to reject, and how much of a concession to make. Decision-making is difficult and time-consuming; it is hard on the personal aspects of the relationship. Soft, cooperative, bargainers are little better. Instead of seeing the other side as adversaries, they prefer to see them as friends. Rather then emphasising a goal of victory, they emphasise the necessity of reaching agreement. The danger in this position is that the negotiator is soft on both the people and the problem. Any negotiation primarily concerned with the relationship runs the risk of producing a sloppy agreement. It also makes the negotiator vulnerable to exploitation by someone who plays a hard game of positional bargaining.

A problem-solving, or principled, approach to bargaining changes the game, the underlying orientation. It focuses on finding solutions to each party's sets of underlying needs, interests and objectives. In attempting to uncover these underlying needs the problem-solving strategy seeks to present greater opportunities for mutual gain.

In the problem-solving strategy the lawyers negotiate with each other as participants in a joint decision-making process – not as antagonists in a battle over the distribution of goods. It is assumed that mutual interests can be found even amongst the most antagonistic adversaries. A problem-solving strategy recognises the legitimacy of the values, positions and interests of the other side. It assumes that most negotiations are made up of multiple issues and that a negotiation strategy that focuses on underlying interests is most likely to uncover those issues. Negotiation as a process should not focus on manifest positions, it should instead explore the underlying concerns and interests of the parties in the relationship. Negotiation itself becomes a means for establishing a positive relationship with the other party.

The problem-solving strategy has been most clearly articulated by Fisher and Ury. Their prescription for principled negotiation is made up of four fundamental points:

(a) *Separate the people from the problems – be hard on the problem not the people.* Most negotiations involve emotional issues for the parties which can be intensified by positional bargaining. These emotional issues can distort communication and divert attention from the problem before them. Principled bargaining requires an approach to negotiation which separates the human dimensions of the problem from the problem itself.

(b) *Focus on interests not positions.* Fixing on positions (demands) can harden differences and make compromises difficult. Negotiators should seek, instead, to redefine and reshape interests (needs, concerns, goals).

(c) *Invent options for mutual gain.* In generating options it is necessary to avoid premature judgment, seeking a single answer, assuming that there is a fixed pie, and thinking that solving the other party's problem is that party's problem.

(d) *Insist on using objective criteria.* The use of standards and objective criteria should enhance the prospect of developing a mutually acceptable settlement. The negotiator should seek agreement on the standards to be applied before even considering possible terms.

Advocates of a problem-solving approach argue that all negotiations should be approached with a view to producing a solution that satisfies both parties. The principled negotiation that follows focuses on basic interests, mutually satisfying options, and fair standards. It is likely to lead to a wise agreement. This method permits the negotiators to reach a joint decision, without all the costs of digging in to positions only to have to dig themselves out. By separating the people from the problem, the negotiators should be able to deal directly and empathetically with each other. They should be able to produce an amicable agreement which provides a positive continuing relationship with the other party.

The problem-solving approach sounds good in theory, but it is not always clear how it should work in practice. The following three examples are given to show how it might work out in particular settings.

Example 24.1 The Egyptian–Israeli border negotiations

The Egyptian–Israeli negotiations over where to draw a border in the Sinai appeared to be an absolutely classic example of zero-sum bargaining, in which each square mile lost to one party was the other side's gain. For years the negotiators proceeded inconclusively with proposed boundary lines drawn and redrawn on innumerable maps. On probing the real interests of the two sides, however, Egypt was found to care a great deal about sovereignty over the Sinai while Israel was heavily concerned with its security. As such, a creative solution could be devised to 'unbundle' these different interests and give to each what it valued most. In the Sinai, this involved creating a demilitarised zone under the Egyptian flag. This had the effect of giving Egypt 'sovereignty' and Israel 'security' (see Fisher and Ury, *Getting to Yes*).

Example 24.2 The sale of a 'lemon'

The sale of a second-hand car, a 'lemon', has led to a dispute. Shortly after the purchase the car ceased to function. The owner sues claiming consequential damages including lost income from the loss of her job due to repeated lateness and absences as a result of the malfunctioning car. The seller counterclaims for the balance due on the car.

If engaged in conventional adversarial negotiation the parties would structure their negotiations around the value of their respective monetary claims. The purchaser's lawyer would evaluate the amount her client had spent on the car, how much she has lost in income, and the cost of the lawsuit itself. The seller's lawyer would compute the balance due on the car, subtract payments made, and add the fees to recover the balance due. Both lawyers might then discount their targets by the costs of achieving the results through adjudication. The solution to the negotiation would be measured in monetary terms.

The difficulty with this approach is that the real goals or objectives sought by the parties might not be accomplished at all. The car purchaser wants a reliable car to take her to work and the car seller a profitable sale and a satisfied customer who will make recommendations to her friends. If, however, the parties considered what they had initially desired from this transaction, they might arrive at other solutions. Alternatives could be found which would more completely and efficiently satisfy their needs, solutions not necessarily arising from compromise. If, for example, the car purchaser's problem is transport to work, the car seller might repair her present car, or substitute another car at little or low cost to a dealer who has a large inventory. At the same time, the car seller could continue to hold the purchaser to her contract, or a new contract could be negotiated (Menkel-Meadow, 'Towards another view of legal negotiation: the structure of problem-solving').

Example 24.3 The concert singer

A singer negotiating with the owner of an auditorium over payment for a proposed concert reached impasse over the size of the fee with the performer's demands exceeding the owner's highest offer. In fact, when the amount of the fixed payment was the issue, no possibility of agreement existed. The singer, however, based his demand on the expectation that the house would certainly be filled with his fans, while the owner projected only a half-capacity crowd. This provided a way out. They reached a mutually acceptable arrangement in which the performer received a modest fixed fee plus a set percentage of the ticket receipts. The singer, given his beliefs, thus expected an adequate to fairly large payment; the concert-hall owner was happy with the agreement because he only expected to pay a moderate fee (see Lax and Sebenius, *The Manager as Negotiator*).

24.4 Selecting an Appropriate Style or Strategy

Negotiation theories, the distinction between different negotiation styles and strategies, are intended to guide the choices that you will make in a negotiation. Although they are defined in opposition to each other, in practice different styles or strategies, or different combinations of style or strategy, may be needed depending on the context, the goals of the party, and the stage of the negotiation. To a large extent the negotiator's success depends upon an ability to choose the most effective style or strategy at each point in a negotiation.

In determining which style or strategy to select the negotiator will need to consider the following factors:

(a) The legal aspects of the negotiation.
(b) The relative power of the parties.
(c) The goals of the client and the configuration of shared needs.
(d) The stage of the negotiation.
(e) The negotiator's preferred style or strategy.

24.4.1 THE LEGAL ASPECTS OF THE NEGOTIATION

All negotiations take place within the 'shadow' of the law. This shadow may be made up of the substantive law, court procedures and sanctions, rules of evidence, judicial involvement in settlement efforts, court standards for the approval of certain settlement efforts, special procedures for particular kinds of litigation, deadlines and rules for determining costs. Hazel Genn's study of personal injury litigation has shown how each of these factors interact to structure the negotiation process (H. Genn, *Hard Bargaining* (1988)).

In personal injury litigation the flexibility inherent in the common law and statutory definitions of negligence opened up a space within which negotiation can take place. This flexibility is caused by a range of questions that need to be asked in any kind of personal injury litigation: Was there a duty of care? Was that duty broken by the defendant? Did the breach cause an injury? Was there any contributory negligence? How much is the injury worth?

But considerations of costs, and questions about the plaintiff's ability to pay the lawyers' fees may constrain the kinds of strategies that are open to the lawyer who is likely to face an insurance company which is itself highly aware of the range of strategies that can be deployed. In the following three situations this context led each of the parties to adopt an adversarial approach to negotiation:

(a) The litigation is privately funded. In this situation the plaintiff risks a lot in litigation. If solicitors are instructed who are not specialists in litigation practice they may be slow to collect evidence and institute proceedings. The solicitors are likely to act cautiously to achieve a settlement and are unlikely to look for creative solutions to the client's problems, though they may act cooperatively. Claims inspectors from insurance companies are aware of the constraints inherent in the position and are likely to exploit those constraints.

(b) The litigation is legally aided. The defendant insurance company knows that it cannot impose the threat of costs so it is likely to respond differently to plaintiff initiatives. Some plaintiffs may still adopt a cautious approach and may need to settle because of the low level of remuneration provided by legal aid work. Specialist personal injury lawyers may adopt a different stance. They make litigation pay by adopting a high case load and a high profile. They adopt a competitive approach and are ready to start and press forward with proceedings to force a settlement in their client's favour.

(c) The litigation is funded by a trade union. In this situation the solicitor has no concerns about costs and will be able to refuse offers that others would find acceptable. If necessary they can risk going to trial. They, too, can take an aggressive stance and adopt the view that a relentless and apparently uncompromising push towards trial is the best way to stimulate early realistic offers from the insurance companies that stand behind the defendant.

In different areas of legal practice a different relationship between substantive law, court procedures, rules of evidence etc. can lead the parties to adopt a range of different styles or strategies.

24.4.2 THE RELATIVE POWER OF THE CLIENT

Differences in resources – money, personnel and time – have an obvious impact on the selection of bargaining style and strategy. Where the other side is more powerful they have more alternatives to a negotiated settlement available to them. They can risk deadlock and breakdown – they can also make threats which will appear credible – but they can also engage in problem-solving to their benefit.

The less powerful negotiator has two options. An attempt can be made to change the perceived balance of power between the two parties or a cooperative problem-solving approach can be adopted.

Changing the perceptions held by the other side involves improving the apparent strength of the negotiator's position. If, at an early stage, the other side can be convinced that the negotiator's evidence at trial will come up to proof, then the negotiator may be able to adopt competitive tactics later on. For negotiators with less power the use of cooperative tactics or a problem-solving strategy will be favoured because the use of competitive tactics will lack credibility.

24.4.3 THE GOALS OF THE CLIENT AND THE CONFIGURATION OF SHARED NEEDS

The goals of the client and the configuration of the parties' shared needs are critical considerations in selecting an approach to negotiation.

Where the client treats the outcome of the negotiation as the equivalent of a monetary sum and has the goal of achieving as much of this as possible then a competitive adversarial stance is likely to be favoured.

Where the client sees the negotiation as having an integrative potential then a competitive problem-solving approach may be favoured. A large part of the skill of the negotiator lies in an ability to identify integrative potential. This may be done by identifying 'bridging proposals', which satisfy both parties' interests, or through the formation of a 'logrolling agreement', in which the parties take concessions on different issues on which they place different priorities.

Where the parties have an on-going relationship this may affect the manner in which they construct their goals. An on-going relationship may be a feature of a dispute where the parties had a prior relationship, e.g., husband and wife, employer and employee, business partners or directors in a company. But many negotiations in a dispute are frequently 'one-shot' negotiations – they are not based, and are not intended to lead to, a continuing relationship.

By contrast many transactional negotiations provide opportunities for the parties to agree voluntarily to the rules that will govern their future relationship. Here cooperative methods are likely to be successful. But not all transactional matters lead to an on-going relationship. Some involve one-off commercial transactions, in which the parties could as easily do business with another party, and at certain stages in the negotiations competitive behaviour may be thought appropriate.

24.4.4 THE STAGES OF THE NEGOTIATION

Most negotiations go through a series of distinct phases or stages. Different forms of negotiating behaviour may be appropriate at different stages of the negotiation process.

Many negotiations go through a stage marked by intense competitive tactics and then move to a stage marked by cooperative tactics and a problem-solving strategy. In some negotiations, attempts to use a cooperative problem-solving approach too early in the negotiation may backfire. The other side may wish to save face and relieve accumulated frustration. They may be too angry to trust cooperative methods; they may be too caught up in their own position to see the value of a problem-solving strategy. They may only be able to move on to adopt another approach when they become frustrated with the failure of competitive tactics.

In many negotiations there are a range of issues. On some a competitive stance may be appropriate, on others a cooperative stance. In other negotiations a competitive approach prevails for a long time. Then as deadlock looms one of the parties typically makes a realistic proposal on one or more of the issues. Competitive tactics early on in the negotiation may, ironically, increase the prospect of success by creating a climate within which a cooperative problem-solving approach is welcomed. Both sides typically make a series of concessions and begin to suggest problem-solving alternatives. Threats and arguments may, though, continue. Some issues may be resolved; others are more open to problem-solving; yet others are still the subject of bitter dispute.

24.4.5 THE NEGOTIATOR'S PREFERRED STYLE

Negotiators need to work out which styles and strategies they can best work with, and they should work out how best to respond to the styles and strategies selected by the other side.

While a particular approach, a style–strategy combination, may be required for a particular negotiation it may not be one that the negotiator is comfortable with. To a certain extent negotiators have to work within the constraints of their own personalities.

Equally there is no point adopting a cooperative problem-solving approach whilst the other side sticks aggressively to a competitive adversarial approach. In this setting negotiators should try some of the techniques advocated by Fisher and Ury, or they should respond in turn, confident that deadlock, or the prospect of deadlock, will lead to a more creative approach as the negotiation moves into another phase.

24.5 The Negotiator's Dilemma

The account of negotiation styles and strategies which has been presented in this Chapter, implies a distinction between two dominant styles or strategies: the competitive and the adversarial, and the cooperative and the problem solver. To a certain extent these styles and strategies are distinct. But they are likely to be present in all negotiations.

Negotiation involves an essential tension between the two distinct sets of approach (see Lax and Sabenius, *The Manager as Negotiator*). No matter how much creative problem solving enlarges the pie, it still must be divided. The added value that has been created by openness, clear communication and creativity must still be divided by hard, tough bargaining. And if the pie has not been expanded the dilemma is even sharper: there will be less to share and the competitive bargaining will be even harder.

This dilemma affects both strategy and tactics.

First, competitive and adversarial tactics can impede cooperation and problem solving. Exaggerating the value of concessions and minimising the benefit of others' concessions presents a distorted picture of one's relative preferences. As a consequence mutually beneficial trades may not be discovered. Making threats or commitments to highly favourable outcomes impedes hearing and the understanding of others' interests.

Second, cooperative approaches to creative problem solving are vulnerable to tactics for claiming more value for one of the parties. Revealing information about one's relative preferences is risky. The information that a negotiator would accept position A in return for a favourable resolution on a second issue can be exploited: 'So, you'll accept A. Good, now let's move on to discuss the merits of the second issue.' The willingness to make a new, creative offer can and often is taken as a sign that its proposer is able and willing to make further concessions.

146

These tensions cannot be magically resolved as the problem-solving, win/win approach seems to suggest. They have to be managed and worked through, but they will be part of any negotiation. Negotiation represents an attempt to reach a joint decision to further each side's interests in a manner that will improve upon each side's best alternative to a settlement. But at the heart of negotiation there will always be 'opportunistic interaction – less than fully open motives and methods, self-interested manoeuvres' (Lax and Sabenius, *The Manager as Negotiator*). Each party will be trying to reach a joint decision, but each will be pursuing their own interests, *some* of which may conflict with interests of the other side, and each side will pursue other interests by seeking to influence the other side, by not cooperating fully, by trying to turn situations to their advantage, and even by outright resistance. Without such strategic manoeuvring the interaction would not be negotiation, it would just be 'problem solving'. Negotiation is more than just problem solving.

TWENTY FIVE

PREPARATION FOR NEGOTIATION

25.1   Introduction

All negotiators, whatever their style or strategy, should prepare for and plan negotiations. The negotiation process itself, when the parties meet to discuss the case, will be quite difficult. Although each side will have come together through recognition of the need to reach a joint decision through cooperation, each will have different needs and interests, and will want to advance their own position in respect of these interests. The negotiation process will be marked by opportunistic interaction as the parties manoeuvre for position, open communication will be difficult, and the difficulties in communication may be amplified by the emotion generated by the process. Negotiation can be complex because it will cover multiple issues, agreement upon one issue may precede and depend upon agreement on another. It is a difficult process with much toing and froing between the two parties. If you have not prepared and planned for the negotiation, the negotiation will control you. Preparation and planning means that at least you stand a chance of controlling the process.

In preparing a negotiation preparation plan, all negotiators, whatever their style or strategy, should undertake five steps:

    (a)   Research the facts and the law.
    (b)   Establish the client's goals and agree a strategy.
    (c)   Identify the client's BATNA (best alternative to a negotiated agreement).
    (d)   Define the informational goals.
    (e)   Plan the agenda.

In establishing the client's goals and formulating a strategy, an adversarial negotiator should, in addition, identify the 'minimum disposition', or 'bottom line', target points and various concession points. These provide a benchmark against which to evaluate the proposals of the other side, and they provide a set of meaningful targets.

As part of the same process, problem-solving negotiators should seek to identify the needs and interests of each party. They should identify issues around which agreement might crystallise, and they should seek to identify constructive agreements which seek to satisfy mutual needs.

These processes will be considered as a sixth step in the planning process.

25.2   Five-step Preparation Action Plan

25.2.1   STEP 1: RESEARCH FACTS AND LAW

Without a sound grasp of the facts and the applicable law, effective negotiation is impossible. The first stage in the preparation of an action plan, therefore, focuses on research into the relevant facts and the applicable law. You will have done a lot of this as the case develops but, prior to the negotiation itself, you should review the case file, consider the history and development of the case, and identify the relevant facts. You should then identify legal issues for each set of facts, and you should review agreements similar to those that will be the subject of the negotiation. In addition to researching the law and facts for your own side you should also review the position of the other side. How do they view the facts, what interpretations of the law favour their standpoint, what strengths and weaknesses are there in their case? You then need to prepare a balance sheet matching the strengths and weakesses in each side's case.

25.2.2 STEP 2: ESTABLISH THE CLIENT'S GOALS AND AGREE STRATEGY

As a negotiator you have a duty to seek an agreement that satisfies your client's interests. You cannot do this unless you have clearly identified your client's instructions. In preparing for a negotiation you need to explore the full range of options that might be available to you, discuss these with your client, and then develop specific objectives for achieving these in the context of a particular negotiation. If these objectives dictate a particular style of negotiation or a particular negotiation strategy then this needs to be discussed with the client.

The client needs to be aware that sticking at a certain point could lead to deadlock. A client who intends to adopt a cooperative strategy also needs to be warned that this could provide an opportunity for exploitation by the other side.

It is particularly important to determine the limit of your own instructions. If you intend to negotiate with a competitive style than it could be to your advantage to have only limited authority to settle. You can use the limitations in your authority both to defend your own sticking point, and to announce that this is your final offer. If, on the other hand, you wish to embark on a problem-solving negotiation you may seek a broad authority. Anything else may constrain your options, put rigid limits on your ability to produce a settlement, and frustrate your broader objectives.

25.2.3 STEP 3: IDENTIFY THE CLIENT'S BATNA

Negotiation is one of several means that might be adopted to realise your client's objectives. Other ways may be available but at the moment a joint decision achieved through negotiation appears to provide the best form of action. The best test of any proposed joint agreement is whether it offers better value than any other solution that could be achieved outside of an agreement.

Consider the following rather simple example. Debby, the owner of a small print shop wishes to sell a printing machine. She has been approached by John who has offered £1,000. She is tempted by this offer. She paid £10,000 for it five years ago, but she has no idea what it is currently worth. Before accepting the offer, Debby makes a number of inquiries. She is told that the new price is £12,000, though the machine has been significantly up-graded since the production of her model. She rings up a scrap dealer, who indicates that he will take it away for £500. At this point she is quite attracted to the £1,000 offer from John. She then telephones a much bigger printer, who says they will pay £1,000 for it, and provide her with work worth a further £1,500 over the next two years. She then discusses the matter with John, and they agree on a price of £3,000. By identifying better alternatives to the intial agreement, she was able to construct a better final deal.

As a negotiator you always seek to identify your client's best alternative to a negotiated agreement (the client's BATNA). Your client's BATNA is the standard against which any proposed agreement is measured. Developing a BATNA protects your client from accepting terms that are too unfavourable and from rejecting terms that it would be in the client's best interests to accept. It provides a realistic measure against which you can measure all offers.

A better alternative to agreement might involve agreement with another party, it might involve unilateral action, it may involve accepting mediation or arbitration, and it may involve going to court. These alternatives may in some circumstances produce a better deal, in others they will incur hidden costs. By evaluating these alternatives you might conclude an agreement on lower terms than you had initially anticipated, but this might be better than any of the alternatives. Working out a BATNA should provide you with a feel for what may be acceptable and what is not. To work out a BATNA you should construct a list of actions that your client might take if no agreement is reached, then select the option that seems best. You should then measure all proposed settlements against this alternative option.

25.2.4 STEP FOUR: DEFINE INFORMATIONAL GOALS

Negotiation is a process in which information is continually exchanged. The information that is exchanged is usually critical to the outcome of the negotiation, because it is through the exchange of information that the parties learn more about the other side. As both parties learn more about each other so they move towards an agreement. Information will be exchanged throughout the negotiation process, sometimes informally and sometimes formally. The initial letters, statements of position, the construction of the agenda, opening statements, subsequent bids and responses, all provide the negotiators with information about the other side's positions, interests, style and strategy.

As a negotiator you should define your informational goals in advance of the meeting. You should identify the information that you need from the negotiation, the information that the other side is likely to protect, and any information that you want to give to the other side.

25.2.5 STEP 5: PLAN THE AGENDA

All negotiations will have an agenda. In some cases the agenda will be implicit, in others it will be explicit. Where the agenda is implicit it will have been determined by one of the parties, but not articulated. Where it is explicit it will have been agreed between the parties.

The agenda should identify, distinguish and illustrate the issues in dispute. A well-defined agenda should distinguish three different dimensions of the negotiation: the content, the procedures and the personal interaction (B. Scott, *The Skills of Negotiating*). 'Content' refers to the range of topics to be settled; in an oil contract, the quality of the oil, the quantity, delivery, terms, discounts etc. 'Procedure' refers to the manner in which the negotiation will take place, the control of the meetings, the matters to be discussed, the preliminaries, the timing of different phases of the meeting. 'The personal interaction' refers to the manner in which the individuals involved in negotiating interact with each other, the order in which people will speak, the manner in which they speak, how they will respond etc. The agenda may be specifically defined and discussed by the negotiators, or it may be implicit, emerging as the negotiators move through the various phases of the negotiation process.

Competitives and problem-solvers have different orientations towards the agenda.

Competitives will seek to control the agenda to dominate the proceedings. They will use it to sort, rank and identify the issues in dispute. The competitive will prefer to work with a hidden agenda, to spring traps, to work with his or her own priorities, and to control the process. The competitive will want to plan the opening moves, anticipate the other side's opening moves, and work out tactical responses.

The problem-solver will use the agenda to construct a framework within which joint decision-making is facilitated. He or she will want to make the agenda explicit, agreeing the agenda with the other side and using the process of agreeing the agenda to emphasise the processes involved in decision-making.

In constructing an agenda for the meeting the problem-solver should seek to identify each of the dimensions of the negotiation by focusing on the four Ps: purpose, plan, pace, and personalities (B. Scott, *The Skills of Negotiating*). The purpose is the reason for coming together: to explore the issues, to identify mutually profitable interests, to agree specific details, to review progress and plans etc. The plan describes the topics to be discussed and the order in which the parties will take them. The pace is the rate at which the parties need to move – the timetable for the meeting. The personalities are the people in the team, and the manner in which they intend to interact. If all the parties share the same thoughts about the purpose, plan and the pace then it is much easier for the personalities to work together in a spirit of joint decision-making. Discussing the agenda can then be used as a means of agreeing the process. Where one party starts a negotiation with a statement of their position, the other can seek to construct a problem-solving structure by agreeing an agenda.

25.3 The Competitive Negotiator's Sixth Step: Identifying the Bottom Line

The negotiation process in an adversarial negotiation can be compared to a tug of war. The rope strung between the two adversaries represents the continuum along which the parties will bargain. Planning in a competitive adversarial approach to negotiation involves plotting moves along that continuum. It involves identifying the party's 'minimum disposition' or 'bottom line', target points, opening offer and concession points (see Bastress and Harbaugh, *Interviewing, Counseling and Negotiation*).

The 'minimum disposition', or 'bottom line', is that point along the continuum beyond which the negotiator and client are determined that they will not pass. At this point deadlock, or an alternative to a negotiated settlement, would be preferable to agreement. Each party will have their own bottom line. The space on the continuum between each party's bottom line constitutes the 'bargaining zone'. Any settlement within this range may be acceptable to each side but the negotiator should also identify a 'target point' – the point at which the negotiator realistically hopes the other side will settle. This may be identical to the other side's minimum disposition, but it may also be above that point. The negotiator should also select an 'opening offer' – the point at which negotiations should begin – and a series of 'concession points' – points at which the negotiator plans to move along the continuum prior to settling.

Bastress and Harbaugh use a simple problem to illustrate the processes involved in constructing a pre-negotiation chart. Two years ago Weber sold a company to Jones. The sale included a non-competition clause that was valued, in the sale, at £115,000. Weber now seeks to go into business again and wishes to be released from the agreement. The maximum that he is prepared to pay for the release, his bottom line, is £70,000. In his lawyer's judgment a realistic target point is £57,500, half the amount allocated to the non-competition clause in the earlier sale. Weber wishes to start with an opening offer of £28,750, on the grounds that his value as a competitor has decreased rapidly because of changing business requirements. They agree to make a concession at £45,000 as a mid-point between the opening offer and the target point of £57,500.

Weber and his lawyer now need to anticipate the other side's anticipated opening offer, target points, concession points and bottom line. Weber and his lawyer assume that Jones will make an opening demand of £92,000 based on simple depreciation. They further believe that Jones expects to get £75,000 – Jones's target point. Weber believes that they will move to a concession point of £57,000. They assume that Jones's bottom line will be £50,000.

The information from this analysis should be plotted on a bargaining chart (see table 25.1). The chart includes a 'bargaining zone' which amounts to the gap between the two overlapping bottom lines. It is in this gap that the settlement will fall.

Table 25.1

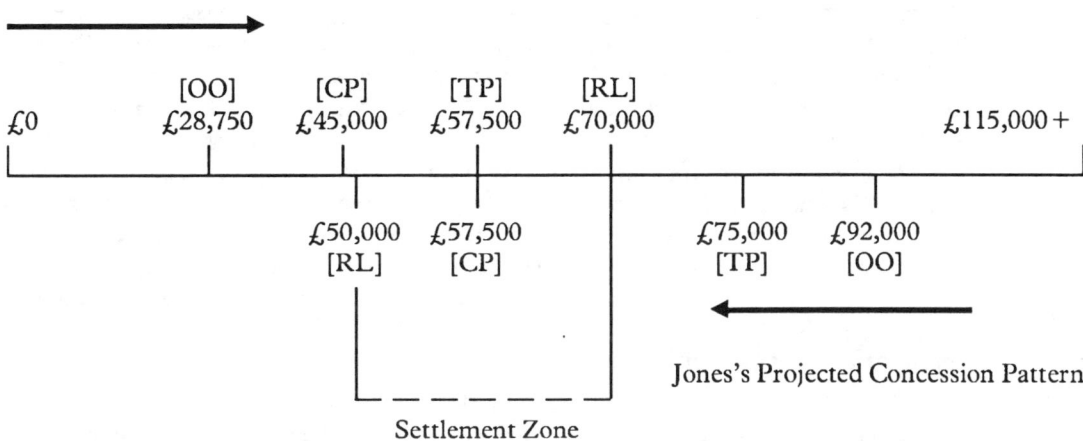

	Opening Offer [OO]	Concession Point [CP]	Target Point [TP]	Resistance Level [RL]	
£0	£28,750	£45,000	£57,500	£70,000	£115,000 +

Weber's Projected Concession Pattern

	[OO] £28,750	[CP] £45,000	[TP] £57,500	[RL] £70,000	£115,000 +

| | | £50,000 [RL] | £57,500 [CP] | £75,000 [TP] | £92,000 [OO] |

Jones's Projected Concession Pattern

Settlement Zone

The value of this kind of chart should increase with the complexity of the negotiation. A similar chart should be constructed for each issue. This should identify issues in which there is a bargaining zone, and the issues in which there is no settlement zone because the parties' bottom lines do not overlap. This should identify the scope for trade-offs between the different issues.

Some theorists are critical of this kind of negotiation planning. It is a time-consuming process, which assumes that each of the issues can be mapped out in a relatively simple format. Many negotiators build up a feel for the issue, and a feel for where a settlement is likely to take place. Fisher and Ury counsel against this form of pre-negotiation planning. They argue that it restricts the negotiator's freedom to react to what can be learnt in the early stages of the negotiation process. A negotiator who has constructed a 'bottom line' may not really listen. Such a negotiator may be inflexible and committed to one position, and may seek to manipulate the other side. The bottom line may have been set too high, forcing the negotiator to adopt too combative a position.

Advocates of competitive bargaining are likely to disagree. Without a negotiation chart it can be difficult to establish points along the continuum, difficult to convey commitment to any position along the bargaining continuum, and difficult to plan tactical moves within the negotiation. Research, moreover, tends to suggest that negotiators who have constructed high target points and who have high aspiration levels do better in negotiations than negotiators with lower aspirations. Negotiators who expect more, tend to receive more.

25.4   The Problem Solver's Sixth Step: Identify the Needs and Interests of the Parties

In preparing a problem-solving negotiation it is necessary to identify the integrative opportunities in the bargaining situation – opportunities that will satisfy the needs of both of the parties. This requires the identification of both parties' respective interests and the consideration of the range of issues that may be present in the negotiation. This is a creative process which requires the parties to expand the options available, rather than close the gap between them. It requires a certain detachment from the party's own position, so that the negotiator can see the negotiation from the other side's point of view. Above all, as in interviewing, it involves holding judgment back. Nothing prevents creativity so much as a critical sense waiting to pounce on the drawbacks of any new idea. The invention of options needs to be separated from the process of judging them. Three techniques can be used to assist this process: 'brainstorming', the circle chart, and inventorying. The first two techniques are suggested by Fisher and Ury in *Getting to Yes*, the third is suggested by Bastress and Harbaugh in *Interviewing, Counseling and Negotiation*.

25.4.1 'BRAINSTORMING'

A brainstorming session is designed to produce as many ideas as possible to solve the problem at hand. All participants in the process are encouraged to articulate whatever possible solutions come to mind – however ridiculous. One idea should stimulate the next. The key ground rule is to postpone all criticism and evaluation of ideas. Brainstorming should not involve a search for the right answer, it should consider a range of potential solutions. Brainstormers should be encouraged to look at the problem from the perspective of different professions. They should seek to expand the agenda, and they should seek to focus on agreements of different strengths. Agreements on procedure may be possible, for example, where agreements on substance are difficult. Partial agreements may be easier to reach than comprehensive agreements. Agreements on principles allow a space for further negotiation, while final agreements foreclose future options.

25.4.2 THE CIRCLE CHART

The circle chart provides a way of categorising four different types of thinking that might be involved in considering options. The first kind of thinking is analytical – it entails thinking about a particular problem, asking what is wrong, analysing the problem. The second type of thinking is descriptive analysis – putting problems into categories, diagnosing the problem. The third type of thinking is strategic thinking – considering what ought to be done, producing theoretical cures, and devising strategies. The fourth and final type of thinking is action thinking – the production of specific and feasible solutions for action.

Table 25.2 The circle chart

	What is wrong	*What might be done*
In theory	*Step 2: analysis* Diagnose the problem: sort symptoms into categories. Suggest causes. Observe what is lacking. Note barriers to resolving the problem.	*Step 3: approaches* What are possible strategies or prescriptions? What are some theoretical cures? Generate broad ideas about what might be done.
In the real world	*Step 1: problem* What's wrong? What are current symptoms? What are disliked facts contrasted with a preferred situation?	*Step 4: action ideas* What might be done? What specific steps might be taken to deal with the problem?

The circle chart maps out these four kinds of thinking (see table 25.2). Its value lies in its circular character. You can begin at step 1 and move through each of the steps to step 4. Or you can start at any point in the circle and move either forwards or backward through the problem. Having thought up a form of action you can move back around the circle to identify the general approach of which the action idea is merely one application. You can then go back one stage further and consider the diagnosis which led to that approach. From there you can move forward again to consider methods for dealing with problems analysed in that way.

25.4.3   **INVENTORY THE NEEDS OF THE PARTIES**

Bastress and Harbaugh's negotiation plan requires the negotiator to inventory, classify, compare and satisfy the needs of the parties. This is a four-step process in which the negotiator and client:

(a)   Identify the needs and interests of all of the parties. The negotiator and the client should independently list the needs and interests on separate pieces of paper, then work together to produce a single list.

(b)   Classify the parties' needs differentiating between absolutely essential, important and desirable items.

(c)   Compare the needs of the parties, by differentiating between shared needs, needs that are independent of each other, and needs that are in direct conflict with each other.

(d)   Search for solutions to meet the shared, independent, and conflicting needs and interests of the parties.

This process should produce a map of the parties' needs and interests. On one side of the map the negotiator will be able to identify the needs that are shared. These needs will be ranked as essential, important and desirable. At the other side will be the needs that are in conflict, which will again be ranked as essential, important and desirable. It may be easier to open up the bargaining process by considering items that are seen as shared, but which are not too important, moving through to consider those that are in conflict but which are important in different ways to each of the parties.

TWENTY SIX

CONDUCTING A NEGOTIATION:
A PROBLEM-SOLVING APPROACH

26.1 Introduction

The high point of a negotiation is the meeting. It is in the negotiation meeting that negotiators establish a basis for communication, exchange information, learn more about each other's concerns, and move towards agreement.

Negotiation meetings tend to follow a basic pattern. In the early stages the parties *explore* each other's position; they form a relationship and seek to understand each other's concerns. They identify the issues and familiarise themselves with the other person's negotiating style. They then begin a process in which they *meet the other side*. It is a process of exchange and persuasion. They make offers and meet offers from the other side; they exchange information, seek to persuade the other side, and each side's stance is modified by what is learned about the other side. Gradually they begin to *narrow their differences*; they agree on some issues and identify fresh problems. They begin to see that agreement is at hand, and move towards closure.

It is important to be aware of these processes and to plan accordingly. It is also important to be aware that different strategies may be appropriate at different phases in the negotiation process. Many negotiations start off competitively, trading bids and counter-bids, but as deadlock approaches there is a shift to a cooperative, even problem-solving stance to reach agreement. It is important, too, to recognise that different strategies involve different sequences. A competitive bargainer in an adversarial negotiation typically exchanges information after trading bids. Bids will then be modified, and concessions made, in the light of the new information. A problem-solving bargainer, on the other hand, seeks to exchange information first, identifying interests, working out solutions, and only then moving to a process of bidding.

This Chapter identifies the steps taken in a problem-solving negotiation, **Chapter 27** identifies the steps taken in an adversarial negotiation.

26.2 Approaching the Meeting: a Problem-solving Perspective

In a problem-solving negotiation your aim is to identify mutual needs and produce solutions that satisfy both parties. You are working to expand the options available to each party in a win/win negotiation. To do this you need to create a climate, right at the start, that is constructive and open. The agenda should focus on procedure. The agenda-setting process itself should seek to facilitate agreement. Information about each party's interests should be exchanged early on in the process. Each side should then seek to construct solutions that satisfy, as far as possible, both sides' interests. Once these solutions are on the table you should argue for your own client's position.

26.3 Opening

26.3.1 CREATING THE CLIMATE

Your aim, when meeting the other side, is to construct a climate that is cordial, collaborative but businesslike. This can take time but you should have learnt some of the essentials whilst interviewing.

You should start off with a neutral non-business topic: the journey to work, things done at the weekend, or, if you have met before, some shared social experience. You should use this period to adjust to each other; to see who you are working with, to work at their pace, to judge their style and approach. If the other side use this period to probe your position then you should aim to deflect these initial probes. Concentrate on being cordial and gradually move to a consideration of the agenda. Attention to climate before you start can help progress. Little things, like the organisation of seating, can make a difference. You should avoid sitting opposite each other and setting up a face-to-face confrontation right from the start.

26.3.2 ESTABLISHING THE PROCESS

You should already have prepared an outline agenda. If you have got the climate right, now is the time to work on the procedures. You will need to agree on the purpose of the meeting, the plan to be followed, the pace at which the parties need to move, and the personal interaction (see **25.2.5**).

To start with you should ask the other side if they are prepared to agree on procedure, then you should establish the procedure and nurture the sense of agreement:

'We would like to use this meeting to explore each other's position, to exchange information. Is that okay with you?'

'Yes, we'd like to exchange views, but I think we'd like to move towards an agreement on some of the issues.'

'That's fine. I assumed this meeting would last for an hour. Shall we see if can agree on a timetable?'

In this kind of dialogue the parties are both emphasising agreement and checking for understanding.

At this stage it is suggested by Bill Scott in *The Skills of Negotiation*:

(a) The dialogue should be shared. Aim to share the talking and listening time – at least until a procedure has been agreed in which one or other leads.
(b) The opening procedures and discussion should take place in a series of short interacting statements; not a sequence of lengthy submissions from each party.
(c) You should be supportive, providing the other side with ample opportunity to make comments and take the initiative. Repeatedly emphasise the need to develop agreement.
(d) Be agreeable. Whenever it is reasonably possible, assent to the other side's suggestions.

These principles apply even where the other side want to move straight to a particular issue. If you stick to substance they are likely to start the bidding process. You are likely to disagree. You both rapidly move into a confrontational position. To prevent this you should keep the focus on procedure: 'Rather than discuss that straight away, why don't we put that on the agenda, and agree a timetable?'

26.3.3 THE ORDER OF BUSINESS

In a problem-solving negotiation it is best to tackle each of the issues across a broad front. This leads to a process in which the overall pattern is cleared and some progress is made on some of the issues. Then the discussion moves on to consider each aspect of the broad pattern. Then, finally, you move into detailed discussion across the broad pattern of issues.

This leads to a process in which each of the issues is put on the table. Each party's interests with respect to these issues can then be considered. The outlines of prospective solutions should begin to emerge and the parties can then begin to shape their positions.

26.3.4 THE ORDER OF DISCUSSION

The object of structuring the discussion is to facilitate agreement. This can best be achieved by following an independent sequence. The first party make a statement; the second party seek clarification and check for understanding. The second party then separately define their own position, and the first party seek clarification. It is up to each party to be clear about the position of the other side before moving on. They should not at this stage challenge the other side. This process enables each party to recognise the other's interests and then move on to focus on potential solutions.

26.4 Meeting the Other Side: Exploring each Other's Interests

26.4.1 OPENING STATEMENTS

Each party should make an opening statement. This should be brief but it should present their view of the overall negotiation, identify the party's interest, specify how each party can contribute to achieving a solution for mutual gain and stress those areas in which agreement has already been reached.

The opening statement should be independent; it should state the position of one party, it should not attempt to state the joint interests of the two parties. It should concentrate on the interests of each party; it should not respond to the statements put by the other side. It should be general, not detailed; it should aim to identify each aspect of the negotiation, and not explore particular issues in detail. It should be brief, to enable the other party to come into the discussion quickly, so that the parties can interact without being overwhelmed by the duration or complexity of the opening statement.

While the other side are making their opening statement, you should listen. You should not waste energy by thinking up counter-arguments; remember you want to build upon their position, not destroy it. You should ask for clarification, and try to get a clear idea of what the other side are trying to say. You should summarise and respond, to show that you have understood. You should then move on to make your own independent statement.

26.4.2 LOOKING FOR SOLUTIONS

Once you have clarified each other's initial positions it is time to move on to identify issues for mutual gain. To do this you need to work creatively and imaginatively, withholding judgment until you have begun to explore concrete proposals. An explicit statement of intent can help to move the discussion on: 'Right, I think we are clear on how we both see the position. Let's look at the creative possibilities.'

It is now that the work done while preparing and planning comes into play. If you brainstormed with your client you may want to brainstorm with the other side. If you found the circle chart helpful, try it again. Consider constructing a joint inventory of each of the issues. In generating ideas it is best to move laterally and interactively through the issues. A lateral process keeps the discussion moving through each of the discussions. An interactive process keeps it moving between each of the parties. If the discussion is too focused it can be difficult to revert to broad and imaginative thinking. It should be interdependent – because each new suggestion by one party should lead to new suggestions by the other. The process of generating new possibilities should generate a number of new and different ideas. Once a number of ideas are in the open, each can be considered in more detail. Again the parties should do this together. While doing this, both should be considering joint interests and joint solutions, not just advancing their own position.

26.4.3 SEPARATE THE PEOPLE FROM THE PROBLEM

To establish the constructive relationships that are essential within a problem-solving negotiation it is necessary to develop forms of communication that are open, trusting and honest. This can be difficult. A negotiator has an interest in making an agreement that satisfies his or her client, and an interest in an outcome that satisfies the negotiator's perception of him or herself as a person. In a negotiation personal perceptions of self necessarily become intrinsically bound up in discussions of substance. A personal interest in the outcome can lead to intense emotions.

To resolve these problems, Fisher and Ury, suggest that negotiators 'separate the people from the problem'. This requires negotiators to address the people problem. Where perceptions are inaccurate they should be changed; where emotions are high people should be allowed to let off steam. When misunderstanding exists, the negotiators should work on communication.

Where the other side resist you need to step back from your own position, withhold judgment and see the problem from their point of view. To do this you need to get them to articulate that point of view. Ask them how they see the problem and ask their help in solving it. Make your own perceptions of the problem explicit and discuss your joint perceptions. If discussion proves difficult you could try using a flip chart to map out your understanding of the problem and compare it with theirs. As you move to solutions, acknowledge the force of the other side's position by using phrases that incorporate their perception of the problem.

If you are to deal with the emotions generated by a negotiation you need to be able to identify them. You should monitor your own performance to check for signs of anxiety; a fluttering stomach, clenched fists, a raised voice. You should not be surprised if you are anxious. Negotiation is a stressful process. Stress can spur you on to a positive performance, but it can also lead you to tighten up, it can inhibit communication. You should then step back and monitor the performance of the other side. Are they expressing stress or emotion. If so, you should ask yourself why. If they get cross, staying calm can help. Sit quietly and let the anger move on. Wait until they stop and then begin to move back into a more rational discussion of the agenda.

26.4.3.1 Developing communication

Active listening is a key tool in negotiation. It improves both what one party hears and the other party says. You should pay close attention to what is said, ask the other party to spell out carefully and clearly exactly what they mean, make encouraging and supportive noises, and ask them to clarify ambiguities. You should check for understanding: 'If I understand you correctly you'd like to . . .', 'Let me see if I'm following. What you are saying . . .'.

26.4.4 WHAT IF THE OTHER SIDE WON'T PLAY? NEGOTIATION JU-JITSU

Creating a constructive climate with a constructive negotiator can be difficult: it can be desperate if you are confronted with someone who is determined to engage in competitive positional bargaining. Fisher and Ury argue that, at first, you should persist with problem-solving tactics. Then, if the other side won't play, use negotiation ju-jitsu. If the other side attack then sidestep, deflect their attack by focusing on the problem, tackle their statement of position by searching for the interest that lies behind it. Treat their statements as only one option, but do not come back with your own counter-attack.

By using competitive tactics the other side are trying to dictate the agenda. You should not allow them to do this. You should seek, instead, to identify the tactic and name it. You should raise the issue explicitly: 'Don't you think that statement is counter-productive? Rather than trade positions which will lead us to disagree, why don't we move on to . . .?', 'I'm not sure that it's constructive to approach the problem in that way. Let's try to move to a solution that could satisfy our client's desires to . . ..'

26.5 Narrowing the Differences and Moving to Closure

It is now time to generate solutions and consider specific proposals. This can be difficult. You have both identified interests and you now need to consider specific proposals. You can do this by making hypothetical suggestions, which may help the other side move, or by identifying constructive proposals.

26.5.1 HYPOTHETICAL SUGGESTIONS

It is easier to float a proposal than put a firm commitment. It enables you to sketch an idea and it allows the other side to back off. By saying 'What if?', you introduce a proposal and invite the other side to develop it further. Neither side need express a strong commitment and neither side need oppose it. A more relaxed discussion can then follow, with adjustments to the original idea arising as a result of the joint discussion.

26.5.2 SUGGESTIONS THAT WILL HELP THE OTHER SIDE MOVE

To achieve a jointly satisfying outcome you need to make it as easy as possible for the other side to shift their position and agree to a compromise. To do this you need to stress the particular and different benefits which a proposed solution offers the other party. You can do this by playing down the benefits to your own side, encouraging moves that they make, and by stressing that a solution has produced a mutual gain.

You might begin to make joint progress if you both stop to consider the following questions:

(a) Can this or that proposal be used to achieve a wider benefit than first seems possible?

(b) Can a new condition be introduced to offset the disadvantages of a pending concession?

(c) Would a change of emphasis or priority secure long-term advantage against short-term loss?

(d) Might a tactical retreat on a narrow issue now provide a better basis for beginning negotiations on another issue later?

(e) Can agreement on an apparently minor issue create a useful precedent for use at some later stage?

(f) Can the negotiation and its outcome be used to create or improve a favourable, more general, relationship with the other party?

26.5.3 IDENTIFYING CONSTRUCTIVE PROPOSALS

It can be difficult to move to a solution if you are not familiar with the kinds of solutions that can satisfy different parties. It may be useful to consider four types of agreements:

(a) Bridging solutions – are the problem-solver's dream. Bridging solutions totally satisfy all of the aspirations and requirements of both parties, without compromise or diminished expectations. It has to be said that these are rare. In most cases agreement requires one or both of the parties to concede on peripheral issues or to some extent have their initial expectations frustrated.

(b) Logrolling solutions – arise when the parties exchange concessions on different issues; each party concedes on the issue that is of less personal importance, thus creating high joint benefit.

Most negotiations involve multiple issues, and in the final bargaining the negotiators frequently offer to concede on one issue in exchange for a concession on another issue more important to the client. This may lead to frustration but this should be outweighed by enthusiasm for the overall solution.

(c)   Cost-cutting – is the name given to any method that reduces the disadvantages to the other party of agreeing to a proposal which benefits the negotiator's client. Two forms of cost-cutting are common. In the first, the negotiator promises not to use a particular agreement as a precedent for the future. In the second, the negotiator finds a way of reducing the loss of image that the other party may experience as a consequence of making the specific agreement.

(d)   Compensation – is a form of agreement which indemnifies the other party for coming to an agreement. In exchange for a particular concession, the negotiator provides the other party with something in return.

These agreements are forms of compromise from which both parties can share a sense of satisfaction and achievement.

26.5.4   THE ONE-TEXT PROCEDURE

In closing a problem-solving negotiation you need to check for understanding, check that the agreement covers every point that is of interest to you and the client. You need to decide how the agreement will be legally enforced and you need to agree who will draft it.

Where the parties are reluctant to agree, a draft agreement can be sketched out as a basis for agreement – this is the one-text negotiating procedure. It is another of the constructive suggestions to be found in Fisher and Ury's *Getting to Yes*. The essence of the one-text procedure is that an initial draft is produced, which does not purport to be complete. It is acknowledged to have faults, but it is to be used as a basis for further negotiation. Each party is encouraged to make suggestions for improvement. These suggestions are noted and agreed suggestions are incorporated into the text. The new text is then presented for discussion. Each party makes suggestions and the agreed ones are incorporated. So it goes on until agreement is reached.

TWENTY SEVEN

CONDUCTING A NEGOTIATION:
AN ADVERSARIAL APPROACH

27.1 Conducting the Negotiation Process in an Adversarial Negotiation

As a negotiator, in an adversarial negotiation, you are concerned to maximise the gain to your client. You have no interest in expanding the cake, it is a win/lose negotiation. You may, though, adopt either competitive or cooperative tactics. As a cooperative negotiator you will seek the best for your client, but you will be willing to make concessions that are acceptable to the other side – to encourage them to reciprocate. As a competitive negotiator you will seek the best for your client by denying options to the other side. You will make concessions if you must, but your priority is to fight for your client's positions – so you will fight and enjoy the fight. The dynamics of the competitive style are, though, risky, and may lead to deadlock. To prevent this you may have to be prepared, towards the end of the negotiation, to adopt a more cooperative stance.

27.2 Opening: Exploring Each Other's Position

27.2.1 OPENING

As a competitive negotiator, you tend to short-circuit the opening phases of a negotiation. You are aware that the first phase sets the tone for the remaining stages but you want to use it to your advantage. You wish to project power and establish a psychologically dominant position.

You should engage in initial ice-breaking, to establish a basis for communication, but you should be pleasant, brisk and businesslike. You should move swiftly on to business. As a competitive negotiator you will not want to discuss the procedures to be followed, but should move straight to the discussion of content. As a cooperative negotiator you may seek to establish the agenda through discussion, but you may prefer to work with a hidden agenda and simply move on to your first item.

27.2.2 PRIORITISING THE ISSUES

In establishing your agenda you will need to make a decision about prorities. You need to decide whether you wish to start with the least contentious issue or the most contentious issue, and whether to start on one issue or a range of issues.

As a cooperative negotiator you may wish to put the least contentious issues first. This may lead both parties to experience success in the early stages and will lead to the development of rapport in the early stages. Once you have achieved rapport, and established a pattern of concessions, you may be able to gain further concessions on bigger, more contentious issues. Another less contentious issue can then be considered to test their bargaining style and strength. Then, without revealing the item as a priority, you should move on to your priority issues.

The strategy of focusing on the smaller issues may, though, backfire. If you have used small items to build rapport, you may be seen as flexible and accommodating. The other side may then make excessive negotiation demands that lead to deadlock. These considerations will lead you as a competitive negotiator to start off with small non-contentious issues to try out the other side's commitment and skill. You can use a range of confrontational tactics on these issues and examine the other side's response. The other side may grudgingly concede and continue to concede throughout the negotiations. By beginning with big contentious issues, you, as a competitive bargainer, will have issued a challenge to the other side. You play on the expectation that the early stages of the negotiation may be marked by civility and trust. You may also use bargaining on the big issues to test the other side's patience. If they are not prepared to bargain then you may be prepared to risk deadlock.

As a competitive bargainer you are likely to bargain on each issue separately and then seek an integrative approach to the final agreement. By establishing that final agreement is only possible when each issue has been resolved you will have served notice that everything is up for grabs until final agreement – thus creating additional pressure on the other side to concede.

27.2.3 BIDDING

The next major decision in the adversarial negotiation concerns the first offer, when to make it, how much to bid, and how to communicate the bid.

Many theorists argue that, as a negotiator, you should aim not to make the first *offer*. This is said to be a sign of weakness, one that shows a willingness to engage in the concession-making process. It is no such thing. It is true that the person who makes the first *concession* tends to do less well in the negotiation process; once one concession has been made, it is only too easy to make another. But the person who makes the first offer has nothing to lose. You gain the initiative and prevent a stalemate arising from offer 'ping-pong', in which both parties skirt around the issues, each refusing to make an offer, and each waiting for the other side to make the first offer. By making the first offer you seize the agenda and clarify the issues at stake. You should make the offer as soon as you have assessed the other side's strengths, weaknesses and bargaining positions. Once you have made the offer you should scrutinise the other side's response.

As a negotiator using competitive tactics, you should begin the negotiation with a moderately high opening position. Empirical research shows that there is a high correlation between the amount of the negotiator's original demand and the ultimate payoff. But the offer should not be unreasonable. The research results only work where agreement has been reached. If the first offer is unreasonable the other side may conclude that the parties are so far apart that it is not worth bargaining – the other side may also decide to engage in high-risk competitive tactics to bring about concessions.

As a competitive negotiator, your initial proposals must communicate 'firmness'. The offer should be specific so as to create commitment. The sum proposed should be exact – not 'around about' or 'in the region of'. You should not communicate hesitancy – by saying 'We'll consider offering'. Nor should you suggest a sum 'in the range of'.

All offers should be justified. By articulating a justification, you convey commitment to that position and call upon the other side to confront the justification. You will have produced a standard against which the offer can be judged, and you show that this offer is not negotiable.

27.3   Meeting the Other Side: Exchange and Persuasion

Negotiation is a process in which the parties learn more about each other's position and adjust their own positions accordingly. In an adversarial negotiation, you as a competitive bargainer may seek to 'educate' the other side by expressing anger, using threats and presenting arguments – the symbols of traditional 'haggling'. These tactics are used as a show of strength, they demonstrate commitment to the adopted position and they are designed to undermine the stance adopted by the other side. You will also seek to enhance your own power by releasing information which suggests that there is no clear alternative to a settlement. You should seek to identify the other side's 'bottom line' and 'concession points', and you should probe for weaknesses in their bargaining stance. You should also seek to conceal information which reveals your own bargaining stance or which points to weaknesses in your own position.

In seeking information, justifying positions, and presenting bids you should use clear arguments and explanations. The best form of argument is rational, detailed and balanced. It brings new facts or interpretations of facts to the other negotiator's attention. Argument should not be one-sided, nor should it be presented emotionally. It is best presented in a conversational tone, reasonably and calmly without displays of anger or sarcasm. This can be difficult if you have chosen to adopt a competitive style and you wish to undermine the other negotiator's confidence in his or her own position. You will be inclined to use anger and threats to achieve your objectives, but such tactics can backfire.

You can use anger to express dismay, to express frustration that the other party are not prepared to change their position, to intimidate, to express outrage, and to indicate that your position should be taken seriously. Your expressions of anger, whether real or feigned, may be effective, but it will probably produce similar outbursts from the other side. The use of anger creates an atmosphere in which real communication is likely to be distorted. Threats can have the same effect. You can use threats to force the other side to make concessions, but the use of threats is dangerous: it can lead to an increase in the level of hostility. Threats frequently lead to confrontations and a breakdown in the negotiation process. They should only be used where they are credible and where the impact is likely to be significant. The ultimate threat is the threat to break off negotiations. This can signal a high degree of firmness but it is very risky. You should only use such a threat where it is really going to produce a concession or where there is a better alternative to a negotiated agreement.

As a negotiator, in an adversarial negotiation, you may, at this stage, be well advised to use cooperative tactics. If you wish to use cooperative tactics you should start your negotiation with a short opening speech. This speech should be carefully planned. It should start with an opening statement, which should present the facts from your point of view. It should present an analysis of the situation, describe and justify your position, and counter potential arguments from the other side. It should be brief. If you speak for a long time you will find it difficult to watch the other side.

In questioning the other side you should use the same techniques that are used in interviewing. Where you seek to secure information you should use the open funnel technique – starting with open questions and moving slowly to narrow and more specific questions. Where you want to control the dialogue you can use the inverted funnel – starting with specific questions and only moving to open questions when you want the other side to 'open up'. You should use probes astutely: the other side have a vested interest in concealing information and unless you seek clarification, amplification and elaboration, you are unlikely to secure the information you need.

You can use blocks to guard access to your own information. You can answer a question with another question; you have not evaded the question but you meet it with a request for clarification or elaboration. You can meet the question with an answer that gives more or less of an answer than that required by the question. You can respond to a particular question with a general answer, or you can respond to a general question with a particular answer. You can answer the question as though it was another question, either by reframing the question or by providing an answer that shifts the focus of the question. If blocks do not work you can rule the question out of bounds, provided you can give a reasonable answer. But you need to take care if you evade questions or block too effectively. You should never lie and you have a professional duty to act towards other solicitors with complete frankness and good faith consistent with your overriding duty to your client (Solicitors' Practice Rules 1990, principle 16.01).

27.4   Narrowing the Differences and Closing

As each party learns more about the other's position the differences between you are likely to narrow. This should lead to concessions in an adversarial negotiation, as both you and the other side move away from your initial target point towards your 'bottom line'. As a competitive negotiator, your tactic is to reach agreement whilst making as few concessions as possible. You see concessions as a cooperative move which leads to the loss of your own position – and a loss of face. You will have tried to 'win' by committing yourself credibly and irreversibly to a preferred position. At times you will visibly risk breakdown by trying to provoke concessions. You will use concessions to prevent deadlock, or to encourage the other side to reciprocate. You can also use concessions to expedite bargaining and to maintain a good future working relationship between the two parties.

As a competitive negotiator, you will concede infrequently and in small amounts. You will only make concessions in response to concessions from the other side. If you adopt a cooperative style, you are likely to take a different stance. You will plan concessions and trade concessions with the other side. You will seek to make concessions on one issue, and then exchange a concession on another issue.

If you continue to use a competitive style, you may find it hard to close a negotiation. By using competitive tactics you will risk a breakdown. You may have to switch to a cooperative style to avoid deadlock, or as the pattern of concessions begins. You may find that the process of information exchange, which developed during the negotiation, provided real insights into the interests underlying the other side's position. This may lead you both to generate a range of solutions as you to seek to resolve your respective problems.

When you reach agreement you should repeat all the elements of the agreement in a summary. You should check for clarification, and confirm the details of the agreement in writing.

ADVOCACY

TWENTY EIGHT

INTRODUCTION: ADVOCACY AND THE SOLICITOR

Advocacy is the skill, or set of skills, most clearly associated with public images of the lawyer. It is the advocate that you see in films, in plays, and on television. It is the advocate's demolition of the key witness, the dramatic confession sprung on cross-examination, the rhetoric used to persuade a jury, that epitomises the popular view of the lawyer.

Yet, in our jurisdiction, the split profession means that the advocate is as often as not a barrister. Why, then, include advocacy in the skills that should be taught on the Legal Practice Course. There are three reasons: first, solicitors already have some rights of audience; second, the Law Society is seeking greater rights of audience; third, the development and understanding of the skills involved in advocacy will assist your work in other domains of legal practice.

28.1   Solicitors' Rights of Audience

Until recently, rights of audience were determined by the practice of the courts and tribunals themselves rather than by the law. This changed as a result of the Courts and Legal Services Act 1990, which puts rights of audience in the courts and certain tribunals and inquiries on a statutory footing. The Act is intended to improve legal services 'by making provision for new or better ways of providing them, while maintaining the proper and efficient administration of justice' (s. 17). The general principle of the Act is that the question whether a person should be granted rights of audience or a right to conduct litigation should be determined only by reference to whether that person is qualified in accordance with vocational and training requirements appropriate to the court or proceedings, and whether he or she is subject to satisfactory rules of conduct.

On the coming into force of the Act, the rights of audience enjoyed by barristers and solicitors, and the right to conduct litigation enjoyed by solicitors, immediately before the Act, were deemed to have been granted. At this stage solicitors had rights of audience, in some cases limited, in the following four courts:

(a)   Magistrates' courts. Solicitor may deal with crime, care proceedings in respect of juveniles, licensing applications and a sizeable domestic jurisdiction.

(b)   Crown Court. A solicitor may appear in an appeal to the Crown Court from a magistrates' court or on committal for sentence, if the solicitor appeared in the court below. Solicitors may also appear, under similar circumstances, where the Crown Court hears appeals from the civil jurisdiction of the magistrates' court. In a limited number of places solicitors have full rights of audience because they had such rights before the quarter sessions became the Crown Court, e.g. Carnarvon, Barnstable, Truro, Doncaster and parts of Lincoln.

(c)   County courts. Solicitors have full rights of audience in the county courts, which have a wide-ranging civil jurisdiction covering debt, breach of contract, personal injury, recovery of land, bankruptcy and insolvency, admiralty, family proceedings and miscellaneous matters such as mental health and sex discrimination.

(d)   The High Court. Solicitors do not have general rights of audience in the High Court, which has long been regarded as the preserve of the barrister, but they may appear when the judge or master is sitting in chambers. They may also appear in bankruptcy matters, and in formal or unopposed matters where the court will not be called upon to exercise any discretion. They may appear in open court to represent a client when judgment is delivered following a hearing in chambers at which that solicitor conducted the case for the client.

Research, conducted for the Law Society, has shown that just over 60 per cent of solicitors had current experience of advocacy (Chambers and Harwood, *Solicitors in England and Wales: Practice, Organisation and Perceptions*). The most likely venues were county court chambers (45 per cent), followed by High Court chambers (39 per cent). Thirty-five per cent of respondents did criminal advocacy work in the magistrates' court, 33 per cent did civil advocacy work in the magistrates' court, and a similar number, 32 per cent, appeared in the open court.

Over half of these respondents (52 per cent) made an average of at least one or two appearances per week, and 27 per cent made three or more per week. In addition to appearing in court as an advocate, a majority of solicitors had current experience of attending clients in the higher courts and Crown Court.

It is clear that solicitors need advocacy training simply to exercise the rights that they currently hold.

28.2   The Application for Fuller Rights

In April 1991, the Law Society made an application to the Lord Chancellor's Advisory Committee on Education and Conduct, to widen clients' choice of advocate in the higher courts by increasing the opportunities for them to be represented by a solicitor where they so wish.

As a result of that application solicitor advocates may be granted rights to appear in the higher civil courts, the highest criminal courts or all courts. The solicitor advocate would have to satisfy the Law Society that he or she has sufficient appropriate experience of advocacy in the courts or tribunals where solicitors are already entitled to appear; would have to pass a preliminary test or tests in civil and/or criminal evidence; and would have to complete courses of training in civil and/or criminal advocacy satisfactorily.

Only 5 per cent of respondents to the Law Society research said that it was very likely that they would seek the qualification for the Crown Court and a further 8 per cent said that it was fairly likely. These figures change, however, when they are seen in the light of current practice. Only 1 per cent of those who currently did not do any advocacy work at all compared with 52 per cent of those who currently appeared more than three times per week said that it was very likely or fairly likely that they would try for Crown Court rights of audience.

A slightly larger proportion of solicitors (16 per cent) were either very likely, or fairly likely, to try for High Court advocacy rights. Again only 1 per cent of those who did not currently appear at all as an advocate were either very likely or fairly likely to pursue gaining a qualification for appearing in the High Court, whereas among those who currently appeared three or more times per week the figure was 39 per cent.

28.3   The Skills of the Advocate

Texts on advocacy tend to suggest one of two things. First, that advocacy is drama, second, that it is an art. As to the first the student is urged to be dramatic, show no mercy, demonstrate commitment and integrity. As to the second it is said to require flair, ingenuity, and perhaps 'breeding'; it is in the bones. Both of these images may be appropriate. They may identify features that distinguish the excellent from the competent. But advocacy is a mixture of art and skills. It is the possession of skills that leads to competence. In this sense, most advocates are made not born. This text is concerned with competence and the first stages of competence can be acquired through learning the skills involved in advocacy. These skills are the skills involved in preparation and planning, questioning and listening that are involved in interviewing and negotiating but now have to be learnt within the specific context provided by the courtroom.

This context has certain critical factors, whether the trier of fact is a qualified judge, a lay judge, or a lay jury. The critical factors are the rules of procedure and evidence that provide a context within which you must work. Unlike interviewing, in which you determine the agenda, or negotiation, when the agenda is defined by both of the parties, in adjudication the agenda is defined for you by the rules of the court, as interpreted by the judge. Your task is to work within this context to develop the story. You need to portray certain events or scenes, stress important details, gloss over unimportant details, zoom in on critical matters, slow down at certain points. In doing this you work with quite limited materials. You can, in certain circumstances, make an opening speech and a closing speech. Here you need to use the skills involved in making an effective presentation. But your primary materials are provided by the evidence, whether in the form of witnesses, exhibits or documents. You have to use these to construct a persuasive narrative. This you can do by the selective use of questions, the careful prioritising of themes, and the ordering of topics within those themes.

28.4   The Law Society's Training Requirements

The Law Society requirements on advocacy training are broken down into four phases. The first three will be required of all trainees, the last will be required of all solicitors who wish to take advantage of the fuller rights of audience.

The first phase is provided by the Legal Practice Course. As a consequence of completing the course you should be able to formulate a coherent submission based upon facts, general principles and legal authority in a structured, concise and persuasive manner. You should understand the crucial importance of preparation and the best way to undertake it. You should be able to demonstrate an understanding of the basic skills in the presentation of cases before various courts and tribunals and should be able:

(a)   to identify the client's goals;
(b)   to identify and analyse factual material;
(c)   to identify the legal context in which factual issues arise;
(d)   to relate the central legal and factual issues to each other;
(e)   to state in summary form the strengths and weaknesses of the case from each party's perspective;
(f)   to develop a case presentation strategy;
(g)   to outline the facts in simple narrative form;
(h)   to prepare in simple form the legal framework of the case;
(i)   to prepare the submission as a series of propositions based on the evidence;
(j)   to identify, analyse and assess the specific communication skills and techniques employed by the presenting advocate;
(k)   to demonstrate an understanding of the purpose, techniques and tactics of examination, cross-examination and re-examination to adduce, rebut and clarify evidence;
(l)   to demonstrate an understanding of the ethics, etiquette and conventions of advocacy.

During the Legal Practice Course you should be instructed in the general principles involved in advocacy through role play and simulation. In Civil Litigation and Criminal Procedure you are also given instruction on the appropriate pre-trial procedures and proceedings and on how to make interlocutory applications before a district judge.

During the Professional Skills Course, which is taken during the training contract, trainees will be given experience, through simulation and role-play, that will enable them:

(a) to use the specific communication skills and techniques employed by the presenting advocate;

(b) to demonstrate the techniques and tactics of examination, cross-examination and re-examination to adduce, rebut and clarify evidence;

(c) to act in accordance with the ethics, etiquette and conventions of the professional advocate.

During the training contract trainees should be given practical opportunities that will enable them to understand the principles involved in preparing, conducting and presenting a case. To help trainees develop these skills they could be required:

(a) to help advise on pre-trial procedures;

(b) to help prepare cases before trial;

(c) in the company of one or more lawyers:

(i) to attend the magistrates' court to observe trials, bail applications, pleas of mitigation or committal;

(ii) to observe the conduct of a submission in chambers or examination, cross-examination and re-examination in open court;

(d) to observe proceedings in family cases, industrial tribunals, planning tribunals or other statutory tribunals or the use of alternative forums of dispute resolution; or

(e) as training progresses, and under appropriate supervision, to take a more active role in the conduct of a case: this could include interlocutory applications before a master or district judge.

Other Legal Practice Guides deal with the specific requirements of procedure and evidence that underpin the work of an advocate (see the *Civil Litigation Guide* and the *Criminal Procedure Guide*). Here we are concerned to introduce the skills that are applicable in any jurisdiction and to any trial, whether civil or criminal and whether before judge or jury. **Chapter 29** focuses on the steps involved in preparing and planning a case. **Chapters 30** to **32** explore the key elements of the trial preparation: examination-in-chief, cross-examination, and opening addresses and closing speeches.

This Chapter concludes with two sections: The first considers two fundamental principles of advocacy, the second considers some basic points of conduct.

28.5 Two Fundamental Principles of Advocacy

Two fundamental principles underpin much advocacy practice:

You do not give evidence yourself. It is the witness who provides testimony: it is your task to construct the theory of the case, the story, from that testimony. It is not your job to give testimony yourself. You should not, therefore, use phrases such as, 'It is obvious that the car was going too fast under the existing conditions', 'I happen to know that piece of road is dangerous in icy conditions'.

You should not give your own opinion of the facts or the law. The court is not interested in what you consider to be the law, but only with what it is. The court is equally not interested in your opinion of the facts, but merely the arguments which indicate possible interpretations. You should, therefore, 'submit' and not 'opine'; 'suggest' and not 'declare'; you 'persuade' and not 'assert'.

These principles underpin the prohibition on leading questions during examination-in-chief. They should guide you when you make direct presentations to the court, in opening speeches and closing arguments, and they should also guide you when formulating questions. It is not your task to speak for the witness but to get the witness to speak for him or herself.

28.6 Some Basic Points about Conduct

Courts and tribunals are formal settings which operate through formal conventions. You need to be familiar with these conventions and explain them to your client and witnesses. This section deals only with the basics: the formalities involved in addressing the bench, other advocates and witnesses; and how to deal with witnesses.

28.6.1 ADDRESSING THE BENCH, OTHER ADVOCATES, WITNESSES

28.6.1.1 The bench

You should address members of the bench in the following way:

(a) Magistrates as 'Sir' or 'Madam'. It is not correct to call a magistrate 'your worship', although you may use 'your worships' when addressing the full bench.

(b) Circuit judges are referred to as 'your honour'.

(c) The district judge of the High Court and the county court registrar should be addressed as 'Sir' or 'Madam'.

(d) A master of the Supreme Court, or a taxing master, should addressed as 'Master'.

28.6.1.2 The other side

You should refer to 'My learned friend' only if the other side is represented by a barrister. Where the other side is represented by a solicitor it would be appropriate to refer to them as 'My friend', 'The plaintiff/defendant', or 'Mr/Miss/Mrs/Ms Brown'.

28.6.1.3 Witnesses

Witnesses should be addressed directly: Mr, Mrs, Miss, Ms, Dr. Except in the case of children, witnesses should not be addressed by their forenames.

28.6.2 THE PLACE OF WITNESSES

You may need to decide whether witnesses should be in or out of court when not giving evidence.

In criminal cases all witnesses, other than the defendant, should be kept out of court until called. In a civil case witnesses need not be kept out of court, but if you want them excluded you will need to apply to have them excluded.

If the defendant in a criminal case is to give evidence, he or she must be called before other defence witnesses. If the plaintiff in a civil case is to give evidence, he or she should be called before other witnesses. If the defendant in a civil case it to give evidence, he or she should be called before other defence witnesses.

The object of excluding witnesses from the court is to prevent them from knowing what evidence is being elicited from others. This principle should be explained to witnesses, who may nevertheless stay in court once they have delivered their evidence. Witnesses should not discuss their evidence with others still waiting, nor should they discuss it with you if the case has been adjourned while they are giving evidence.

You should always arrive at the court with sufficient time to explain the physical set-up to your client and witnesses.

28.6.3 INTRODUCTIONS

If opening a case you should always introduce yourself and the other side to the court, for example:

> May it please you (your honour, madam/sir, master), in this case I appear for the prosecution/ plaintiff and Mrs Smith (or my learned friend, if the other side is a member of the Bar) appears for the defence.

You should always arrive at court in plenty of time to fill in a slip stating who you are. If you have not had time to do this, after explaining who you appear for, you should add your name.

28.7 Further Reading

Appleman, J. A., *Preparation and Trial* (Vienna Va: Coimer, 1967).
Bellow, G., and Moulton, B., *The Lawyering Process* (Mineda NY: Foundation Press, 1978).
Bennett, W. L., and Feldman, M. S., *Reconstructing Reality in the Courtroom* (London: Tavistock, 1981).
Bergman, P. B., *Trial Advocacy in a Nutshell* (St Paul Minn: West, 1979).
Hegland, K. F., *Trial and Practice Skills in a Nutshell* (St Paul Minn: West, 1978).
Mauet, T., *Fundamentals of Trial Techniques*, New Zealand edition edited by T. Eichelbaum (OUP, 1989).
Murphy, P. and Barnard, D., *Evidence and Advocacy*, 4th ed. (London: Blackstone Press, 1993).
Napley, D., *The Technique of Persuasion*, 4th ed. (London: Sweet & Maxwell, 1991).
Stone, M., *Cross-examination in Criminal Trials* (London: Butterworths, 1988).

TWENTY NINE

PREPARATION

29.1   Introduction

Preparation, not eloquence, is the key to successful advocacy. With thorough preparation you should be so familiar with every aspect of the case that by the time you arrive at the door of the court you will have developed the confidence to make an effective presentation. Without preparation, even the most eloquent advocate will have difficulty presenting a case. If you have not prepared you will be at the mercy of the other side. You will have to adopt a purely responsive strategy: you will be living by your wits. This is not advocacy, and it is not a comfortable place to be. You need to prepare carefully and you need to plan your case.

Preparation and planning involve some quite practical considerations. You will need to review the file and be completely on top of the facts, the law and the procedural steps taken to date. You will need a thorough understanding of the pleadings, or charges, and you will have to review the probable testimony of all anticipated witnesses. You should organise your work in a case file and prepare a trial notebook.

Preparation also involves decisions about strategy and tactics. Decisions about strategy flow from the manner in which you construct your overall perspective of the case. Decisions about strategy lead on to important decisions about case tactics; decisions about how you will present the case, the order in which you will present witnesses, the flow of questions, the determination of priorities. It is these decisions that will be considered here. In the next two sections we will consider two key concepts: the 'theory of the case' and the 'story' behind the case. Each of these may be useful in developing a case plan. A process for developing a case plan will be considered in the final section of the Chapter.

29.2   The 'Theory of the Case'

One form of case planning, recommended in Murphy and Barnard's *Evidence and Advocacy*, bases case planning around the concept of the ideal closing speech; the speech that you as an advocate would ideally like to make, if the evidence given in your case were actually to justify it. By focusing on the ideal closing speech you are forced to think about the case in terms of the evidence that will lead to the effective presentation of your case.

American trial strategists approach the topic of case planning in a similar but more systematic, if slightly grandiose, manner. They suggest that the key to successful case planning lies in the development of a 'theory of the case'. (This concept is to be found in many American 'trial handbooks'. The account here draws heavily upon the work of Thomas Mauet, whose *Fundamentals of Trial Techniques* has been used extensively in the preparation of this section.)

The 'theory of the case' is your position and approach to all the undisputed and disputed evidence which will be presented at trial. A theory of the case is used to integrate the agreed facts with your version of the disputed facts to create a cohesive, consistent, logical and persuasive position at trial.

A 'theory of the case' is another way of describing your overall argument on the facts. Your theory need not be complex and sophisticated, it should be simple, but it should guide the construction of your argument throughout the presentation of the evidence. Consider the following examples:

(a) In a murder case, the prosecution's evidence will show that following an argument, the victim was shot by a man some witnesses will identify as the accused. As advocate for the defence, is your theory:

(i) the accused did not do the shooting (wrong identification); or
(ii) the accused did do the shooting, but was using reasonable force in his own defence (self-defence)?

(b) In a 'running down' case, the plaintiff pedestrian was struck by the defendant's car at a crossroads. Some evidence will place the plaintiff within a zebra crossing with the traffic lights providing a green signal for her to walk. Other testimony will show the plaintiff was outside the zebra crossing, jaywalking across the crossroads. As the plaintiff's advocate, is your theory:

(i) the plaintiff was on the zebra crossing; or
(ii) the plaintiff was not on the zebra crossing but was injured because the defendant could have stopped but did not?

Both of these examples provide simple illustrations of the theory of the case. Your choices clearly affect the manner in which you will examine and cross-examine witnesses. Developing a theory provides you with an orientation towards the facts; it provides you with a consistent and logical position throughout the case. It informs your questioning of witnesses on direct examination and cross-examination and it provides the structure to your opening and closing arguments. Failure to develop a theory will be immediately apparent. Your questioning will be opportunistic and inconsistent. Your courtroom contributions will lack direction.

A theory of the case should enable you to identify the focal points in a trial. These are the moments at which, in an evenly balanced case, the trial turns – the admissibility of an exhibit, the impression made by a witness. Identifying these points is a key element in preparation. Identifying them is easier when you have a well-developed theory of the case.

To develop a theory of the case you need to take several analytical steps. Where you are acting for the plaintiff:

(a) Review the elements of each cause of action you have brought in the case.
(b) Analyse how you intend to prove each of the required elements through available witnesses and exhibits.
(c) Analyse the contradictory facts that your opponent has available to determine what facts will be disputed, and anticipate the witnesses and exhibits your opponent will probably present in order to put those facts in issue.
(d) Research all the possible evidentiary problems that arise so that you will be able to maximise the admissibility of your proof and minimise that of your opponents.
(e) Review the admissible evidence you and your opponent have on each element of required proof to determine the greatest weaknesses on both sides.

Once you have completed these steps, which can be presented in the form of a chart, you should be able to identify the areas where the admissible evidence is in dispute. You then need to develop as much additional evidence as you can to strengthen your version of the case, as well as to attack your opponent's version. The process of developing logical, consistent positions on the disputed facts and harmoniously integrating them with the undisputed facts is what Mauet means by developing a theory of the case.

Do not be misled by the term 'theory of the case'. It provides you with a means for constructing an account, from the evidence, of 'how it really happened'. It also provides you with a device for planning your case. If your case rests on an alibi, you know you must search for facts that make that alibi as credible as possible. If an important piece of evidence consists of hearsay, you must find a basis for an exception to the hearsay rule that makes it admissible.

The formation of a theory of the case is an important aid to advocacy. It changes an amorphous search for truth into a specific line of argument that you can build upon (P. Bergman, *Trial Advocacy in a Nutshell*). But as Bergman points out the formation of a theory is not without risks. If you lock into a particular theory of the case too early, you may discard alternative and stronger theories. If you become committed to a particular theory of the case, pre-trial preparation becomes a roller-coaster ride. Every time you unearth evidence that supports your theory of the case, the case is wonderful and the client is wonderful. The discovery of negative evidence, on the other hand, turns the case into an unmitigated disaster. To safeguard this you need to develop alternative theories, or theories with sub-themes, variations that allow you to adopt a flexible approach both to trial planning and to the trial itself.

Once your theory of the case is developed you should perform the same analysis to determine what your opponent's probable theory and position on the disputed facts will be. This will be important when you prepare to cross-examine your opponent's witnesses.

29.3 Developing a 'Story'

A different approach to trial planning involves constructing your case in the form of a 'story'. This might sound trivial: there is a lot at stake in any trial, and it is, moreover, governed by a series of formal rules. But you should be able to see the relevance of this approach if you think about the way in which a case is presented.

A case is presented primarily through the testimony of witnesses. An opening speech provides an outline of the case to come, and the closing speech provides a persuasive argument based on the testimony given. But, for the most part, evidence is provided either in the form of the testimony given by witnesses, or in the form of real evidence, exhibits, documents etc.

Evidence that is poorly structured can appear meaningless and disconnected. Effective evidence works not through its force as argument – it rarely presents an argument as such – but instead through its structure as a narrative, and narrative works through *implication*. This is a form of argument which does not appear as an argument; it proceeds through the power of a series of propositions which accumulate, and as each proposition accumulates so it connects with other propositions and produces a form of truth. The truth arrives as the lines set out in the propositions gradually converge and as it becomes compellingly evident that the propositions add up to only one thing – the conclusion towards which an approach has been made from the beginning.

This is how narrative works. The author introduces characters, events and descriptions of place and mood. The characters will display their feelings, take part in dialogue, and engage in activities. A story will be more or less credible depending on the manner in which the details are sketched. The story will be made up of a series of elements. Each element implies the other elements, and implies them in movement towards the end. The story, and the various themes that make up the story, will emerge not in the form of a simple statement, but in the form of the connections drawn between each of the elements within the narrative. The coherence of the story will depend upon the general end of the story and upon the manner in which the action of the story is developed from a beginning, through a complicated middle, to an inevitable end.

The concept of trial arguments as a 'story', a narrative structure that links the key elements in a case, was given empirical foundation in Bennett and Feldman's analysis of trial strategies in American courts (Bennett and Feldman, *Reconstructing Reality in the Courtroom*). A story, or narrative, functions to provide a plausible link between each of the elements in the case. It provides a persuasive structure that defines different elements in the case and builds connections between them. A narrative links five elements: the scene, the act, the agent, the agency, and the purpose.

This is most clearly demonstrated in a criminal case where the judge's instructions to the jury emphasise the prosecution's obligation to construct a structurally complete story:

In order to convict the defendant of the crime of . . ., the prosecution must prove beyond reasonable doubt that:

(Actor)	The said defendant, . . .
(Scene)	did on the charged date/time/place/occasion etc.
(Purpose)	wilfully/knowingly with intent etc.,
(Agency)	use force/cause the victim fear of bodily harm/offer for sale etc.,
(Act)	to take the property of/ to cause the death of etc.

The basic prosecution or plaintiff task is to represent the defendant's action within a coherent set of scenes, agencies and purposes as the action develops over time. To satisfy the minimum structural criteria of a story, you need to establish that the actor and act must be connected over time through scenes, purposes and agencies. The first *situates* the actor and action in time and space, at the scene. The second establishes the actor's purpose or *intent*. The third concerns the behavioural mechanics or *execution* of the act. Establishing a story provides consistent definitions for actors and acts that are constant across the scenes, agencies and purposes, thus yielding a consistent and clear interpretation for the actor's act.

While the prosecution or plaintiff have to construct a whole story, the strategy of constructing a complete story of its own is only one option for the defence.

First, the defence can simply *challenge* the prosecution's story: they can show that there are missing elements in the prosecution's story, or that definitions of various scenes, acts, actors, agents or purposes do not support the same interpretation of the defendant's behaviour.

If they fail to challenge the prosecution story they can seek to *redefine* the story. Here the defendant's advocate redefines particular elements in the story to show that a different meaning emerges when slight changes are made in the interpretation of the evidence.

Finally, the defendant's advocate may *reconstruct* the evidence, and tell the defendant's own story. Here the defendant's advocate introduces the defence's own evidence in order to tell a completely different story about the defendant's behaviour.

Constructing the case in the form of a story enables you to make tactical decisions about how to place evidence, order witnesses, structure questions and present arguments. The concept of a story can be used to develop the argument in a case through the manner in which it informs three key elements in the case:

(a) Definitions. Facts are constructed into a story line through the specific language used by witnesses (and elicited by lawyers) to *define* pieces of evidence.

(b) Connections. By locating or placing a particular piece of evidence in relation to the other elements in the story, *connections* are established for the trier of fact.

(c) Validations. The integrity of a story depends on whether the definitions and connections can be *validated* through supporting definitions or whether they can be invalidated by showing that alternative definitions and connections are equally plausible.

The 'story' is an extension of the 'theory of the case'. It develops the theory into a particular narrative and helps to make sense of the tactical decisions that you need to make during a trial. Having constructed a 'theory of the case', or a case 'story', the next stage is to determine tactics. This involves two sets of decisions: a relatively formal, but important, set of decisions about the witnesses that you will call, and the order in which you put them, and a set of 'narrative' decisions, about how you will make your story plausible. We shall consider the question of plausibility or credibility here, while tactical considerations about which witnesses you call will be considered in **30.3**.

29.3.1 CREDIBILITY

In planning your tactics a key concern is to establish the credibility of your 'theory' or 'story'. To do this you need to ensure that your evidence is consistent with common sense, consistent within itself, and consistent with the established facts (see Bergman, *Trial Advocacy in a Nutshell*).

29.3.1.1 Is the evidence consistent with common sense?

To be effective evidence needs to accord with common conceptions of credibility, with common sense, with our experience. Evidence will not be credible if it is counter-intuitive, and to be credible it will need to be established. Thus, if you wish to introduce a witness who claims to identify X, whom they saw running away from them a hundred yards away, on a dark, badly lit night, you will need to introduce evidence to show that claim is credible. Similarly, if your client claims that he had left his house at 3.00 a.m. to return a book to the library, you will need to introduce extra evidence to make it plausible. We *know* from our own experience that these claims are unlikely.

A key stage, then, in the construction of tactics is the determination of plausibility or credibility. You need to consider whether the *definitions* of behaviour that you are making, or the *connections* that you are making are credible. Do they make intuitive sense? If not, you need to consider introducing *validating* evidence. Consider the following testimony:

Q1. At what point did Mrs Brown step out?
A1. Twenty yards beyond the zebra crossing.
Q2. Where was the bus at this point?
A2. Approaching the zebra crossing.
Q3. Where was the defendant's van?
A3. In the outside lane passing the bus.
Q4. What happened next?
A4. Mrs X crashed into the defendant's van.

The fourth answer seems implausible because we tend to think of a van crashing into a person, not vice versa, particularly where the person was killed in the accident. To make it plausible you need to ask other questions, to make it consistent with common experience. So evidence that Mrs A was late for work, that she was running along the pavement before running into the road, that she was distracted by a friend calling on the other side of the road would make *connections* between the statement and common experience. Note, too, that by moving from fairly closed questions to an open question the advocate is able to *validate* the evidence by having the witness volunteer the phrasing. This whole sequence of questions was planned to produce that effect.

29.3.1.2 Is the evidence consistent with itself?

People who describe the same event in different ways tend not to be credible: they cast doubt not only on the inconsistent evidence but on the remainder of their evidence. Consider the following example. George Kelly is identified by a witness as the person at the scene of the crime. The witness says that George was wearing a red T-shirt. George then gives evidence. In response to questions he denies being present, it could not have been him, he does not have a red T-shirt. The prosecution then introduce a photograph of him wearing a red T-shirt. Not only does this cast doubt on the first inconsistent statement – it *invalidates* it – but it also undermines the whole of his testimony.

In preparing your case you need to search the expected testimony for inconsistencies and capitalise on them or, if they are working against you, de-emphasise them. You also need to determine the persuasive effect of inconsistent statements. Is the point crucial or relatively minor? How great is the inconsistency? Does the witness have a good explanation for the inconsistency? To what extent does the inconsistency at one point infect the rest of the witness's testimony?

29.3.1.3 Is the testimony consistent with established facts?

In developing a theory of the case you will seek to integrate disputed facts with agreed facts to produce a consistent and coherent argument. When questioning witnesses you should seek to establish agreed facts and avoid inconsistencies. If you have agreed with the other side that your client was wearing a red T-shirt, and that a person with a red T-shirt was identified as the thief, there is no point in one of your witnesses saying that your client was wearing a white T-shirt. The evidence on that point is not only irrelevant, it also undermines the credibility of the evidence on the disputed facts. The witness appears to be making up evidence to assist the defence case. The lesson is that in preparing your questions you need to avoid disagreements on agreed facts and make *connections* between the agreed facts and disputed facts.

29.4 Constructing a Case Plan

The concept of a case plan has been developed by Sir David Napley (see Napley *The Technique of Persuasion*). He urges advocates to develop, not a 'theory of the case', or a 'story', but 'an appreciation of the situation'. This is a military concept which involves a review of the problem or situation, based on all the available information, culminating in a plan of action. The plan should be in the following logical sequence:

(a) the object to be attained;
(b) the factors which affect the attainment of the object;
(c) courses of action open to the commander and the enemy;
(d) the plan.

The preparation of a case plan is then described using the simple example of a Nigerian lady who has been charged with shoplifting.

She denies the charge. She says she had gone to a large chemist's to purchase presents for her return home. She had often shopped at the store, spending £120 that morning. She is the wife of a government official and is scheduled to leave at 2 p.m. that afternoon.

She was in a great hurry; she had to visit a sick relative, make other purchases, change a considerable quantity of money, collect her luggage and get to the airport by 1 p.m.

The store was busy. She selected some ornaments from the first floor, worth about £13, and queued to pay. Because of the queue, she decided to pay downstairs. She saw there was a queue around this till, too, and so decided to save time by crossing the road to a bank, to change her money, with every intention of returning to pay. As she reached the pavement, she was challenged by a store detective, who then called the police. She gave her explanation of having intended going to the bank before returning to the store. On further questioning you find that because she was in such a hurry she had arranged with a car hire service to have a taxi waiting for her at 12 noon at the back of the store. She was arrested at 11.50 a.m.

29.4.1 THE OBJECT TO BE ATTAINED AND THE FACTORS WHICH AFFECT THE ATTAINMENT OF THE OBJECT

You commence to develop your theory of the case, or appreciation of the situation. Your primary object is to secure an acquittal; your subsidiary objects are bound up with the second phase, the factors which affect the attainment of that object. These are:

(a) The vast majority of shoplifting cases are properly charged and convicted. Magistrates tend to become case-hardened and store detectives know what the magistrates expect to hear. Your task is to convince them this case is the exception rather than the rule.

(b) The store detective will be an experienced witness and you have no material with which to refute her evidence. But . . .

(c) Your client had just enough money on her to pay for her purchases and a great deal more in dollars. But this is common in many shoplifting cases and may not help.

(d) The sole issue is whether the client was leaving the shop having stolen the articles, or whether she intended to return and pay.

The following factors need to be taken into account:

Against her	*For her*
1 She did not at once say she was going to the bank and returning to pay.	1 She had a taxi waiting at the rear entrance. If she was making a getaway she would more easily have dashed into the taxi and departed.
2 She knew she had not paid for the goods when she left the shop.	2 When stopped she was about to cross the road in the direction of the bank.
3 She told no one before leaving what she intended to do.	3 She told the store detective and the police officer, on the latter's arrival, what had been her intentions.
	4 She was of excellent character and standing.
	5 The bank revealed on investigation that no one had made inquiries about whether she was known there and changed currency there.

The next stage of the analysis is to decide the course of action open to the defence and to the prosecution. The defence must call the taxi driver to prove he was waiting for the accused at the rear of the shop. Two strong and impressive character witnesses should be available. The shop must be viewed in advance of the hearing to familiarise yourself with the layout. If possible, someone from the bank should be called to prove she was known to change currency there. The prosecutor should be asked whether there are any facts which are unknown to you.

29.4.2 THE PLAN

There is no real prospect of persuading the magistrates that your client is innocent. Your objective, therefore, is to persuade them that there is a doubt about her guilt, which means that they must acquit.

The essence of your tactics must be to impress the bench into accepting that your client acted foolishly and not wickedly, and that she was proceeding in the direction of the bank and not in the direction of the taxi. Cross-examination and the argument should be limited to that one issue. As the case develops, however, you get a bonus. The police officer proves to be young and inexperienced and in his evidence in chief describes how he told the accused she had committed a crime by leaving the shop with goods for which she had not paid. It was thus possible to suggest that she had been charged without any regard being paid to the true state of her mind at that time and the need to establish dishonest intent.

Producing a plan like this, with clear objectives, helps you plan tactics within the major set pieces: examination-in-chief, cross-examination etc. In the shoplifting case your main objective is to satisfy the court that your client may well be telling the truth when she says that she was walking across the road or in that direction in order to go to a bank where she could change money. If you put this directly to the store detective she is likely to deny it, or, at best, say that she had no idea where your client intended to go. You need to lay a proper foundation for your questioning. You would first ask her whether there is in fact a Barclays Bank on the side opposite the shop. As you know there is one, she will confirm this. You then ask whether she was present when the police interviewed the defendant; you know that she was. You will then remind her that your client had said that she was going to the bank to cash some money. She will agree with that. You might then ask her whether she had been to the bank to see whether the defendant was known there. You know that no such inquiries were made.

You must take care in phrasing your next question. The witness might think that she should have gone to the bank, and she may now not want to help you in your line of questioning. Your next minor objective is to get the prosecution witness to concede before the court that there was a strong possibility that the client's account was a true one. If you simply ask her if she agrees that your client was going in the direction of the bank, she will justifiably say that she has no idea. But if you put the question in this form: 'You of course are not able to dispute the possibility that this lady was intending to go to the bank?', then you may get an answer that she cannot contest it.

Napley's account of this case demonstrates both the pre-thinking which is necessary to lay a tactical foundation for even the most commonplace cross-examination. It also illustrates the importance of making an intelligent appraisal of the witness's likely answer to any of the questions that you might put.

THIRTY

EXAMINATION-IN-CHIEF

30.1 Introduction

An examination-in-chief is the process in which you elicit evidence from your own witnesses. This is a challenging process. You cannot give evidence yourself, you can only ask questions and develop your case through the answers given. Yet, you need to develop through these answers a case that clearly, logically and forcefully presents the facts of the case in accordance with your case strategy. Your case, in addition, needs to be memorable and persuasive.

How are you to do this? Principally through questioning. An examination-in-chief is the process in which you elicit evidence through questions. You will use different forms of questions at different times in the examination with different kinds of witness. Questions are used to get the story out, to emphasise different elements in the story, to zoom in on particular pieces of action, and, sometimes, to slow the evidence down. There are, though, other techniques. You need to make decisions about structure, about pace, about detail and relevance, you also need to make decisions about the order in which you will present your testimony. Most of the decisions will have been made when you constructed your case plan, but they are considered here as they are all a part of the process.

30.2 General Principles

The conduct of an examination-in-chief presents a dilemma. If you provide too much detail the trier of fact may be overwhelmed and bored. If you provide insufficient detail you may not establish your case.

The difficulty arises because the trier of fact usually hears your story for the first time not in the form of a continuous narrative but in the form of a series of answers connected only by your questions. It is, moreover, difficult to present a story in words. Diagrams, visual aids, and real evidence are needed to flesh out the account. By providing too much detail you compound the problem.

How then can you resolve the dilemma? By presenting only that evidence which is relevant, organising it logically, and using language to control the pace and vary the action.

30.2.1 RELEVANCE

The trier of fact wants to hear evidence that is relevant. It is the recitation of numerous details that overwhelms the trier of fact, not the recitation of relevant details. But how do you ensure that your evidence is relevant? Paul Bergman, in *Trial Advocacy in a Nutshell*, provides three suggestions:

(a) Ask yourself if a line of questioning is important enough to be included in your closing argument? If it is not think again. You may still want to include the evidence. It may add flavour to your case, it may have a cumulative effect, it may create a climate in favour of your case and add to the credibility of your argument.

(b) View the situation from the standpoint of your opponent. If you were in your opponent's shoes, is it the kind of evidence you would bother to contest?

(c) Ask how the testimony is linked to the desired conclusion. Is there a direct link? If so keep it in. Is the link circuitous? Have you attacked an issue obliquely for a reason, or simply for effect? If the link is too circuitous, then leave it out.

At the end of the day it will be a matter of judgment, but you will need to develop a fine eye for relevance.

30.2.2   A LOGICAL STRUCTURE

A logical structure should provide the right balance between evidence which is too general, and an account which is too detailed. A chronological presentation of the evidence is usually best. If you have constructed your case in the form of a 'story' it is best to produce it in a chronological narrative. A chronological narrative should achieve two goals. It will stimulate a witness's memory and the witness should, therefore, tell a fuller and more credible story. It should also stimulate the fact-finder's memory, so that the fact-finder is more likely to remember and be persuaded by the evidence.

Sometimes a chronological structure is not appropriate. If the most interesting thing a witness has to say happened in the middle then be flexible. Start the examination at that point, then backtrack and proceed through the rest of the testimony in chronological order. Then try to finish on the same strong point.

30.2.3   USE LANGUAGE AND PACE TO VARY YOUR APPROACH

When you phrase your questions you should choose simple words and phrases. You should plan your questions carefully. If you ask a witness 'how fast' a car was moving, you may get a different answer than if you had asked 'how slow' it was moving. Phrasing can be difficult. In **29.3.1.1**, we gave the example of a case in which a woman was said to 'crash' into a van. This is counter-intuitive but it was the witness's testimony. To elicit that testimony it was necessary to ask a series of directed questions, then move out into an open question. To continue with a direct question, 'At what point did the van hit her?', might have produced a very different response.

You should use questions to control the testimony. Carefully directed questions can lead to a detailed account produced in a series of short answers. The effect is to slow the action right down and move into the salient action in a series of carefully delineated stages. By using broad open questions you may get a very different response, a quick account of the action, which conveys an impression of the speed with which it developed.

30.2.4   USE POINTS OF REFERENCE AND TRANSITIONS

Points of reference and transition questions can be used to change pace and structure the examination.

A point of reference is an inclusion in a question of some matter already testified to by a witness. The matter is included to provide a context for your question. The third question in the following sequence includes a point of reference:

What happened next?

Please go on.

What happened directly after the car swerved?

Points of reference can be used to emphasise important facts, clarify confusing testimony, obtain greater detail, or provide a transition from one episode to another. Points of reference add variety, even drama to your questioning.

Transition questions are used as signposts. They move the witness along from one episode to the next. When a witness has provided evidence on one topic, a transition question lets the trier of fact know that questioning on that topic has finished and the evidence on the next topic is to begin:

Let's turn now to what happened when you arrived at the hospital.

30.3   Order of Testimony

You now have to make decisions about which witnesses to call and the order in which they are to produce their testimony. In making these decisions you will need to remember that you are presenting testimony in the form of a narrative. You are using evidence to develop a *story*. As an advocate you will contend that certain things took place but you will prove that they took place through facts that emerge from the testimony of your witnesses. In total these facts should add up to a story. You will only succeed if your witnesses' story is believed.

30.3.1   SELECTING AN ORDER FOR WITNESSES

In examination-in-chief you aim to produce testimony in a form that is clear, logical, coherent and persuasive. To do this you need to produce evidence within a clear structure, you need to produce witnesses according to plan, and you need to provide a structure for their evidence.

Three principles should help provide a structure:

(a)   Follow the principle of primacy and recency, according to which people tend to remember best what they hear first and what they hear last. This accounts for the general advantage of the plaintiff, who presents evidence first, and argues last. It supports the view that the defendant should make an opening statement, so that the fact finder learns of the defendant's case as soon as possible. It also supports the view that strong witnesses should be called first and last, and that each witness should begin and end on a strong point.

(b)   Do not over-prove your case. By calling too many witnesses you bore the fact finder. In general you should call one witness and not more than one corroborative witness on any one point.

(c)   You are only required to prove the elements of your cause of action and any background necessary for their proper understanding. You should call the witnesses who will secure that objective and you should select those that are likely to be clear, accurate and reliable.

You should then present witnesses in an order that will logically and forcefully present your evidence to the trier of fact. The following order is suggested in Mauet's *Fundamentals of Trial Techniques*:

(a)   Present your case in chronological order or in some other logical order that will make sense to the trier of fact.

(b)   If your client is to give evidence it can help if you call him or her first. This is to provide credibility, which may suffer if he or she has been in court while other witnesses have presented testimony.

(c)   Follow the rules of primacy and recency. Start and finish with a strong witness.

(d)   If you need to call an adverse witness, it is usually safer to call him or her during the middle of the case. You will not have started on a bad note, and you will be able to limit the damage done.

(e)   An important corroborative witness should normally be called immediately after the primary witness to the facts.

(f)   Have proper regard to the convenience of witnesses, particularly experts. Do not keep witnesses at court unnecessarily.

The primary purpose of the order of proof is to present your theory of the case in a logically progressive way, so that it is easy for the trier of fact to follow and understand your case. But you should be flexible. Last minute problems arise often and you will need to adjust your schedule accordingly.

30.3.2   THE ORDER OF EVIDENCE

The basic principle, when eliciting evidence, is to set the scene first, then hear the action. All necessary preliminary descriptions and information should be elicited before reaching the action because action evidence is most effectively and dramatically presented in an uninterrupted manner.

So a witness, the plaintiff in a case arising out of a car collision, could testify in the following order:

(a)   his background,
(b)   description of collision location,
(c)   what occurred just before the collision,
(d)   how the collision actually occurred,
(e)   what happened immediately after the collision,
(f)   emergency room and initial treatment,
(g)   continued medical treatment,
(h)   present physical limitations and handicaps,
(i)   financial losses to date.

Where possible, particularly where you are trying to elicit evidence about an event, you should try to develop descriptive narratives. The witness's response should paint a picture that the jury can actually visualise.

30.3.3   GETTING THE TESTIMONY MOVING

Getting the witness started is always a difficult moment. Simply asking the witness to tell the court all she knew about the break-in at . . .', is not likely to be fruitful. The witness will need to be introduced to the court, and the witness will need time to settle.

The best way to start, with a series of questions that identify the witness, put the witness at ease, and increase the witness's credibility:

Mrs Smith, what is your full name?
Mrs Smith, where do you live?
How long have you lived at that address?
What do you do for a living?

With a few simple questions you may be able to establish that the witness is married, has children, is a long-standing member of the community and holds a respectable position; all this shows that she is a mature, responsible and, therefore, credible person. They also allow the witness to settle down.

You must now move on to connect the witness with the case. The easiest way to do this is to use a pointed, leading question, which provides a point of reference. How you do this depends upon the extent to which the facts are in dispute – because leading questions can only be used where the facts are not disputed.

Where there is no dispute it is easy to lead:

Did you witness the car accident in Brooklands Avenue on the morning of 10 May 1993.
Are you the landlord of the premises at . . .?

If the identify of the person is not in issue, you can begin the testimony there:

How long have you known Mrs Smith?

If the identity of the person is in issue, because of an alibi defence, for example, you can start by considering location:

On 10 May were you in the Safeway supermarket at the bottom of Eccleshall Road?

You then move to focus the questions more precisely on the testimony that you wish to develop, first setting the scene, then describing the action.

30.4 Questioning

30.4.1 GENERAL CONSIDERATIONS

Up to this point you should have decided on the evidence you will present and on the order in which witnesses will appear. Now you have to decide what you want the evidence to sound like. The evidence will be presented in the form of a set of answers: it is your questions that will shape the testimony. Your questions will provide the structure, pace and emphases in much the same way that a conductor's baton shapes the sound of an orchestra. But, as with a symphony, the focus should be on the answers produced, not the questioner.

In the parts of this guide concerned with interviewing and advising, we discussed how questions range along a continuum, from a very wide form to a very closed form. The more open the question the more it allows the witness freedom to respond using his or her own words. The more direct the question, the greater the control exercised by the advocate. Within the continuum are a whole series of questions which you can use to seek clarification, gain more details, and probe for understanding.

You need to select a questioning strategy for each witness. You can either examine a witness using closed questions, which keeps the witness under control, or you can use open questions to elicit evidence through a free narrative, in which the witness provides all or part of the story in his or her own words.

Marcus Stone suggests that in practice, in criminal cases, the controlled method is favoured (see M. Stone, *Cross-examination in Criminal Trials*). The witness is taken through the evidence by tightly framed questions, in small steps, and in an orderly and deliberate way to ensure that all material facts are covered, and to avoid inadmissible, irrelevant, harmful or prejudicial evidence.

It is suggested that a decision to use controlled questioning should depend on the witness, and the nature of the evidence. It is the preferred method where the evidence is important, where caution is advisable, or where the witness might be unable to sustain an account of the facts without detailed prompting.

Too much control in questioning may lead to stark, impoverished forms of testimony, unleavened by rich factual detail or personal involvement. It is for this reason that some writers dislike controlled questions. They believe the witness should be encouraged to tell the story in his or her own words. The best way to achieve this is to use open questions which let the witness tell the story and reveal the important evidence personally. You can then move to elicit more details and greater emphasis by using more directed questions.

Paul Bergman, in *Trial Advocacy in a Nutshell*, provides the following example of an ideal questioning pattern:

(a) Closed questions to establish background and set the scene.
(b) Open questions which allow the witness to tell part of the story freely. 'Please tell us everything that happened before she pulled out a gun.'
(c) Closed questions to bring out details and emphasise that portion of the story.
(d) Open questions which allow the witness to tell the next part of the story freely.
(e) Closed questions to bring out details and emphasise that portion of the story.

The following sections provide a more detailed consideration of question types. The classification and examples are drawn from *Trial Advocacy in a Nutshell*.

30.4.2   THE OPEN NARRATIVE QUESTION

The open narrative question calls a witness's attention to a certain subject and then asks the witness to talk about that subject. The narrative question provides little direction and it imposes no structure. As the following example demonstrates, the narrative question allows the witness to tell the story in his or her own words, making the testimony seem more real and giving it greater dramatic effect.

And what happened after your arrived at the wall?

Well, this funny-shaped person kept saying things like, 'I'm going to jump. I'm going to jump.' After a few minutes he pitched forward and fell all the way to the ground. By that time the king's men had arrived on their king's horses, but it was too late.

As in a conversation, it provides a basis for a more natural form of communication. An added value is that it can be coupled quite naturally with more specific questions to bring out omitted details: What did the funny-shaped person look like? How long after the witness's arrival did Mr Dumpty pitch forward?

With a responsive witness narrative questions can be used at the beginning of the testimony, so that the witness can narrate an overview of a story, and the advocate can fill in details with more specific questions. Narrative questions should not be used with partisan witnesses, or with witnesses who are prone to digress and fill answers with discrepancies.

30.4.3   OPEN QUESTIONS

As narrative questions become more limited, they become merely open questions. Open questions leave to the witness the particular words to be used to describe something, but in this case the advocate selects the specific subject-matter for the witness to talk about:

Why did you approach the wall?

What did he say to you?

What was the next thing that happened?

Open questions move the testimony along. Once you have directed the witness to a certain area, open questions can be used to break up the evidence and to control its pace. Open questions, such as those below, are short, broad, and non-leading, they do not detract from the witness's own account:

What did you see (next)?

What did you hear (next)?

What did you (he, they) do (next)?

Did anything happen?

What happened (next)?

Then what happened?

Using only short open questions can become boring, so you need to vary the form by using specific, explanatory and follow-up questions where appropriate.

30.4.4 CLOSED QUESTIONS

Closed questions are those which pointedly ask a witness for a particular fact. They do not suggest the desired answer, but they leave the witness no room to use his or her own words:

What colour was the car?

How long did the incident last?

What are the names of the people you were with?

Each question calls for one bit of information. The benefit of closed questions is that they allow the advocate to control the testimony. Closed questions can be used to 'set the scene', and clarify and emphasise testimony. They can also be used to supply transition points between narrative parts of an examination.

30.4.5 LEADING QUESTIONS

A leading question suggests, in its phrasing, its own answer.

Was the man five feet ten inches?

Did he take the purse after he said he would rob you?

The light was on red, wasn't it?

These questions lead to a yes or no response. They usually assume facts that have not yet been established. This is fine when the facts are not in dispute. You have seen above how leading questions can be used to elicit basic details before moving into the body of the evidence. You should, though, use leading questions sparingly. Not because they are prohibited, but because they undermine the witness. By suggesting the answer you diminish the impact of the witness. You put the answer in the witnesses mouth and give evidence yourself. If a witness simply answers yes or no, then you and not they have provided the testimony.

30.5 Special Considerations

30.5.1 REFRESHING MEMORY

Sometimes a witness will need to refer to a statement, or notebook, to refresh his or her memory. The witness may be nervous, and not be able to remember the testimony, or, if a policeman, may deal with so many cases that he or she could not be expected to remember. Referring to a notebook or a statement is permitted provided the record was made at the time of the incident or shortly thereafter. You need to establish this and then confirm that the notes can be used:

Q. Can you recall what happened after the car swerved?

A. No. It was too long ago.

Q. Do you recall making a statement to the police shortly after the accident?

A. Yes

Q. How soon after the accident did you make it?

A. About an hour, while I was at the police station.

Q. Was the accident still fresh in your mind at that time?

A. Yes.

Q. Your honour, may the witness refresh her memory by referring to her evidence?

30.5.2   REAL EVIDENCE

Real evidence, evidence which is in a tangible form, can often interest, and may have unshakeable credibility. It provides, quite literally, something real and memorable, which can be got hold of. It has a permanence that oral testimony lacks. It corroborates simply by its presence. It makes the testimony of a witness more graphic, it adds substance that words alone cannot provide. Real evidence can be, for example, a weapon, a piece of clothing, a photograph, or a document.

Before real evidence can be admitted you need to ensure that the evidence is admissible, see the Civil Evidence Act 1968, ss. 1 to 9, the Criminal Justice Act 1986, ss. 23 and 24 and RSC, ord. 38. You also need to ensure that the evidence has been disclosed to your opponent and/or that your opponent has had a chance to inspect it. You also need to establish continuity of possession and demonstrate that the evidence produced is the same item that was used in the matter under consideration.

Where the item is not already in an identifiable bundle, it will need to be marked. This will identify the person introducing it and enable the exhibit to be distinguished during the trial. The bundle should be number P1 or D1, depending upon whether it has been introduced by the plaintiff/prosecution or the defendant. You should ask the judge for the exhibit to be marked.

It is necessary, finally, to introduce the evidence.

Where there is no dispute, you may lead the exhibit, as in the following example:

A. I saw the defendant with a bloody knife in his hand.

Q. Please look at this knife. Is this the knife?

A. Yes.

Q. Your Honour, may that be marked P1?

Where the item is in dispute it may be necessary to lay a proper foundation for its admissibility or to establish continuity:

A. I saw the defendant with a bloody knife in his hand.

Q. Please look at this (*handed to the witness*) – have you ever seen it before? *or*, Could you describe the knife?

Q. Is this that knife?

30.6   Re-examination

When the cross-examination of a witness has been completed, the advocate may re-examine his or her witness. The purpose of the re-examination is to explain or further develop matters that were raised during the cross-examination. This means that the scope of the re-examination will be limited to what the cross-examiner chooses to raise during his or her examination. It does not provide just another opportunity to go through the evidence provided through examination-in-chief.

Before re-examining a witness you should consider carefully. If you have nothing substantial to develop arising out of cross-examination, do not re-examine solely to rehash already existing evidence. You should certainly not re-examine simply to develop something that you have previously held back. Because you are limited to what was considered in cross-examination, you may not have the opportunity to develop the evidence that you held back. The safest approach is to bring out the entire evidence during the examination-in-chief.

The most common re-examinations arise where the cross-examination has:

(a)   called into question the witness's conduct;
(b)   brought out only the parts of a conversation or event favourable to the opponent;
(c)   highlighted inconsistencies in a witness's testimony or impeached the witness with a prior inconsistent statement; or
(d)   shown the witness's testimony to be muddled and confused.

The following two examples illustrate the correct use of re-examination.

The cross-examination of a rape victim has stressed the fact that the victim waited two hours after the rape before she called the police. The implication is that no rape occurred. On re-examination the following question is appropriate:

Q. Why didn't you call the police for two hours?

A. I was upset and afraid. He said he'd come back and kill me if I called the police.

The cross-examination has elicited part of a conversation, that part which helps the cross-examiner. On re-examination the following question is proper:

Q. Other than 'I'm sorry this whole thing happened?' did you say anything else to Mr Smith at that time?

A. Yes, I also said, 'However, if you don't pay me the money you owe, I'll have to hire a lawyer to collect it'.

THIRTY ONE

CROSS-EXAMINATION

31.1 Introduction

Cross-examination is the process of examining your opponent's witness. It is a process that is frequently shrouded in mystery. It is cross-examination which is said to reveal the great advocate, the artist, who is able to win the case through a series of inspired questions. It is the process in which a series of questions or the inspired question brings the opponent's case collapsing like a house built of cards.

For the novice, cross-examination produces uncertainty and misery. Direct examination has now come to an end, and it is your turn to cross-examine. What are you to do? Two responses are common. In the first, you aimlessly rehash the direct examination, except that you ask the questions in a sneering voice. In the second, you probe minute aspects of the testimony, in an attempt to challenge the witness's memory or perception of the event in question.

A better approach is available. You use cross-examination in a structured manner to achieve one of the two purposes of cross-examination, and you use cross-examination to advance your theory of the case and achieve the objectives you formulated in your case plan. You may not be adopting an inspired approach to cross-examination, but you will be carefully organised and well prepared. It is on this platform that artistry can grow.

31.2 Purpose

The purpose of cross-examination is basically twofold:

(a) To elicit favourable evidence and advance your own case. This involves getting the witness to agree with those facts which are consistent with your theory of the case.

(b) To construct a destructive examination which undermines your opponent's case. This involves asking the kinds of question which will discredit the witness or the witness's evidence.

If you wish to elicit favourable evidence and advance your own case you will engage in a constructive cross-examination. You will attempt to elicit favourable or indisputable facts. You will seek to develop new emphases and new meanings, and to present an alternative case.

If you wish to construct a destructive cross-examination you will either challenge the evidence as inconsistent, improbable or unrealistic, or you will challenge the witness as a mistaken or untruthful source of evidence.

If you are going to conduct a cross-examination which is designed to undermine your opponent's case, you should always elicit favourable evidence first. This is because the credibility of a witness should be high at the end of his or her examination-in-chief. This is, therefore, the time to extract favourable testimony, not when you have discredited the witness.

If you decide to conduct a constructive cross-examinatioin the opening should reassure the witness, showing that he or she is to be trusted. If you have managed to extract favourable testimony you may decide not to undermine the witness. If you do, the favourable testimony may be less plausible.

Before embarking on cross-examination, you should consider whether it is right to do so. You should not cross-examine a witness whose testimony has not been harmful. Nor should you cross-examine a witness whose evidence was not credible.

You should not cross-examine where a claim or a defence consists of more than one element. You may be prepared to concede that two of the elements exist, but that three other elements do not. In a case of theft, for example, you may be prepared to concede that a theft took place but you contend that your client has an alibi. In such a case it would be inappropriate to cross-examine a witness whose testimony simply established that a theft had taken place.

Whatever tactic you decide to use you should always cast it in the light of your theory of the case, your objectives or your 'story'. The main way in which you will elicit a narrative is through your own witnesses, but you should seek confirmation of and support for your story by constructive questioning, and use destructive questioning to challenge competing versions of the story. You should try to do more than just score isolated points. Your cross-examination should always be informed by a clear sense of purpose.

31.3   Elements of Cross-examination

Mauet, in *Fundamentals of Trial Techniques*, argues that successful cross-examinations follow a preconceived structure that gives the examination a logical and persuasive order. He argues, further, that your chances of conducting a successful cross-examination are maximised when you follow certain rules. The following two subsections of this Chapter focus on the structure and the rules, while the third considers the key element in all cross-examinations, the leading question.

31.3.1   STRUCTURE

To establish a cross-examination that has a clear, logical and persuasive order you need to follow four basic guidelines:

(a)   Cross-examination should be restricted to three or four basic points, each of which support your theory of the case. Attempting much more will invariably create two problems: the impact of your strongest points will be diluted, and the less significant points will be forgotten.

(b)   Make your strongest points at the beginning and end of your cross-examination, because first and last impressions are likely to be the strongest.

(c)   Vary the order of your subject-matter. The best cross-examinations follow a structure in which your theory of the case is kept implicit rather than explicit. By varying the order of your subject-matter you should be able to achieve your purpose without the witness becoming too aware of the point that you are trying to establish.

(d)   Do not repeat the evidence-in-chief. Advocates repeat the examination-in-chief in the vain hope that the witness's evidence will somehow fall apart in the retelling. This invariably fails. It is likely to work only where the witness's evidence appears memorised.

31.3.2   RULES FOR CROSS-EXAMINATION

The following rules are for guidance, they are not prescriptive but they provide a safe approach.

(a)   Know the probable answer before you ask the question. Cross-examination is not a time to fish for interesting information: its sole purpose is to elicit favourable facts or minimise the impact of the evidence-in-chief. Be sure, then, that you have an idea of the probable answer every time you pose a question.

(b)   Listen to the witness's answers. This is crucial. You need to watch for the nuances and gradations in the witness's evidence; you need to gauge the witness's reaction to your question and the tone of the answer; you also need to look for reluctance and hesitation on the part of the witness. This can be difficult to avoid if you are caught up in your notes or worrying about the next question. The best way to cross-examine it is to organise your notes into cross-examination topics. This way you do not have to try to follow a preordained script of carefully constructed questions; rather you formulate questions as you respond to the witness.

(c)   Do not argue with the witness. This is both improper, unprofessional and it will damage your own credibility. It can happen if you are frustrated by answers which are not to your liking. You can avoid this with careful organisation and a good structure.

(d)   Do not let the witness explain. This provides the witness an opportunity to be expansive and slip in a damaging answer. It can arise if you use open-ended questions which ask how or why something happened.

(e)   Keep control of the witness. You can do this by asking precisely phrased leading questions that never give the witness an opening that may damage you. You can also do it by demonstrating to the witness, before asking important questions, that you know the facts.

(f)   Do not ask one question too many. This rule should not be taken too far. It could really be phrased slightly differently: do not make your argument explicit. This flows from the proposition that you should ask only enough questions on cross-examination to establish the points you intend to make during your closing argument. The questions you ask in cross-examination should merely suggest the points that you wish to make. Your questions in cross-examination may imply a theory of the case, but they should not articulate it. You should not, therefore, ask the last question that explicitly drives home the point. Leave this question to your closing speech, when you can rhetorically pose the question yourself.

This rule is usually demonstrated by some examples, usually apocryphal, of the famous last question. Two are provided here, the first from Mauet, the second from Bergman:

Example 1. The accused was charged with unlawful sexual intercourse with a girl under 16 and there had been corroboration. The witness giving that corroborative evidence was a farmer who said he had seen the pair lying in the field and the cross-examination was as follows:

Q.   When you were a young man, did you ever take a girl for a walk in the evening?

A.   Sure, that I did.

Q.   Did you ever sit and cuddle her on the grass in a field?

A.   Sure, that I did.

Q.   And did you ever lean over and kiss her when she was lying on her back?

A.   Sure, that I did.

Q.   Nothing improper about that, all perfectly natural and proper?

A.   Yes.

Q. Anybody in the next field seeing that might easily have thought you were having sexual intercourse with her?

A. Sure, and they'd have been right too.

Example 2. This case involves a defendant who allegedly committed assault by biting off a victim's nose. The cross-examination was of an alleged eyewitness to the assault, whose testimony, succinctly stated, was, 'The defendant bit off the victim's nose'.

Q. Where did the fight take place?

A. In the middle of the field.

Q. Well, where were you?

A. I was on the edge of the field.

Q. How far away?

A. About 50 yards.

Q. What were you doing there?

A. Just looking at the trees.

Q. You had your back to the fight didn't you?

A. Yes.

Q. So the first you knew that there was a fight was when you heard the victim scream?

A. Yes.

Q. And it was not until after the victim screamed that you turned around?

A. Yes.

Q. How can you say, then, that the defendant bit off the victim's nose?

A. Because I saw him spit it out.

In both examples the last question is the one question too many. But in both cases, as Paul Bergman suggests, it is impossible to imagine that the last question would not have been asked of the witness during re-examination, or even during the examination-in-chief. The real purpose of the rule is to keep the argument implicit. Avoiding one question too many is simply one way of doing that.

31.3.3 LEADING QUESTIONS

In attitude and verbal approach, cross-examination is the opposite of examination-in-chief. With examination-in-chief, you need to develop testimony in an orderly fashion, and to frame your questions to allow a witness to tell a story in his or her own words so that the testimony will have maximum credibility. In cross-examination your emphasis is entirely different. You have isolated the points that you want to make and you want to make these points clearly and directly. You do not want a witness to tell you the story in his or her own words: that has already been done in the examination-in-chief. You want the witness to verify matters that you have put in your own words. The key to doing this is to use leading questions.

Q. On 13 December 1992, you owned a Ford car, didn't you?

Q. You had two drinks in the hour before the collision, right?

Q. You were looking away from the scene of the accident, isn't that correct?

Leading questions are valued on cross-examination because they take attention away from the witness and give it to the advocate. If leading questions are being used, facts are being supplied by the advocate, not by the witness. The witness's role is limited to affirming or denying a matter stated by you. Leading questions are the mechanism through which you control a witness.

The most appropriate form of leading question is the one in which the advocate makes a series of assertions and statements of fact. By phrasing your questions narrowly, asking only one specific fact in each question, you should be able to get yes, or no, or short answers to each question. You should also put your points with a series of short, precise questions, each of which only contains one point. It is through a series of cumulative short questions that you lead up to the point you want to establish.

31.4 Advancing your Own Case: Eliciting Favourable Testimony

One of the key purposes of cross-examination is to advance your own case, both by eliciting facts from the witness that will support your case and by putting your theory of the case to the witness. Where you wish to elicit favourable testimony from the witness you should do this first. If you are pleasant and courteous, the witness should relax and cooperate.

It is important to approach each witness's testimony with an open mind. Usually the witness will give evidence upon a number of points that are either neutral to your position or which are directly helpful. The witness may have identified your client but may agree that the crime was committed on a dark night and that the lighting was poor. A witness to a motor accident may agree that the road surface was wet and that both parties were driving fast.

You should review the evidence of each witness and ask:

(a)   Are there areas of consensus between the witness's testimony and that of my client?
(b)   Has the witness said anything which can be expanded upon to help the case?
(c)   Is there anything in a prior statement, which, though not included in examination-in-chief, may help the case?
(d)   Has the witness said anything which runs contrary to common sense?
(e)   Will the witness cooperate?

The main constructive techniques progress along a continuum. At one end of the continuum you will accept the evidence-in-chief but seek to give it a new emphasis. At the other end you will seek to challenge it by putting your alternative case. You may, alternatively, seek a fresh interpretation of the evidence by giving it a new meaning (see Marcus Stone, *Cross-examination in Criminal Cases* on which the following section draws).

31.4.1   EMPHASIS

In the most constructive forms of cross-examination you find something in the evidence-in-chief which favours your case. You accept the evidence, but you make the witness repeat it for emphasis.

The technique could be illustrated by the cross-examination of a sales assistant who witnessed a robbery. The sales assistant claims to have recognised one robber as a customer, by his build, his hair colour and typical way of walking. In his evidence-in-chief, he says, 'It was all over so quickly'. In cross-examinatioin you might seize on the brevity of the event for emphasis, eliciting further details to build up a picture of how many things the witness seems to have attended to in a short period of time, leaving little time to study the robber. The emphasis on one element, the brevity of the event, supports the cross-examiner's theory of the case: that the identification is either unreliable or wrong.

31.4.2 NEW MEANINGS

Cross-examination can be used to give a new meaning to any adverse and material impression evidence or to any circumstantial evidence which may otherwise yield an adverse inference.

You should start with friendly and indirect tactics which proceed gradually, step by step. By careful leading questions, the witness is made to accept minor adjustments to the evidence here and there, stressing this and toning down that, so that the balance and pattern are subtly altered in the direction of the new meaning.

This is where you need to take care in posing the final question. Your new interpretation of the evidence may be accepted by the witness, in which case putting the final question should favour your case. But the new interpretation might be denied, in which case you should not put the question.

31.4.3 PUTTING YOUR CASE TO THE WITNESS

Whether or not you use any other constructive method you should put your version of the case to any witness who knows the facts, giving him or her a chance to accept or deny it. This is a general rule of tactics. If you have led, or intend to lead, evidence to contradict a witness, you should give that witness a chance to explore the contradiction. Sometimes you may do this directly, and be met with a yes or no response. At other times you move subtly, using a series of short, leading questions.

31.5 Challenging the Opponent's Case

The main aim of cross-examination is to challenge the opponent's case by weakening or destroying harmful evidence. This can be done in one of two ways, discrediting the evidence and discrediting the witness.

31.5.1 DISCREDITING THE EVIDENCE

It is important, when planning a cross-examination, to remember that most witnesses are not lying. They are genuinely seeking to provide an objective and truthful account of the events as they saw them. Attacking them as untruthful rarely helps. You need to focus, instead, upon the manner in which they saw an event. Most people only see an event from their particular standpoint. As they only see a part of the event they tend to fill in the gaps in their observations. They make inferences, make connections and draw conclusions. Once they have done this they come to believe their version of events, and no other version seems tenable. It is your task in cross-examination to explore the gaps between what was seen and what was inferred, to show that the witness is not as reliable as he or she just appeared. The basic methods used for exposing a witness's reliability focus on the witness's perception, memory or ability to communicate.

As you are not suggesting that the witness is lying you should adopt a reassuring tone. You should use suitably phrased leading questions to suggest that you sympathise with the difficulties that may have led to mistaken evidence and allow the witness to save face.

31.5.1.1 Perception

Here you are seeking to show that the witness did not really have the opportunity to see the event in question. This is usually done by suggesting that the event occurred quickly or unexpectedly and that the witness was too far away to observe accurately what happened.

In a case involving a car accident, for example, cross-examination may demonstrate that the witness was too far away to see what was really happening, that she could not see the cars involved until just after the point of impact and that her view was obscured.

31.5.1.2 Memory

It can be difficult to remember the precise details of an event that occurred some time ago. A witness in court may have to deal with events that happened years ago. It can be particularly difficult where the event occurred during the normal course of a person's experience and when it had no particularly distinguishing features. Here cross-examination may establish that because of the similarity between this particular event and other ones like it the witness cannot really distinguish this particular event.

As an example take the evidence of a plaintiff's secretary who has given evidence that she mailed the defendant a letter which accepted a previous offer the defendant made to the plaintiff. The defendant has denied receiving the plaintiff's letter. The cross-examination should demonstrate that because the secretary types and processes so many letters, she cannot possible remember how this particular letter was handled.

31.5.1.3 The witness's ability to communicate

A common cross-examination technique focuses on the witness's ability to describe details and directions, to estimate distances and time, and to demonstrate that he or she cannot accurately recreate a picture of what actually happened. By pinning the witness down to specific estimates of distances, time and speed you can often reveal internal inconsistencies.

31.5.2 DISCREDITING THE WITNESS

You should always exercise caution when seeking to discredit a witness. For the most part witnesses are genuinely seeking to be helpful. Attempts to attack the witness can, therefore, backfire. Nevertheless, if you can show that the witness is not to be believed it can have a devastating effect. There are three ways of discrediting a witness: discrediting the witness's conduct, exposing inconsistencies in the witness's testimony, and impeaching the witness to show that he or she is not worthy of belief.

31.5.2.1 Discrediting a witness's conduct

In this instance you are seeking to show that there is a contradiction between the evidence given and the conduct of the witness. The witness may have given a perfectly reasonable account but may have acted inconsistently. The actions are then invoked as speaking louder than their testimony.

A typical example arises where the defendant in a motor accident has given evidence that he was not negligent, but cross-examination reveals that he left the scene of the collision without calling the police or subsequently reporting it, and without talking about it to his wife. A defendant charged with rape but who alleges consensual intercourse, provides another example. Cross-examination may reveal that after he left the woman he did not return home, that he stayed off work, and that no witnesses were available to describe his demeanour during those three days.

In each of these cases the witness has acted inconsistently. The witness has not done what common sense suggests he ought to have done. It is this gap between their behaviour and common sense that leads to the suggestion that their testimony is not to be believed.

31.5.2.2 Exposing inconsistencies in a witness's testimony

One of the most frequently used methods of challenging a witness at trial is by showing that his or her testimony is inconsistent with a prior statement. The witness's testimony may contain a fact which is inconsistent with prior testimony; it may contradict other facts contained in the same testimony; or it may exaggerate or embellish facts. In each case the technique is the same: repeat, build up and contrast (see Mauet, *Fundamentals of Trial Techniques*).

First, ask the witness to repeat the fact which he or she asserted in evidence-in-chief, the one you plan to challenge. Use the witness's actual answer when you cross-examine since the witness is most likely to agree with the actual answer, rather than a paraphrase. Then, build up the importance of the statement. Direct the witness to the date, time, place and circumstance of the prior inconsistent statement, whether oral or written. Finally, read the prior inconsistent statement to the witness and ask the witness to admit making it. Use the actual words.

An example, from a civil motor vehicle accident case, illustrates the technique:

Q. Mr Jones, you say you were about 15 metres from the accident when it happened?

A. Yes.

Q. There's no doubt in your mind about that is there?

A. No.

Q. Weren't you actually *over 30 metres* away.

A. No.

Q. Mr Jones, you talked to a police officer at the scene a few minutes after the accident, didn't you?

A. Yes.

Q. Since you talked to him right after the accident, everything was still fresh in your mind?

A. Yes.

Q. You knew the police officer was investigating the accident, didn't you?

A. Yes.

Q. And you knew it was important to tell the facts as accurately as possible?

A. Yes.

Q. Mr Jones, you told that police officer, right after the accident, that you were *over 30 metres* away when the accident happened, didn't you

A. Yes.

This demonstrates the basic techniques – repeat, build up, and contrast – by picking up a simple fact, 15 metres, which was singled out for challenge, then contrasted clearly with the contradictory earlier oral statement – 30 metres.

31.5.2.3 Impeaching the witness

In some cases, you may be able to impeach a witness in order to show that he or she is unworthy of belief or that little weight should be attached to his/her evidence.

A witness may be discredited by showing that his or her evidence was affected by:

(a) bias;
(b) interest in the outcome of the proceedings;
(c) motive for testifying in a particular manner;
(d) previous convictions or bad acts.

Bias and prejudice are usually established by exposing a family or employment relationship which suggests that the witness is incapable of being impartial and objective. A witness may be thought to be impartial where he or she has a financial or other interest in the outcome of the proceedings. Greed, love, hate and revenge, are all recognised as compelling emotions. If you can suggest such a motive it is likely to taint the witness, even if the evidence itself is quite plausible.

If you wish to discredit a witness it is best to do it subtly, bit by bit. If you simply suggest to a mother, who has been asked to appear as an alibi witness, that she is lying to protect her son she is likely to deny it. If you gently build up an impression of partiality, as in the following example, it is much more believable.

Q. Mrs Jones, your son was living with you on the date this robbery was committed, wasn't he?

A. Yes.

Q. In fact he's still living with you now, isn't he?

A. Yes.

Q. So you see him every day?

A. Yes.

Q. You talk to him?

A. Yes.

Q. You talk to him about his problems, don't you?

A. Yes.

Q. Wouldn't it be fair to say that you've talked to him about this case?

A. Yes.

Q. You were surprised when he was arrested?

A. Yes.

Q. As far as you are concerned this must be an awful mistake?

A. Yes.

Q. Did your son ask you to come to court?

A. Yes.

Through this gradual lead-up the advocate has managed to suggest the closeness of the relationship, the fact that they had talked about the case, and the fact that the mother is unlikely to believe ill of her son.

THIRTY TWO

OPENING AND CLOSING SPEECHES

32.1   Introduction

Although they have different purposes, the opening address and closing speeches are discussed together here for two reasons. The first is that in both you have a chance to talk directly to the trier of fact. The second is to de-emphasise their importance.

The opening address is often overemphasised because it is that strategic psychological moment at which you can set the scene, capture the jury and dominate the proceedings. The closing address, meanwhile, has a similar symbolic importance. It is the point at which the final denouement is given. The brilliant advocate addresses the jury, links the final threads together and produces a sobbing confession from the well of the court.

Both the opening speech and the closing address are important but magistrates, judges nor juries are likely to be too swayed by glowing rhetoric. It is their job to decide the case as best as they can on the evidence before them. It is your task in the opening to make that task easier by providing a structure that frames the evidence.

This Chapter is in three parts. The first is technical, it sets out the right to make an opening speech and closing argument, and it describes the order of speeches. The remaining two sections consider the opening and closing speech in turn.

32.2   Who Makes Opening and Closing Speeches

In criminal matters the prosecution always have the right to make an opening speech, while the defence do usually make an opening speech.

In the magistrates' court only one speech is allowed for each party. The prosecution should make their speech at the beginning. In simple cases, and when appearing before a stipendiary magistrate, the right to make a speech is often waived. It may be appropriate in a complex case or where you want to introduce a plan or map in the evidence.

In the Crown Court the defence can only open a case if they intend to call a witness to fact, and not in cases where only the accused and witnesses to character are called. The defence opening speech is rare. It should be made after the prosecution have given evidence and before calling witnesses.

In civil cases it is usually the plaintiff who begins. In the county court the defendant's advocate may make an opening speech but he or she is not then entitled to make a closing speech except with the leave of the court. As the practice differs between courts, it is wise, if you wish to make an opening speech, to check on the practice in that court.

In criminal matters it is usually only the defence who will make a closing speech. Where the defence exercised the right to make an opening speech then the prosecution will be allowed to make a closing speech. The defence always address the court last.

In civil cases the plaintiff always has the final word.

32.3 The Opening Speech

32.3.1 PURPOSE

The principal purpose of the opening speech is to provide an outline and guide to your case. It has been described, by Paul Bergman, as a form of road-map, made on the assumption that the fact finder will be better able to follow the road of evidence knowing where the road will eventually go. The evidence is provided with a context, which it makes more meaningful, and therefore more persuasive (P. Bergman, *Trial Advocacy in a Nutshell*).

32.3.2 OPENING FOR THE PLAINTIFF OR PROSECUTION

The opening statement should provide a summary of the evidence that will be produced by the maker of the statement. It should be a summary not an argument.

It should provide a summary that is both long enough to introduce the case but not so long that the actual evidence produced is boring and an anticlimax. You should save details for the actual testimony: after all your case is not circumscribed by the evidence predicted in your opening statement. The summary should, though, be relevant. Although it will only provide a summary it should still be well-structured: it should be a cohesive whole in which one thing should lead logically to the next.

You should start with a statement of the nature of the case before the court, go on to state the issues that will need to be decided, and then summarise the facts which you will seek to establish during the trial. The summary of the facts should provide a chronological account of what happened. You should then describe the harm or loss suffered. You should then move onto a consideration of the pleadings or the counts in the indictment.

If you are opening on behalf of the plaintiff in a civil case, you could, for example, start by saying: 'May it please your honour, this is a case for damages for breach of contract'. As a next step you should then hand the judge the bundle of agreed documents and then take him or her through the chronology tying up the relevant dates with the document to which it relates. As you move through the chronology you will build up for the judge a picture of the events in the case. Before you move on to the pleadings you should preface your remarks with a short account of the issues in the case. You then move on to the pleadings, any schedule of events, and any orders that might have been made. If you wish to amend the pleadings you should do it now. It is best to provide a draft of the amended pleading and to give appropriate references to the *County Court Practice*.

In a criminal case, the prosecution will often forgo an opening speech, especially where it is a simple case. Most writers recommend that an opening speech should still be made, but the speech should be kept brief. Magistrates will not need an exhaustive explanation of all the facts. In a criminal case before a jury, the prosecution should give a more detailed account of the evidence that will be introduced. The penultimate step is a summary of the relevant law, followed by a conclusion which indicates why, on the basis of the law and facts to be established, you should succeed. In a criminal case before a jury, you will need to explain the law in non-technical language. Your account will need to be plain and simple.

The opening statement introduces the court to your theory of the case, the set of propositions which incorporates all the agreed facts with your party's version of the disputed facts. It provides a clear, coherent, integrated overview of the evidence, which spells out the inferences that you contend should be drawn from the primary facts (Mauet, *Fundamentals of Trial Techniques*).

The summary of the facts should not be overstated, it should not go beyond what the witnesses will actually say. The failure to live up to a promise made during an opening statement may make a case appear far weaker than it actually is. The summary should not be contentious. It should summarise the potential evidence, not the conclusions you want to be drawn or the arguments that you want to make on the basis of the evidence. Conclusions, inferences or judgments of credibility are matters of argument.

The statement should only include a summary of the facts that you can actually produce. If you suspect a witness may not come up to proof, or even not appear, you should not introduce that witness's testimony, nor should you introduce testimony that you hope will be introduced by the other side.

Where appropriate you should anticipate the defence. You must work out their theory of the case and try to rebut it. If there are obvious weaknesses in your own theory acknowledge them and explain why, in spite of the weaknesses, the plaintiff or prosecution is entitled to a verdict.

Where possible, you should make your opening lively and interesting. This is not always going to be easy in a routine case on breach of contract or a dispute about rent. But you should, if you can, try to engage the court's interest. Use plain language, try to tell the story as you would to a group of friends. Use eye contact to build rapport. Try to personalise your client, by using his or her name, while referring to the other side as 'the respondent'.

Finally, you may want to conclude with a summary that provides a series of questions which need to be answered in the proceedings. By doing this you will establish a clear agenda. You should, therefore, conclude, by identifying those questions: 'In my submission, the questions you will need to consider when you have heard the evidence are five, and are as follows . . .' (D. Napley, *The Technique of Persuasion*).

32.3.3 OPENING FOR THE DEFENCE

As an advocate for the defence you are in a different position to the prosecution or plaintiff. The trial will already have run much of its course. Witnesses will have appeared and you will have disclosed your own position through the questions that you asked in cross-examination. You do not need to establish a background to the case, you need to challenge the case put forward by the other side. But you do not need to destroy their position in opening, you can save arguments about the credibility of the evidence produced, and the inferences to be drawn from it, to the closing speech.

If you do decide to make an opening you should start with a comment on the evidence given so far, provide an outline of the evidence which is to come, state your theory of the case and anticipate defects in your argument. You should conclude with a summary of the questions that you think need to be answered.

32.4 The Closing Speech

32.4.1 PURPOSE

The closing argument is the chronological and psychological culmination of the trial. It provides your final attempt to address the court. It should not, though, be a separate moment. It should form an integrated whole with the evidence you introduced and, where you made one, your opening speech. The closing argument should provide a shape to the evidence. It should pervade the trial (P. Bergman, *Trial Advocacy in a Nutshell*).

The primary purpose of the closing speech is to present the argument that underpins the case. In presenting this argument you seek to persuade the fact finder that the case should be decided in your favour and you do this by presenting your theory of the case. This may have been apparent from the testimony, but it may not. Now you can interweave your theory with the evidence to produce a coherent and convincing account.

The final speech also provides a point at which you can address the evidence that weakens your case, and a point at which you can respond to evidence presented by the other side. It also provides an opportunity to address the law. Here you need to exercise caution. If you are addressing a jury, you will need to remember that the judge will follow, and that he may present a different account of the law. You will need to explain your points clearly and in plain terms.

If you have defined your theory of the case and developed clear objectives for the trial your closing speech should develop logically. If you formulated questions in your opening, now is the time to return to them, to present them again and show how the evidence has provided the answers in your favour. Although you should have planned your speech, you will still need to prepare, to respond to the evidence given, and to deal with unanticipated arguments.

It will be some time before you present a closing speech to a jury, but the closing speech to a jury trial provides a good model. It will provide a basis for your future work, and it will provide insight as you observe closing speeches made by others.

32.4.2 STRUCTURE

The closing speech should have a clear, logical structure. It should be easy to follow, yet encapsulate the major points. Each case will require a different argument, but many will have a similar structure. The following structural outline provides a simple guide:

(a) Introduction.
(b) Issues.
(c) Narrative.
(d) The argument
(e) Confirmation and refutation.
(f) Result.

This structure is in two parts. The first part reviews the evidence, using a narrative approach. It provides a logical approach to the testimony, using the structure that informed your examination-in-chief; context first, then the action. The second part reviews the evidence. It is essentially argument, using only those witnesses, exhibits, inferences and techniques that will persuade the trier of fact to decide in your favour.

This approach does not review the evidence witness by witness, exhibit by exhibit. This can be tedious. You will end up repeating aspects of the evidence throughout your speech and you will find it difficult to compromise by selecting isolated portions of the evidence. It provides a structured overview, which organises the evidence around the issues and summarises the evidence that applies to each issue. It situates the evidence in a meaningful context and frames it for the trier of fact, to support your standpoint.

32.4.2.1 Introduction

The introduction provides a preview, a road-map that highlights the most significant and favourable aspects of your evidence. It should not be too detailed, but it should provide a set of prompts. It gives advance notice of the points you will make and it gives the fact finder a checklist. This should help retain interest as you move from point to point.

32.4.2.2 Defining the issues

In constructing a story for the case you will have been concerned to *define* the issues, make *connections* between the evidence, and used evidence to *validate* your argument.

In this section you will use your definition of the issues in an attempt to control the decision-making process. An implicit definition of the issues will have been provided in the evidence. Now is the time to make it explicit so that the trier of fact can move easily to *connect* them to the evidence. Your questions in the opening address provide a useful starting-point. Return to them and use them to frame the evidence.

The following two examples, taken from Paul Bergman's *Trial Advocacy in a Nutshell*, show how you can define the issues. Although set in rural America they provide a good example of how the selection of standpoint can lead to a different perspective on the same set of facts. The plaintiff claims that he was injured as a result of the negligence of the defendant, who claims that he swerved across the road to avoid a small flock of chickens.

The first lawyer, adopting the standpoint of the plaintiff, framed the issue as follows:

> The issue you have to decide is whether the safety of a bunch of chickens has a higher priority than the life or property of a human being.

The second lawyer, adopting the standpoint of the defendant, framed the issue in its rural agricultural context:

> The real issue in this case is whether every chicken farmer in this country has an obligation to erect chicken barricades around his entire property.

The issues which you define may be either legal or factual, or a mixture of both. Often you will define the issues in terms of the legal basis of the claim or defence. In a civil case this will be found in the pleading, in a criminal case in the indictment. In defining the issue you will seek to connect the central question with the particular facts.

In defining the issue you may keep certain issues out, or minimise the damage caused by the negative effect of another issue. Consider the following example, again from Paul Bergman, which in a brutal criminal case confines the issue:

> In this case, there is no question but that a particularly brutal crime was committed. Our purpose during this entire trial has never been to claim anything to the contrary. But the issue that is presented to you is the identity of whoever committed such a foul crime. The evidence is overwhelming that it was not my client, Mr Attila.

32.4.2.3 Narrative

It is now time to provide an account of what happened, following the order that you used in conducting your examination-in-chief. Describe the parties, then the scene, then the action. This personalises the issue, provides a context and then moves on to describe the action. Again, you should describe the action from your standpoint, which at this point can incorporate the inferences that you will seek to establish.

Two examples, adapted from Mauet's *Fundamentals of Trial Technique*, demonstrate the technique. First the prosecution:

> The pub was well-lit. There were lights over the bar, lights over the front entrance, lights in the street that shone through the front windows, and lights from the jukebox. There was more than enough light for the customers to observe accurately and identify the robbers.

Now the defence:

> The pub wasn't well-lit. It was pretty much like any other pub you've ever seen. Successful pubs create moods in large part through dim lighting. This pub was no exception. It had only a few small lights spread throughout the pub. This is hardly the kind of lighting you would want to have when correctly identifying the robbers is critically important.

32.4.2.4   The argument

Here you provide a summary of what happened. You have defined the issues and provided a narrative, now you move on to connect the issue and the narrative:

> Did the police have reasonable grounds for believing that the person driving the car was Tom Jones. The evidence is quite clear. The police had no reasonable grounds for believing the driver to be Tom Jones. At the time of the arrest Tom told them he had not been driving the car. You have heard that the police harassed Tom Jones. You have seen that they gave inconsistent evidence. Do you really believe that Tom was driving the car?

32.4.2.5   Confirmation and refutation

Having provided a summary, which again defines the issue, you move on to review the evidence, repeating critical testimony that supports your side and refuting evidence that does not. Selectivity is crucial. Pick the significant parts of the important evidence and argue your case emphatically.

When confirming your case introduce your witness, build him up and then review the critical evidence:

> You remember Mr Brown. He was standing at the junction by the Astra. He has been employed at the Post Office for 18 years. He has no interest in the outcome of this case. He does not know Tom Jones. Wasn't he in the best position to see who was driving? Didn't he get a full view of the driver? Wasn't he, in fact, the only person really to see who was driving that car? What did he say? He said . . .'

The refutation or rebuttal is done in the same way. Select the other side's evidence, minimise it and belittle it. It is now that you challenge the witness's background or qualifications, his or her recollection, or knowledge of the facts.

32.4.2.6   The result

In conclusion you move to a summary and request a proper verdict.

This structure follows the broad three-stage approach advocated in Anthony King's *Effective Communication*. The three parts are:

(a)   The introduction in which you tell your audience in outline what they will hear.
(b)   The main body in which you develop your themes.
(c)   The conclusion in which you will summarise the key message.

The introduction alerts the listener; the body of the presentation develops the main theme or themes; the conclusion should repeat your main message and suggest the action to be taken.

32.4.3   PRESENTATION

Closing arguments should be short, but they should be long enough to cover the ground. To help the trier of fact both understand and hear your argument you need to cultivate a slow and clear delivery. Allow yourself time to phrase your submission so that the trier of fact will understand what you have to say. Taking time as you speak is not the same as wasting time. This happens when you cross-examine to no purpose, or present four witnesses when one will do. Try to maintain eye contact, watch for signs of boredom and respond accordingly. If addressing a judge, see that he or she is keeping up. If the judge is writing notes slow down; if he or she is content for you to move along, keep to a conversational pace. Keep your head up, not buried in notes, and keep your voice up throughout the sentence.

Try, too, to adopt a conversational tone. Present your story in the manner that you would tell it to a group of friends. Generate interest by being enthusiastic. Use themes, raise questions, introduce analogies, slow the topic at appropriate points, make contrasts, provide pointers,

A theme can be used to describe your theory of the case: 'The real victim is Tom Jones. He is the victim of unreliable identification and the victim of a vindictive campaign.' You then return to this point as you review the evidence.

Rhetorical questions can be used to supplement the questions that you have used to define the issues:

> Why should Tom Jones risk conviction? He knows the consequences. As you have heard he has just been promoted at work, he has been married a month, and he has just moved into a new home. Why, at this golden moment in his life, should he risk so much? As you have seen the evidence supports his case.

Analogies and stories can define and crystallise an idea. An analogy that draws upon common experiences connects your ideas with the fact finder's own experience. Analogies do not have to be complex to be effective. Consider the following example, from Bergman's *Trial Advocacy in a Nutshell*:

> We have all had the experience of walking down the street and calling to someone we thought was a friend, only to discover we have made a mistake.

or

> We have all seen movies and read books in which innocent people were convicted as a result of mistaken identity.

In presenting evidence you should present the strongest part of your argument first, then volunteer and deal with your weakness, before finally confronting the weaknesses in the position put by the other side.

INDEX

INDEX